# CANADA, NATO AND THE BOMB
## The Western Alliance in Crisis

# Tom Keating and Larry Pratt

SO-BBE-803

Hurtig Publishers Ltd.
Edmonton, Alberta

Hurtig Publishers Ltd.
10560-105 Street
Edmonton, Alberta
Canada  T5H 2W7

**Canadian Cataloguing in Publication Data**

Pratt, Larry, 1944-
  Canada, NATO and the bomb

Includes index.
ISBN 0-88830-332-7

1. North Atlantic Treaty Organization—Canada.
2. Canada—Military policy.   I. Keating, Thomas F.
II. Title.

UA646.5.C3P72   1988      355′.031′091821      C88-094299-1


*Editorial*/Maryhelen Vicars
*Design*/David Shaw & Associates Ltd.
*Cover design*/**word**and**image**
*Cover photograph*/Canapress
*Composition*/Howarth & Smith Limited
*Manufacture*/Hignell Printing, Winnipeg


Printed and bound in Canada

# Contents

*The characteristic danger of great nations
is that they may at last fail from
not comprehending the great institutions which
they have created.*

WALTER BAGEHOT

*For Sam and Amy
and for Trish, Rebecca, Kate, and Shaun*

# Preface

Canadian security policy is approaching a crossroads. One road open to us is to follow the current trend toward regionalism and isolationism within the Atlantic Alliance and to opt for Fortress North America and closer strategic co-operation with the United States. A second path leads us away from formal participation in NORAD and NATO to a policy of neutrality and the establishment of an understanding with the United States comparable to that between Finland and the Soviet Union. The third road is to resist these continentalist and neutralist options (which may in practice be more similar than different) and to renew our commitment to the collective defence of the North Atlantic security community; that is, to the defence of "the West". Canadian interests in the protection of sovereignty and territorial integrity and the security of our European allies all point in the direction of a multilateral rather than bilateral strategy. The third road is still our best option.

Why should we defend "the West"? Twenty or thirty years ago, few Canadians would have questioned the need for western security, and even fewer would have challenged the concept of "the West". Today, however, it is more fashionable to describe the North Atlantic region pejoratively as the heartland of advanced capitalism, as "the North", or simply as a group of more-or-less anti-Communist states bound together by this negative ideology. The consensus which underpinned nuclear deterrence and support for the North Atlantic security system has eroded.

In Western Europe itself, deterrence and NATO's security policy have been brought into question in the past six or seven years by defence professionals and by a broadly based peace movement. An altogether artificial crisis of confidence in the stability of the deterrence system has been generated by Right and Left; and many Europeans now appear to believe that, far from being in Europe to defend their allies, the Americans are there in order to launch a "limited" nuclear war from European territory. Political consensus concerning the system of "extended deterrence" (deterring attacks against allies) has disintegrated to the point where cautious European strategists such as Michael Howard advocate a shift away from reliance on U.S. nuclear weapons to a conventional defence buildup.

The isolationist Right in the United States, harking back to the thirties, is unabashedly hostile to the Europeans on the grounds that the latter have failed to support America in Afghanistan, the Middle East, and Central America and have carried on commercial relations with the Soviet bloc while failing to carry their share of the Alliance's defence burden. Richard Pipes, an influential anti-Soviet author and former member of Ronald Reagan's National Security Council, argues, for example, that the U.S. cannot meet the global Soviet threat when the bulk of its forces is allocated to the defence of Europe. "An alliance kept in place long after the circumstances that shaped it have either profoundly changed or disappeared, is a monument to the shortsightedness of American diplomacy. NATO really is not so much an alliance as an insurance policy, extended by the United States to Western Europe at low expense to the insured but at an immense cost and risk to the insurer. As such, it offers Moscow superb opportunities for driving wedges between the United States and Western Europe." (The Russians could not hope for a stronger ally than Mr. Pipes.)

Similarly, those who would reorient Canada away from its postwar strategy of support for NATO sometimes suggest that this country went to war in 1914 and 1939 because of sentimental ties to Crown and empire. Pierre Trudeau was to lament that "NATO had in reality determined all of our defence policy. We had no defence policy . . . except that of NATO. And our defence policy had determined all of our foreign policy. And we had no foreign policy of any importance except that which flowed from NATO." In fact, Canada went to war and entered NATO because its vital interests were threatened. Canada could not (and cannot) stand by and watch any hostile power gain a hegemonic position in Western Europe and control of the North Atlantic, for that would threaten our security, weaken our trading and commercial position, and force us to make the best terms we could get from the United States. The same reasoning lay behind our initial support for the North Atlantic Alliance: we wanted to help deter the Soviets, to reassure the Europeans, and, not incidentally, to pursue a multilateral security policy. The alternative, it was clear, was strategic continentalism. In short, we have interests in Western Europe—political, strategic, economic, and cultural—and we have fought to defend those interests. States go to war over such interests and create alliances to protect their interests short of war.

This book examines Canadian defence policy in NATO through a broad political and strategic perspective. It reviews the evolution of Canadian defence policy since 1945 in the context of the shifting strategic and political conditions within NATO and the international system at large. It begins with an analysis of the origins of NATO and proceeds to consider the subsequent shifts in Canadian defence policy with the intent of identifying the factors that led to these shifts and their implications for Canadian national interests. In the late 1940s, Canadian policy makers were convinced that a multilateral approach to western security was of fundamental importance and were instrumental in bringing the Americans and the Europeans together to establish NATO. They also sought to ensure that the Alliance would be more than just a military pact and would in addition help to solidify western co-operation in other areas.

A great deal has changed in the intervening years and the book will examine the forces that have led to these changes and have caused the current crisis that plagues the Alliance. By reviewing the historical evolution of Canadian defence policy with special reference to this country's involvement in NATO, the authors intend to show that despite some significant changes in the international strategic environment, a multilateral approach to western security remains the most viable approach to protecting Canadian interests.

Defence of "the West" is still Canada's best alternative to a myopic, introverted future inside the North American bunker. This book will attempt to make the case that our national interest, broadly conceived, is larger than continental defence; indeed, that we have an interest in opposing certain trends in U.S. military policy, such as the Strategic Defence Initiative. Within NATO, we will argue, Canada should support those who wish to reduce the Alliance's dependence on American nuclear forces and to build up conventional defences, especially in central Europe. Contrary to some opinion, the prospects for successful conventional defence and deterrence are by no means hopeless; resources allocated to nonnuclear deterrence and defence would be well worth the political effort and economic burden.

The authors view strategy and security policy in the broadest sense: as inseparable from the political, economic, and social dimensions of policy. The German philosopher of war Carl von Clausewitz viewed war as a great societal activity, a "continuation of politics by other means," and this is how we must view strategy as well. Part of our difficulty in recent years is that the study of strategy has in the West been dominated by abstract, apolitical calculations in which the most implausible scenarios are taken seriously and addressed through technological solutions. Neither political motivations nor the societal dimensions of strategy and armed conflict figure in such calculations. The reduction of strategy to "threat analysis" and debates over high-tech weapons systems is manifestly absurd. As a small power with limited resources and wide-ranging interests, Canada has a special interest in viewing strategy in the classical manner: as the art of applying military means to fulfill the ends of policy.

# Getting Out?

## NATO and Canada's Interests

Forty years ago, Canada came under very strong pressure from the United States to realign her economic and security policies on a North American basis. A deepening international economic crisis and fears of a Third World War seemed to be driving Canada inexorably toward continental commitments in which the price of her solvency and safety would be the loss of her independence.

As a way out of Canadian economic difficulties caused by Europe's postwar crisis and a worsening dollar shortage, in late 1947 the Americans offered Mackenzie King's government commercial reciprocity—free trade—and even a North American customs union. Seizing on Canada's weakened situation, one American negotiator called it a unique opportunity "of promoting the most efficient utilization of the resources of the North American continent and knitting the two countries together—an objective of United States foreign policy since the founding of the Republic." Prime Minister King, who soon came to the same conclusion, authorized his top officials and cabinet colleagues to explore in great secrecy the American initiative; most were enthusiastic, partly because they saw little prospect of Europe's recovery and thus favoured North American economic integration, and partly because they could smell war and supported closer U.S.-Canadian relations. Fortress North America was better than no fortress at all. But after consulting his ancestors on the meaning of 1911—the last Canadian election fought on the free trade issue—the Prime Minister, having received his customary "guidance from Beyond", turned the U.S. initiative down in favour of a less risky multilateral approach.

It was security and the threat of another terrible war that preoccupied Mackenzie King, a tired and aging politican in his last year in office, when he arrived in Britain in November 1947 to attend the wedding of Princess Elizabeth. There he was given a most gloomy account of the deteriorating international situation by the Labour government's crusty foreign secretary, Ernest Bevin, who confessed to feeling "more pessimistic than he had felt at any time in his life." Bevin was a tough, realistic union leader and politician who was becoming convinced that Stalin's intention was to bring the whole Eurasian land mass under Russia's sway, and that only a western coalition led by the United States could prevent him. The Americans, British, and French must make a stand to save Western Europe. The Russians would try to make this impossible, and there would be conflict. "What he feared," King recorded, "was not an open declaration of war, or the intention on the part of Russia to bring on a war immediately, but rather that the Americans with their sense of power might become impatient at Russia's behaviour and that matters would drift unintentionally but quickly into overt acts which would lead to war." The Canadians, too, worried about the American sense of power, a sense of Manifest Destiny that had again revealed itself in a number of military encroachments on Canadian territory and sovereignty during and immediately after the Second World War; now the worsening international situation posed the same grim alternatives as the U.S. bid for a North American customs union—Fortress North America or no fortress at all.

That war might indeed be coming, whether Stalin wanted it nor not, was borne in on Canadians by the Communist *coup* in Czechoslovakia in March 1948 and the prolonged crisis over the Soviet blockade of Berlin later that year. The fear of war was all over Europe that summer, and with it grew a conviction that the real danger was not so much one of an imminent Russian invasion but of a political and psychological collapse in Western Europe, following which the Communists would simply mop up. Britain and several other European states were anxiously seeking security guarantees from the United States and Canada. Mackenzie King remained morbidly afraid of being drawn into faraway European quarrels, but his secretary of state for external affairs (and, by November, his successor), Louis St. Laurent, favoured an activist's diplomacy to create a North Atlantic security system "to confront the forces of communist expansionism with an overwhelming preponderance of moral, economic and military force," (with the emphasis on the moral and the economic, to be sure). St. Laurent's view prevailed. The idea of a collective regional pact was greatly preferred by Canadian politicans and diplomats to that of a bilateral security arrangement with the United States for three central reasons.

In the first place, Canada had a vital interest in preventing another war in Europe and she was therefore driven—in spite of Mackenzie King's frettings—into supporting guarantees and other measures that would help restore confidence and a balance of power in Western Europe. A Russian conquest of Western Europe would mean war, and war on most unfavourable terms; the states of that region were now viewed as Canada's first line of defence. An Atlantic security grouping, it was hoped, would also help forestall the growth of neutralism in Europe and contain any revival of German militarism. Canadian interests, not sentiment, lay behind the decision to support an alliance of North Atlantic states. The same interests would prompt a wider commitment, made in 1950 after the outbreak of the Korean War, to station a Canadian brigade group in Europe as a tangible and visible symbol of Canada's commitment to the Alliance.

In strategic terms, Canada's commitment was not crucial. The crux of the matter was to secure the firm commitment of *American* military power to the multilateral Atlantic project, and it was to this goal that Canadian diplomats devoted much of their energies and considerable skills after the West Europeans signed their Brussels security pact shortly after the events in Czechoslovakia. Traditional American isolationism, a dislike of entangling alliances of any sort, was still to be found at the highest reaches of the American government, including the State Department and, of course, the Senate. Why should the United States, the world's strongest power, give up its unilateral freedom of action, its right of unilateral decision, and bind itself to the Europeans through formal treaty obligations? The State Department's most influential opponent of an Atlantic military alliance, policy planner George F. Kennan, argued that the challenge to Europe from Soviet Russia was a political or psychological one against which weapons and security commitments would be of little use, and that the proposed anti-Soviet coalition would reinforce the permanent division of Europe. But even Kennan—the object of much of Canada's diplomacy in 1948—reluctantly came to agree that Europe's recovery depended on something tangible in the way of external security guarantees, and that these should be offered on a multilateral basis.

Second, a regional security pact was viewed by Canada and the British as an instrument with which the more intemperate side of American unilateralism might be restrained. America's monopoly over atomic weapons (until the first Soviet atomic test in August 1949) and that "sense of power" alluded to by Bevin must have greatly worried Stalin; it worried America's friends as well. There was genuine fear by 1948 that Soviet probings and anti-Communist hysteria might prompt the U.S. to issue nuclear threats, even to launch a preventive war that would automatically involve the whole Western bloc.

And third, a multilateral Atlantic pact was a far more acceptable option to Canadian policy makers than the prospect of an unequal and unpopular continentalism in military affairs. There is little doubt that Canadian politicians and diplomats eagerly sought such an alliance as a counterweight that would help offset the preponderance of the United States. They also saw that if Canada opted for isolationism in the hope of avoiding commitments to Europe, it would in effect be choosing Fortress North America and sacrificing a vital interest of any state —its independence in foreign affairs. An old formula was at work: safeguard Canadian independence by choosing multilateral over bilateral arrangements. Canada could retain its independence only by subsuming its unbalanced relationship with the U.S. in a wider organizational framework—NATO. Domestic political concerns worked in the same direction. Some military co-operation with the U.S. was going to be inevitable but, politically, it would be easier to deal with U.S. requests to conduct military operations or maintain bases and facilities in Canadian territory if these were seen as part of a multilateral coalition. "The North Atlantic treaty proposal," James Eayrs has written in his definitive account of Canada's role in the creation of NATO, *Growing Up Allied,* "appeared attractive to the policy community at Ottawa for a reason additional to that of helping Canada deflect ill-timed proposals for reciprocity. A multilateral treaty was seen as well as a device for reducing the pressure of the Pentagon. A United States administration pledged to co-ordinate its defence policies with those of allies in Western Europe as well as those of its ally in North America would be less likely than a United States administration going it alone to lean as heavily upon its northern neighbour. Canada, allied to the United States within the North Atlantic coalition, would have more room in which to breathe and manoeuvre than would be hers if locked into a stifling bilateral embrace."

These three interests—preventing another major war through the creation of a regional system of collective security; binding the U.S. to multilateral rather than unilateral guarantees and decisions; and the need for a broader Atlantic security grouping as a counterweight to American dominance in North America— underlay Canada's very strong diplomatic support for the North Atlantic Treaty in the late 1940s. Canadian statecraft was based implicitly on the assumption that the country's independence could be secured only through a coalition strategy that would involve some sacrifice of all its members' autonomy in military affairs. Ottawa's clear preference for multilateral approaches in both economic and security affairs arose from a realistic view of the consequences of the only practical alternative— continentalism. Like any other state confronting its prospects in a rapidly changing system of world politics, Canada realigned in April 1949 (when Parliament ratified the North Atlantic Treaty) on the basis of a calculation of its national interests and the available options. It did not realign out of sentiments of friend-ship, for it was understood that alliances are not the friendships of international relations. Any decision to withdraw from NATO or to stay in must pass the same test of national interests. Have our basic interests in security and independence changed? Would our interests be better served by getting out?

## Erosion of Commitment

Much has changed since 1949. Around the NATO Alliance a new generation of politicians, mandarins, military planners, and aca-demic strategists has come into power. It lacks historical attachment to the older ruling "Atlanticism" that bound the architects of the Alliance—Bevin, Acheson, Pearson, Monnet, Adenauer—to one another. That in itself is not to be regretted: alliances that depend on ideology are unlikely to contribute anything positive to international order; and in any event, the Atlanticism of the fifties and sixties represented the values of a rather exclusive transatlantic elite whose moment has clearly passed with the era of American dominance. The newer leaders of NATO have a view of the Soviet Union that is probably at least as harsh and ideological as that held by the postwar architects of the Alliance, but what—with very few exceptions—distinguishes them as a group is their insularity, their inward-looking mentality, and their preference for thumbing their noses at their allies through unilateral acts. President Reagan's violent bombing raid on Libya's cities in April 1986, which we discuss in Chapter Five, was symbolic of what the American Right proudly calls "global unilateralism": a belief that America needs to shed her entangling alliances and use her power in whatever manner necessary in any remote corner of the globe. To the global unilateralist, NATO and other multilateral alliances and institutions are expensive encumbrances on America's freedom to pick its own friends and enemies, not to mention its own fights.

In NATO Europe, unilateralism is a coat of many colours. The British Labour Party's ideas on defence, nuclear weapons, and NATO derive from the "Ban the Bomb" movement of the 1950s, particularly from the Campaign for Nuclear Disarmament and its push for unilateral disarmament. It was unilateralism, not the Bomb, that Labour's Shadow Foreign Secretary was speaking of when he warned the party conference in 1958 not to force Britain to go "naked into the conference chamber." French unilateralism is associated with the acts and legacy of General Charles de Gaulle, whose rejection of America's hegemony led him to withdraw France's forces from the military structure of NATO and to pursue an independent policy based on the nuclear *force de frappe*. Yet de Gaulle forged a domestic consensus on security that has allowed his successors to play a far more positive role in Europe and the Alliance. Alas, the same cannot be said of the Federal Republic of Germany, perhaps the pivotal ally in NATO: buffeted between cold war and detente, incoming missiles and outgoing missiles, a strong America and an unreliable America, the leadership and the people of West Germany seem increasingly anxious and ambivalent about their status in the Alliance. Since the early 1980s German public opinion has reflected a growing alienation from the policies of the U.S., a deepening sense of vulnerability and dependence, and fears over the future of East-West relations. Germany's insecurities have fostered a romantic pacifist neutralism, (still confined to a minority, to be sure), that could evolve in a few years into a romantic pronuclear nationalism with real mass appeal unless its fears of abandonment by its allies—Canada among them—are calmed.

## Unilateralism: NDP Style

What of Canada, postwar champion of multilateral approaches to international security questions? At first glance unilateralism in Canadian defence appears to be confined to the left of the political spectrum, for the New Democratic Party and most sections of the peace movement favour withdrawal from NATO and all military agreements with the U.S. and an exclusive focus upon defence of Canada's own territory and sovereignty. This pursuit of military independence or of armed neutrality would not only fail to protect Canada from nuclear attack or involvement in a major war, it would quickly reduce our status from a voluntary ally to a simple dependent of the United States. Because Canada's only practical alternative to multilateral or collective regional security is a continental military arrangement, the visions of the NDP and most peace groups tend to overlap with the isolationist, "Canada-first" opinions on the Right of the Conservative Party.

The New Democratic Party was founded in 1961 amidst a great debate over whether Canada should withdraw from NATO and all military co-operation with the United States. Two groups of activists opposed any military alignments. The first was pacifist, antinuclear and antimilitarist, and found its roots in the party's social gospel tradition and the acts of conscience of leaders such as J.S. Woodsworth, whose unyielding opposition to war had, in 1939, gone as far as opposing Canada's involvement in the coming struggle against Hitler. Woodsworth's was a minority view—neither the NDP nor its predecessor, the Co-operative Commonwealth Federation, ever embraced pacifism—but in 1939 many in the CCF objected to Canada's automatic involvement in "European wars which brought no peace." It was time to discard the colonial mentality and recognize that Canada was an independent, self-governing *and* North American state. Thus, the CCF rejected Woodsworth's pacifism in September 1939 but gave only qualified approval to the war effort: "Canada should be prepared to defend her own shores, stated the party, but her assistance should be limited to economic aid and must not include conscription of manpower or the sending of any expeditionary force." This statement, which closely resembles recent NDP policy toward NATO, represents the nationalist position of many Canadian social democrats, and this second group is much more significant than the pacifist wing of the party. Whether directed against Britain, as in the interwar years, or, as in the postwar period, against the U.S., left-nationalism rejects both multilateral and bilateral defence alignments on the grounds that such ties require the sacrifice of too much autonomy and involve Canada in great power conflicts in which she has no direct interest. Therefore, it is argued, Canada should still "be prepared to defend her own shores"—whatever that means—but *only* her shores, her territory, her sovereignty. It is a view that can only be described as isolationist, yet it must be admitted that it is probably the majority view of Canadian social democrats.

The NDP initially agreed to back Canada's participation in NATO, a position supported by its first leader, Tommy Douglas, and his successor, David Lewis. But this was only on condition that Canada itself was nonnuclear in every sense and that the Alliance supported democratic regimes in Europe. Much of the internal debate over NATO turned on the involvement of various Mediterranean dictatorships—Portugal, Spain, Greece, and Turkey—in the coalition, and it was only by holding their noses that many NDP members could live with the party's policy. (Spain was kept out of NATO until after the death of General Franco). In 1969, as part of a radical anti-American attack from the Waffle faction on Canada's complicity in the Vietnam War, an NDP convention voted to withdraw from NATO and that decision has been overwhelmingly ratified by party committees and conventions in the intervening years. It is supported by about half of the party's parliamentary caucus. Although the NDP position on NATO may be modified before the federal election expected in 1988, we cannot expect electoral expediency to outlast the fundamentalist views of party militants—for whom getting out of NATO is akin to one of Martin Luther's theses, to be nailed to the door of the Church as a statement of theological purity. If the NDP shifts on NATO, it will be a purely tactical move—to be overturned when the party is returned to opposition after an election.

What underlies the NDP's majority view on defence policy is a complex mixture of nineteenth century liberal ideas about war and disarmament, a vitriolic dislike and fear of the United States, and a traditionally isolationist view of Europe. Above all, New Democrats recoil from the idea that Canadian security can be best obtained in military alignments with the great powers. It is alleged that NATO ties Canada to military spending levels, to first use of nuclear weapons, and to various policies and institutions of the United States. Party spokesmen argue that, in place of NATO, the first principle of Canadian defence policy should be protection of territory and sovereignty, a view also held by the peace movement, the British Labour Party, and other European social democratic parties, though not by most voters. Asked during the 1987 British election how territorial defence would work against a nuclear-armed aggressor, the Labour Party leader, Neil Kinnock, argued for a guerrilla resistance to make a Soviet occupation untenable. He lost the election, partly because of the defence issue. The NDP's present leader, Ed Broadbent, is said to be personally opposed to his own party's stance on the Alliance, but he cannot overturn the policy without risking the alienation of many party activists. By default, then, the party line on defence policy is made by the militants who want unilateral withdrawal from all military commitments. The leadership is reduced to making convoluted and damaging rationalizations of a policy that is untenable in every sense. As one example, the party's defence critic, Derek Blackburn, told us in a 1987 interview that "the Europeanization of NATO" could only lead "to a greatly revitalized western defence":

They already would have two independent nuclear forces, the U.K. and France. Germany is a very iffy thing, I admit. Let the Europeans handle that, I think they can. Plus the fact that when the Americans withdraw . . . I can't see anything but good coming from it on the Eastern side. There will be tremendous internal pressure from countries like Hungary and Poland, even East Germany, for Mikhail Gorbachev to come clean with them and say, "Okay I think maybe it's time to lift the military presence out of the East Bloc."

"Let the Europeans handle that." Now there is the authentic voice of the North American isolationist. If Germany turns toward neutralism or an arrangement with the Eastern bloc when the North Americans disengage from Europe, not to worry: let the Europeans look after themselves. And how should the Americans and Canadians leave? Even the most sweeping plans for military disengagement from Europe always saw this happening as part of a multilateral political and military settlement, not in the form of a unilateral withdrawal by the West—an event which would very likely force Western Europe into the kind of uncertainty and instability it has not experienced since the late 1940s. Critics on the Left in Europe and Canada, together with the New Right NATO-bashers in the United States, anticipate a happy outcome from military disengagement: if only Europe could push back the superpowers, the entire continent would pull together in tranquility. The "Europeanization of NATO", which is to succeed the period of American hegemony, begins with the withdrawal of North American forces from the continent, an event that is to induce the Europeans, led by France and Germany, to resolve their own problems of military co-operation.

Our view of the matter is quite different. Western Europe has enjoyed forty-five years of prosperity and peace, but this in itself is hardly evidence that the Alliance has outlived its usefulness. On the contrary, the postwar Western European order owes much of its remarkable stability not to the deterrent effects of nuclear weapons, but rather to the entanglement of outside powers—the U.S., Britain, and Canada—in the affairs of continental Europe. It was, first, the extension of the North

American security guarantee via the ratification of the North Atlantic Treaty in 1949 and, second, the British-orchestrated integration of West Germany into NATO in 1955 that permitted the Europeans to set aside their ancient feuds and rivalries. The entanglement of the Americans, the British, and the Canadians in Europe defused the Hobbesian fear and insecurity that underlies most interstate military competition. By protecting Western Europe from the Russians, NATO also protected the Germans from the French, and vice versa: European integration and co-operation, however halting, would not have been feasible without the presence of external security commitments. Remove or seriously weaken those commitments and what will happen? At a minimum, each European state will look to its own security, and there is nothing in international history that would lead us to predict that the outcome will be co-operative. Without external guarantees, Josef Joffe argues, "Western Europe might revert to the pattern of interaction resembling the prewar period rather than surge forward toward true integration. The weak would once more worry about the strong, and the strong—such as Great Britain, France, and West Germany—would once more worry about one another. In such a system, the Soviet Union would not necessarily loom as the great federation but as a key player that could use its overweening strength to play one West European state against another and to dictate the terms of its relationship to them all.[1]

If the costs of remaining in NATO and Europe seem large, they should be weighed against some of the possible costs of withdrawal. The costs of preventing a war should be balanced against the costs of fighting one. A nonaligned or "Finlandized" Canada would have to spend several times what it currently does on defence merely to satisfy the Pentagon that it was not a security threat to the U.S.; and nonalignment is no guarantee of either independence or safety. A more likely outcome—it is almost a certainty—is that without the multilateral North Atlantic pact, Canada would simply have to make the best terms it could get in a far-ranging security agreement with the United States. In a sense, we would be back in the position faced by Mackenzie King's government in the first years after the war, but we would no longer have the buffering effect of the Alliance between ourselves and the U.S. This unappealing prospect would be visited upon Canada by an NDP leadership whose defence policy has hitherto been the creature of internal party politics.

## Continentalism: Tory Style

A more gradual approach to the same end—one draped in the banner of "Canada First"—is to be found in the policies of the Progressive Conservative government headed by Brian Mulroney. What we have termed in this book the ruse of sovereignty is everywhere at work in the Tory approach to security and alliances.

Canada's 1987 defence white paper argues that the country can retain and even strengthen its forces in NATO Europe and also embark on the building of a fleet of ten or more nuclear-powered submarines for the protection of the Arctic and our other two coasts. While the Conservative white paper makes a great deal of the gap between commitments and real capabilities, it adds a new and very costly obligation on a defence budget already strained to the limit. Successive reports by Senate committees, the Auditor General, and other agencies have shown that the Canadian armed forces are seriously undermanned, ill-equipped, overcentralized at the top, and lacking in reserves. The forces chose to implement the economies of the Trudeau era by centralizing and unifying, and the impression given by many of the studies is that Canada is not only unable to add new commitments, it cannot fight to protect those it already has. In particular, we have allowed our commitments in NATO to deteriorate along with the equipment: Canada's land involvement in Europe is the visible symbol, the ticket of entrance, that supports our policy of providing for our security through multilateral coalitions—a far less costly option than any feasible unilateral posture—and yet we have permitted it to rust out like an obsolescent piece of military hardware.

White papers are nothing more than statements of intent. The proof lies in what gets implemented or dropped, how many scarce dollars are devoted to which service, or which equipment project (the army alone has 164 such projects underway or in the planning stages) is selected within the budget. The Conservatives plan to increase Canadian defence spending by a minimum two per cent annually in real terms over a fifteen-year period; but even if economic conditions and politics permit this, Canada will be unable to acquire much of the new military equipment it will need if the forces are to carry out their missions. For instance, resources devoted to the nuclear-powered submarines (whose true cost is grossly underestimated in the white paper) will compete with the army's need to replace its Leopard tanks with a couple of hundred main battle tanks for use in European conventional defence, and so on. For a small power such as Canada, the sheer cost and rapid obsolescence of modern military hardware can rapidly overwhelm the defence budget. Commitments must be abandoned, and it is here in the realm of economics and technology that withdrawing to Fortress North America begins to make sense. The "hidden meaning" of the white paper lies in Prime Minister Mulroney's apparently innocuous foreword in which sovereignty and self-interest (not the prevention of war) are enshrined as the ultimate goals of Canadian policy.

In the concluding chapter, after we have completed our review of political and strategic trends across the Western Alliance, we shall return to Canada's defence debate. The point we wish to end on here is an ironic one: in the late forties, Canada helped to create NATO and rejected free trade with the United States; in the late eighties, Canada is weakening its commitment to NATO while actively seeking free trade. Can there be any real doubt about where we are going?

## CHAPTER ONE

# NATO: The Counterweight

We must therefore make it clear to the world, and especially to Great Britain, that the poppies blooming in Flanders fields have no further interest for us. We must fortify ourselves against the allurements of a British war for democracy and freedom and parliamentary institutions, and against the allurements of a League war for peace and international order. And when overseas propagandists combine the two appeals to us by urging us to join in organizing "the Peace World" to which all British nations already belong, the simplest answer is to thumb our noses at them. Whatever the pretext on which Canadian armed forces may be lured to Europe again, the actual result would be that Canadian workers and farmers would shoot down German workers and farmers, or be shot down by them, in meaningless slaughter. As the late John Ewart remarked, we should close our ears to these European blandishments and, like Ulysses and his men, sail past the European siren, our ears stuffed with tax bills. All these European troubles are not worth the bones of a Toronto grenadier.

Frank Underhill, 1939

It is obvious now that we could not afford to see Britain and France go under, and that we had to come to their help, whatever we might think of their particular policies before 1939. So, today, we cannot afford to see the United States go under, whatever we might think of the madness of Dulles and the Pentagon militarists.

Frank Underhill, 1960[1]

## Getting Involved

Prime Minister Mackenzie King had gone to Britain to attend a royal wedding but his thoughts were on war when he returned to Ottawa to brief the cabinet in December 1947 on his discussions in London with British Foreign Secretary Ernest Bevin. Bevin had compared the current European situation with that which existed in 1936. There were many ominous signs and the memories of Hitler and Munich were difficult for the British to shake. For King the thought of Europe breaking down yet again into war was "just too terrible to contemplate." The efforts to maintain the wartime unity had failed and the British acknowledged in March 1947 that they no longer had the capability to balance the shifting power in the Mediterranean. The United States took up the gauntlet. The Truman Doctrine along with a package of military assistance to Greece and Turkey was proclaimed in March. Two months later the Marshall Plan of economic assistance to the war-torn economies of Western Europe was launched. The United States was settling into its newly acquired role of superpower but the Soviet Union showed no inclination to go along. Co-operation between these two dominant states became ever more difficult and Bevin expressed his concern to King that the Council of Foreign Ministers meeting would be unable to resolve the outstanding issue of Germany and that Russian obstruction would feed American impatience and the two would soon be enjoined in battle. As Bevin predicted the council adjourned *sine die* before the end of the year with Germany still unresolved. Two months later the "coup" in Czechoslovakia confirmed its place within the Soviet sphere of influence. The ghost of Munich had come back to haunt. Developments moved even more quickly after this. Pressure mounted on Norway which, along with Denmark, approached Britain with requests for military assistance in the event of a Soviet attack. The Berlin blockade set up by the Soviets in June 1948 added to the darkening storm clouds that were gathered over Europe in that fateful year. For Lester Pearson, then a member of the Department of External Affairs, these events were foreboding. "Here we go again, it's the third time we'll be over in Europe fighting and, by God we've got to do something about it."[2] These were the seeds of the North Atlantic Treaty Organization (NATO).

The Second World War made it clear to Canadians that the isolated neutrality they had sought to protect in the prewar years was not easily reconciled with their widespread economic interests or the technology of modern warfare. To paraphrase Trotsky, Canadians may not have been interested in war but war was interested in them. The end of the war confirmed the shifts in power that would dominate the next forty years of international politics as the supermen of Europe were replaced by the superpowers, one of which lived next door and both of which were becoming linked with the weapons of modern technology; atomic bombs and intercontinental delivery systems. Canadians could not afford to be as sanguine as they had been in the twenties, when oceans and indifference separated them from the centre stage of international power plays. The United States had become the principal player and the North American continent would never be as comfortable again. The temptations of isolationism and neutrality had been replaced by a different attraction. In his Grey Lecture, Secretary of State for External Affairs Louis St. Laurent made it sound as if it had always been that way.

It has never been the opinion of any considerable number of people in Canada that this continent could live unto itself. We have seen our own interests in the wider context of the Western World. We have realized also that regionalism of any kind would not provide the answer to problems of world security. We have realized that a threat to the liberty of Western Europe, where our political ideas were nurtured was a threat to our own way of life.

The war marked a fundamental shift in global politics and Canadian foreign policy responded accordingly. In a proposal designed to cure many ills, St. Laurent, aided by his undersecretary of state for external affairs, Lester Pearson and inspired by Pearson's assistant, Escott Reid, took a radical departure from isolationism and led the country into its first alliance, a mutual security pact that would link Canada with the very states of Europe so readily disparaged in the 1930s. The European order would now receive more direct attention.

17

Canadian interests demanded the security of Western Europe and the prevention of a Soviet-American military conflict, but policy makers were still faced with some hard choices. Confronted with a public that was anxious to forget the sour taste of warfare and the misery of the regimented life of the military, Canadian forces in Europe were returned home, war assets were sold off or dismantled, and defence budgets were slashed. The Canadian armed forces, which had swelled to nearly 750,000 men and women in the midst of the war, were quickly depleted to less than one-tenth that size in 1946. Flushed with the success of victory over the Fascists, the allies had begun to forge the postwar order that would secure peace. A more activist breed of Canadian foreign service officers favoured involvement because of their belief that the country both could and should contribute to shaping the postwar order to protect Canada's vital national interests.

A continuation of the peace was foremost among the objectives of the government but there were other pressing concerns. In the reorganization of the postwar balance, Canadians clearly favoured multilateral associations that would not leave Canada subject to the overwhelming influence of her former colonial master nor to the emerging hegemony of the United States. Initially, the United Nations received all the attention. Canadian policy makers embraced it with an enthusiasm that was nowhere to be found when the League of Nations had been established a generation earlier. Whereas Canadians had worked diligently in the 1920s to limit the powers of the League, in 1945 they supported enforcement measures for the UN as the best possible means for ensuring the continuation of the fragile postwar peace. The UN could not escape the East-West conflict that degenerated into the cold war, but its failure to preserve the peace did not alter the basic multilateralist orientation of the Canadian government as Canada along with Britain and the United States began to devise alternatives that would satisfy their security needs.

Once the war fears intensified in 1947, officials in Ottawa turned their attention to a postwar alliance that would substitute for the UN without destroying it and link Canada with the United States and the countries of Western Europe. Another war in Europe would not leave Canada untouched. In the 1930s,

Canadians had avoided getting involved in European politics in the hope that they would be excused from the next war. Noninvolvement provided little security, however, and in 1939 Canadians had gone off to another European war because Canadian interests could not survive without European powers in balance and at peace. In the late 1940s policy makers were once again confronted with the prospects of war but this time they recognized that only by being actively involved in furthering European security and stability would this country have any chance of preventing that next war from occurring. As the historian J.B. Brebner wrote at the time, Canadians "knew that they could not cut themselves off from the rest of the world. Its health was their health; its disease their destruction."[3] The willingness to make a commitment to a transatlantic security pact was rooted in a recognition of the necessity for stability through deterrence. This was, of course, the premise of the United Nations, that potential aggressors would be deterred through the collective action of the member states. The failure of the general scheme of collective security through the UN gave way to the more limited objective of collective defence through the North Atlantic Alliance to ensure the security and stability of the West. Economics, politics, and culture all supported the transatlantic connections but the original motivating factor was the fear of war and the need to make a military commitment to support the fragile peace.

The first reaction to the Soviet coup in Czechoslovakia came from the states of Western Europe who on March 17, 1948 signed the Brussels Treaty; a collective defence pact of fifty years duration between Britain, France, Belgium, the Netherlands and Luxembourg. The participating states saw the treaty as a first step in deterring possible Soviet pressure. The treaty guaranteed "all the military and other aid and assistance in their power" in response to an armed attack. The primary objective, however, was to convince the Americans that the Europeans were willing to work for their own defence. Well aware of their limited capabilities and with one wary eye looking across the Atlantic at the United States, the British saw the treaty as the first step in getting the Americans to support Western Europe. British Prime Minister Clement Atlee worried that American access to bases in Canada would undermine the United Nations and encourage American isolationism because "she would thereby strengthen an important sector of the defensive glacis with which she is at present clearly bent in surrounding herself."[4] Like British policy makers of the late sixties, Atlee and Bevin realized that American isolationism would be more difficult with a Canadian commitment to Europe. In the late 1940s Canadian policy makers shared this assumption. Britain was anxious to extend the mutual defence pact across the Atlantic and Canadian leaders shared this anxiety. In fact, Canadians had already started the process.

Seven months before the Brussels Treaty was signed, Assistant Undersecretary of State for External Affairs Escott Reid had defended a collective security pact among western states as fully consistent with the UN Charter. After a public relations campaign to drum up support for the UN, policy makers were unwilling to abandon the organization or to be seen to be undermining it, but they were willing to acknowledge its failure. James Eayrs' analysis of this period concludes that "by the fall of 1947 there existed within the policy community of Canada a consensus that the time was approaching when it would be prudent and expedient to create a Western security alliance of some kind to meet the threat of Soviet imperialism and to prevent the outbreak of war."[5] Not just any sort of an alliance would do. Regional arrangements were to be avoided for fear that they would either return Canada to the fold of the British Empire or leave it encased within a North American fortress dominated by the United States. The long-standing aversion to domination from Downing Street was now blended with the sour aftertaste of American activities in Canada during and immediately after the Second World War. Concern for possible American encroachments on Canadian sovereignty was widely shared and demands for access were to be resisted. A North Atlantic alliance might help limit the pressure.

In addition to the overwhelming security considerations, Canada's commitment to NATO was strongly motivated by its relationship with the United States. The primary concern for security was informed by an equally compelling concern for Canadian independence. A policy of complete isolation would do little to secure Canadian interests in prosperity, peace, and independence which were (and continue to be) linked to a stable European order. A policy of neutrality or nonalignment carried the risk of leaving Canada fully exposed to American pressure. By getting the United States involved in a multilateral alliance the Canadian government thought it could limit American pressure on Canadian territory by making it part of a collective activity. Canada's ambassador in Washington in 1948, Hume Wrong, used this argument in his successful effort to convince a reluctant George Kennan, then an advisor in the U.S. State Department, to support American involvement in NATO.

> It would be far more difficult for Canada to collaborate in planning defence against Soviet aggression on the basis of a unilateral U.S. assurance than it would be if both countries were parties to an Atlantic agreement. Furthermore, under such an agreement the joint planning of the defence of North America fell into place as part of a larger whole and would diminish difficulties arising from fears of invasion of Canadian sovereignty by the U.S. It would be easier to advocate a policy of Canadian aloofness if the present state of affairs was maintained. An Atlantic pact would go a long way towards curing our split personality in defence matters by bringing the U.S., the U.K. and Canada into regular partnership.[6]

The active participation of Canada and the United States in the North Atlantic Alliance not only extended our defence perimeter to Western Europe, it also worked to fend off what was by the late 1940s becoming excessive American pressure for Canadian contributions to continental defence. Not only would the Americans be reassured that Canada would remain faithful to the cause but the Alliance itself would help to limit the need to secure the North American continent in response to European instability.

> The close military alliance of the United States and western Europe is of paramount importance to Canada as it removes Canada from the front line of the American defence perimeter (and) by discouraging the development of new threats to American security which, besides posing a direct military col-

lateral threat to Canada, could terminate American toleration of the independent policy of Canada.[7]

Paradoxically, in light of the repeatedly expressed concerns about American domination within the Alliance, NATO was viewed from the very beginning as the counterweight to a narrower American-dominated continental defence scheme in which the United States would hold preponderant power. You were less likely to get raped, said one Canadian diplomat, if there were fifteen in the bed. This remains one of the most compelling rationales for Canadian involvement in NATO.

It is common today to view NATO as little more than an American-dominated military arrangement in which member states respond to the demands of the Pentagon. When NATO was first established, however, the United States was at best a reluctant partner. Many Americans in the late 1940s, including Kennan and his colleague Charles Bohlen believed that European security could be guaranteed by a statement by the United States president that the Americans would come to the aid of Western European nations if ever they were confronted with a Soviet attack. They believed that a verbal commitment would both reassure the Europeans and deter the Soviets. After watching the Americans wait on the sidelines at the start of the last two wars, Canadians and Europeans alike were less than reassured by a mere declaration of intent. They also thought it unlikely the Russians would be effectively deterred. Well aware of the earlier reticence of Americans to jump into the fray, both Canadians and Europeans for their own peace of mind and to unsettle the Soviets, wanted the Americans to make clear beforehand their willingness to get involved from the start. NATO was designed not only to deter the Soviets but also to link the United States as directly as possible to Western Europe, to compel them to get involved in the next war from the beginning. Conditioned by their experiences during the last war, the member states supported an Alliance that would make clear to the Russians that the states of Western Europe, Canada, and the United States would consolidate their capabilities in any future conflict and fight together from the start. Stalin was to get the message that had never been delivered to Hitler.

Deterring the Soviet Union was not the only problem; nor was ensuring an American commitment. There was also the need to impose some restraints on the United States. Policy makers in Ottawa expressed concern that the Americans might push too hard and too fast in trying to roll back Soviet advances in Eastern Europe, or that they might undertake a "preventive war" while they enjoyed a monopoly of nuclear weapons, to rid Europe of the Soviet menace. "It seems to me," John Holmes cabled from his post at the Canadian embassy in Moscow in 1948, "of desperate importance that we use our considerable influence in the coming months to prevent the United States from taking heady action without calculating the consequences."[8] NATO was seen as the instrument by which militant militarism in the United States would be constrained in the early years of the cold war. The British and French shared these concerns and the Canadians played on these fears to press the latter to join the Alliance. Everyone concerned realized that if the Soviets and the Americans went to war Canada could not avoid being involved. In Ottawa, war-avoidance took precedence over an anti-Communist crusade and a desire to limit Soviet expansion was tempered with the recognition that the ideological animosity that divided the superpowers might cause either one of them to light the fuse that would touch off the next war. The Soviets were to be deterred, not goaded into a war.

The European members of the Alliance were another matter. They were not immune to continentalist pressures of their own. Just as Canadian officials tended to concentrate on their biggest problem, the United States, Europeans concentrated on theirs—Germany. Twice in the century Canadians had been called to Europe to help the continent control German power. They did not want to be called upon a third time. The European balance of power had to be managed and while a minor power could do little on its own it might be of some use in supporting like-minded states. The Alliance provided Canadians with their best chance to get involved before the shooting started. Although relegated to a seat on the bench as the occupying powers attempted to define an acceptable settlement in Germany, Canadians were not ambivalent to the settlement. European stability had to be maintained and those revolutionary states who wished to upset the balance had to be constrained. Unilateralism would need to be muted and security no longer left for states to decide on their own terms. The opportunities for war were to be limited by linking the European states in an arrangement for collective defence.

Security was, however, not the only issue. Canadians also worried about economic conditions. Britain was still an important trading partner and the states on the continent were potential markets. Europeans would provide the alternative to the American economic and political absorption that so worried MacKenzie King. King rejected the free trade agreement concluded with the United States in 1948 on the grounds that Canadian interests were best served through a wider free trade arrangement with the European states. A security pact would, in his view, facilitate such an arrangement. It would not be a simple matter, however, as Canadian leaders were aware that the Europeans would need help in looking beyond their own continent.

> European economic integration could very easily mean the creation of new trade barriers against Canadian imports; and military co-operation amongst the countries of western Europe could mean a great growth in neutralist sentiment. Both these possibilities would imperil the success of the North Atlantic treaty. They would be particularly dangerous for Canada since we would be left to deal with the United States on our own and almost inevitably would sink into a policy of simple continentalism.[9]

The fear that increasing European economic and military integration would lead to a growth in neutralism in Europe has been the scourge of two generations of Canadians. Containing the continent's power politics and assuaging its nationalist aspirations were central objectives of the treaty. The potential integration of the continent might swing the pendulum too far in the other direction. Europe's importance to Canada was and remains much more than a potential source of global disorder. By maintaining security and economic links with the nations of Western Europe, Canada can withstand some of the more disconcerting aspects of American strategy.

Membership in NATO was seen as a way to enhance Canada's ability to assert its own interests effectively "not by a strategy that defends these interests in a vacuum of sovereign isolation but by one which seeks to influence the wider interdependent environment to which it feels bound by common interest and sentiment."[10]

## Being There

The North Atlantic Treaty was signed in Washington on April 4, 1949. Canada, the United States, and Britain had initiated secret negotiations in July of the previous year. They were joined by France, Norway, Denmark, Belgium, Luxembourg, and the Netherlands at the signing. The signing of the treaty did not lead to rapid changes in Europe or in North America. The treaty had been concluded to counter the potential threat of Soviet expansion in Europe. It was very much the product of fear, but it was initially viewed more as a means of psychological and political reassurance to the member states than as a military deterrent to the Soviets. Neither was the Alliance designed as a vehicle for an anti-Communist crusade. Such a crusade may have been of interest to some and there is little doubt that the St. Laurent government in 1948 realized that the threat of godless communism would win support for the Alliance in the isolationist parishes of rural Quebec. For the most part, however, policy makers were not motivated by anti-Communist zeal and had little interest in reforming Soviet society. The threat of war was enough to bring the treaty into effect.

In negotiating the treaty some Canadian officials and particularly Escott Reid favoured an agreement that would go beyond military co-operation and commitments. Reid and others successfully pressed for the inclusion of Article 2—the so-called Canadian article—in the final treaty draft. Article 2 called on the signatories to "encourage economic collaboration" among themselves and to strengthen their "free institutions" and "the principles upon which these institutions are founded." Including these commitments in the treaty would, in Reid's view, emphasize the strongest element of the Alliance—the liberal democratic character of its founding members. As a longer-term objective, Reid and others thought that co-operation in these nonmilitary fields would ensure a more permanent transatlantic security community. It was also believed in some quarters that the political, economic, and social links among Alliance members would be the most effective deterrent to the threat of Soviet subversion within the war torn societies of Western Europe.

The reluctance on the part of Canadian officials to describe NATO as a military alliance was also in part an indication of their fear of public opposition to Canadian participation. From the government's perspective Canada's unmilitary people were not likely to support an alliance that rested on brute force alone. It is evident, for example, that Pearson was attempting to quell potential opposition to the treaty when he told the House of Commons in February 1949 that: "NATO must not become merely a screen for narrow nationalist suspicions and fears, an instrument of unimaginative militarism or an agency of power politics or imperialistic ambitions of any of its members." The appeal for public support was one obvious reason why the government had negotiated the inclusion of Article 2 in the treaty and emphasized this in presenting the treaty to the Canadian public. The appeal was successful; the treaty was widely supported within Canada with only two dissenting votes when it was brought before the House of Commons for approval. This widespread popular support for the Alliance only began to fade when Canada and other allies were called upon to make their military commitments tangible.

During its first year in existence the Alliance operated as a mutual support system. If it meant anything for levels of national military spending, it was seen as the most likely method for limiting military expenditures because the capabilities of member states would be pooled and adversaries would be matched against the collective forces of the member states. Deterrence would be achieved by the political commitment of mutual support, not by large stockpiles of weapons. Within fourteen months of its founding, however, this political commitment placed demands on Canadian forces and defence expenditures that were not expected when the treaty was signed in 1949.

The militarization of NATO occurred in the wake of the outbreak of hostilities in Korea in June 1950. Until this time members of the Alliance were resting, however uncomfortably, with the view that the primary threat was one of domestic subversion of the weakened states of Western Europe. The proper response to this was economic and political support for the reconstruction of Western European economies and societies, with some military aid for the depleted reserves of the European members of the Alliance. The Korean War changed this. There was now a widely shared belief that peace was threatened and that the Soviets would use force to redistribute the postwar balance of power. While there was some concern for the conflict in Korea most Canadians continued to view Europe as of primary importance. As Pearson and Brooke Claxton, the minister of national defence, consistently repeated, the main front was in Europe. And Europe did not look good. "All in all, there isn't a great deal over here with which to wage war," was how Canada's representative in Bonn described the situation in a memo to Ottawa.[11] There was widespread fear that the Russians were simply instigating conflicts in peripheral areas as a diversionary tactic to draw attention and troops away from the central European front. Despite profound differences with the United States over the conduct of the war in Korea, Canadians shared with them the view that the danger of Soviet aggression was now in need of a response.

The war had a major effect on western thinking and generated support for higher defence expenditures, unprecedented large peacetime armed forces, and, for the first time in peacetime, the deployment of Canadian forces to Europe. Canadian defence expenditures rose rapidly to postwar levels never before imagined, rising from $385 million in 1950 to $1.7 billion four years later. This marked a watershed not only in Canada's involvement in the cold war but in the membership and organization of the Alliance as well. Membership was expanded to include Turkey and Greece, discussions began on West Germany's rearmament and potential contribution to the Alliance and the formal organization of NATO was established. The focus of the Alliance's concerns became primarily military in character and an integrated military command Supreme Headquarters Allied Powers Europe was established. American General Dwight Eisenhower was appointed the first Supreme Allied Commander of NATO's integrated multinational force. All subsequent commanders have also been American. One of the largest peacetime collective military forces began to take shape. What had previously been viewed as a struggle that was best fought with economic and political weapons now became a military confrontation and a test of nerves between two heavily armed blocs. The cold war was now on in earnest and the shift in temperature and NATO's response brought Canadian troops back to Europe. In the autumn of 1951 the 27th Infantry Brigade was dispatched to the central front. Eisenhower maintained that the deployments were in response to an emergency but that "on a long-term basis, each important geographical area must be defended primarily by the people of that region."[12] Despite this, Canadian forces have remained in Europe ever since. They have also remained a major point of contention.

The militarization of NATO brought on by the Korean War continued at the North Atlantic Council meeting of February 1952 in Lisbon. Frightened by the prospects of a conventional war and less convinced of the credibility of American atomic weapons in light of the Soviets' demonstrated nuclear capacity, NATO members were pressed by Eisenhower to increase their conventional forces dramatically from about twelve divisions in 1952 to ninety-six divisions by 1954, with twenty-five of these at battle readiness on the central front. The "shield" of conventional forces had to be strengthened to enhance the "sword" of NATO's nuclear deterrent. The Alliance's new military mandate was greeted with disdain by some in Canada. M.J. Coldwell, leader of the CCF, spoke for many who had supported the Alliance in 1949 when he informed the House of Commons in 1952 that "the policy outlined at Lisbon jeopardizes the peaceful and defensive objectives which brought the Organization into being."[13] Co-operation in nonmilitary areas had not materialized and the concentration on the military aspects of the Alliance even worried Pearson. As Alliance members, including Canada, failed to meet the conventional requirements requested by NATO headquarters in 1952, concern grew within allied headquarters about the alleged "gap" between the forces available to deter the Soviets and the forces required. The gospel of a conventional imbalance was proclaimed and the Alliance became even more reliant on the nuclear guarantee. This only made matters worse for many Canadians.

Canadians have never been comfortable with the military aspects of NATO. This is especially evident when it involves the nuclear strategy of the Alliance. The criticisms which greeted NATO's military response to the Korean War intensified later in the 1950s when the United States began to deploy "tactical" nuclear weapons to Europe to be used by NATO forces. This deployment raised opposing fears among NATO governments. A fear of abandonment by the Americans in the face of growing Soviet nuclear capabilities was countered by a fear of being trapped in a limited nuclear war confined to the European continent; an option that was being widely discussed by American strategists in the late 1950s. At a NATO heads of government meeting in Paris in 1957, the United States proposed to increase its stockpile of nuclear warheads in Europe and to place these weapons and some intermediate-range missiles at the disposal of NATO's Supreme Commander. The proposal was not widely applauded because of its potentially destabilizing consequences and according to an *Economist* leader in January 1958, Canada "was just about the first to object to Washington's proposal." Despite the concerns expressed at the Paris meeting, within two years Canada had "accepted without question its tasks under the 1957 'overall Strategic Concept for the NATO Area' . . . and consequently acquired and deployed in Europe the CF-104 Starfighter nuclear strike aircraft and the Honest John surface-to-surface missile."[14] It had been much easier to ignore matters of nuclear deterrence when Canadians were not in a position to pull the trigger, but when NATO commitments combined with the deployment of nuclear weapons in Canada, Canadians had their own nuclear role to condemn along with the nuclear strategies of the Alliance.

By the early 1960s opposition to Canada's Alliance membership began to spread. James Minifie, a Washington-based correspondent with the CBC, in a widely read book *Peacemaker or Powdermonkey* first published in 1960, argued that Canada should withdraw from its alliance with the United States and the nations of Western Europe and cancel its bilateral agreement with the United States for the joint air defence of North America. By pursuing this option, Minifie argued that Canada could then act as the shining light of nonalignment that would lead the Third World out of the darkness of the cold war. Minifie viewed

NATO as nothing more than "an excuse for maintaining American forces in Europe." Like many of the critics that followed, he had difficulty separating NATO from NORAD and saw both as mere extensions of American foreign policy. Arguing that the United States had now become the world's dominant imperial power, Minifie suggested that Canada had little to choose between a world ruled from Washington and one ruled from Moscow. Minifie cast a plague on both their houses. The nonaligned option for Canada in the cold war was not a new proposal and its advocates have since the late 1940s voiced their concerns, not about being caught on the sabre of Britain's imperial ambitions or dragged into wars on the European continent, but about the possibility of being dominated and ultimately overwhelmed by too close an association with the United States. In the late 1940s Harold Innis wrote that: "Whatever hope of continued autonomy Canada may have in the future must depend on her success in withstanding American influence and assisting in the development of a third bloc designed to withstand the pressure of the United States and Russia."[15] A nonaligned Canada would not be isolated from the corridors of international power but instead would act as a trenchant voice in support of the oppressed peoples of Latin America in their resistance against American imperialism. Discounting pacifist responses as unrealisitic, Minifie acknowledged that Canada would have to maintain sufficient military capabilities with which to reassure American security concerns but once this task was completed would be able to roam free, unshackled by the binds of alliances, to influence the course of international politics.

Minifie's solitary cry flourished into a crescendo during the 1960s as he was joined by a number of articulate Canadians who opposed the government's defence policies. Encouraged by the nuclear weapons debates during the last days of the Diefenbaker government and further incited by the excesses of the Vietnam War as it began to appear on television screens in the late 1960s, Canada's foreign and defence policies were subjected to a sustained critique. For most, however, the main problem was the United States. Andrew Brewin, who during this period was the NDP's defence policy critic in the House of Commons, correctly observed that those who opposed a continuation of

Canada's Alliance commitments were "really not so much concerned with (NATO) as they are with disentangling us from the partnership with the United States."[16] The emerging antiwar movement in the United States generated much sympathy in Canada and was influential in convincing Prime Minister Pearson to be among the first of the United States' allies to criticize the American military campaign in Vietnam. Despite his concerns, Pearson made it clear that he would not sever all military ties with the United States when he informed a group of University of Toronto professors that Canada could not stop arms shipments to the U.S. under the Defence Production Sharing Agreement because it would be tantamount to abandoning Canada's Alliance membership. Many thus saw Canada's relationship with the United States within NATO as leaving the country little choice but to collaborate with the American war effort. For them the conclusion was simple—if the Alliance dragged Canada into such complicity with the United States then Canada should abandon the Alliance.

Growing domestic criticism of the country's Alliance membership was matched by the government's interest in realigning Canada's armed forces. Since the early 1950s Canada's armed forces had been designed to serve NATO and NORAD commitments. The nuclear weapons debate of the early 1960s had demonstrated the need to reassess if and how the country should support these commitments. Canada's nuclear angst began to subside after Pearson's Liberal government accepted nuclear weapons for the armed forces in 1964 with a commitment to get out of these nuclear roles as soon as possible. There were also other interests that needed to be served. Canadians had become active supporters of United Nations-sponsored peacekeeping forces and a white paper on defence policy presented in 1964 identified peacekeeping as the priority role for the Canadian armed forces. Military contributions to NATO and NORAD were considered of secondary importance at the time. Realigning force commitments was also encouraged by a desire to reduce defence spending in response to the pressure placed on the federal purse from an expansion of social programs. In an attempt to meet these priorities the government favoured military commitments which would limit the forces needed in Europe and would complement the interest in peacekeeping. The preferred alternative appeared to be mobile forces that could be sent to NATO's northern or southern flanks in times of crisis and in 1967 the government assumed a commitment to reinforce Norway in a crisis with the Canadian Air Sea Transportable Brigade (CAST).

This did not entirely satisfy domestic critics of Canadian defence policy. Some thought the government should leave NATO and concentrate on peacekeeping. Eric Kierans, a member of the Trudeau cabinet and a vocal opponent of Canadian involvement in NATO, pressed for the removal of Canadian forces from Europe to assist in peacekeeping operations in places like Vietnam. The emphasis on peacekeeping was also challenged after Egyptian President Gamal Nasser dismissed the UN Emergency Force from the Sinai Peninsula in 1967 before launching an attack on Israel. This had been one of Canada's largest and most successful peacekeeping operations but its dismissal by Nasser and the ensuing war in the Middle East intensified criticisms of peacekeeping and Canadian involvement in such operations. The emergence of detente in East-West relations provided an additional motivation for Canada to reconsider its Alliance membership and the need for Canadian forces in Western Europe. With the election of the Trudeau government in 1968, European commitments were subjected to additional challenges by what were seen as more pressing domestic and continental concerns. James Eayrs maintained that "With the St. Lawrence as turbid as it is today, it is blind to keep watch on the Rhine . . . the imperatives of classic isolationism—can be justified if it means putting our house in order."[17] Trudeau himself expressed concern about the prospects of American urban violence spilling over into Canada's metropolitan areas. The gist of all of these arguments was that the main threat was no longer across the Atlantic; it was right here at home and the military would be needed to deal with it.

Although many commentators considered it significant that the Trudeau government decided to remain within NATO, it did signal a significant shift in defence policy when it halved Canadian force levels in Europe in 1969. The reduction was made to meet allegedly pressing defence requirements at home. Sovereignty had become the government's top defence priority. The withdrawal implied that continued Canadian participation in

NATO was no longer considered essential. Instead, as Bruce Thordarson concluded in his authoritative account "the decision to emphasize sovereignty appears to have been inspired by the belief that defence policy had to be based on national interests that were more North American-oriented than were contributions to world peace and security through participation in NATO. Mr. Trudeau explained that the redefinition of the roles of the Canadian Armed Forces that this implied was intended to reassure the CAF personnel, and 'especially' to convince the public, that there was a valid role for armed forces in Canada."[18]

The Trudeau government's realignment of defence priorities substantially diminished Canada's military contribution to NATO. In addition to halving the size of the Canadian contingent in West Germany, the government also withdrew the RCAF from the nuclear strike role in central Europe. Finally, in decommissioning the HMCS *Bonaventure*, the government erased its most significant contribution to the Alliance's antisubmarine warfare tasks. These cuts were only partially compensated for by the commitment of the CAST Brigade for deployment to Norway. General Paul Manson, the chief of Defence Staff outlined the problems this created for the military in a presentation to the Senate Committee on National Defence in May 1987.

The effect of the (1971 White Paper) on the land forces was to reverse the priority of its missions, with all that that implies. Its presence in Germany was reduced from approximately 6000 troops in a mechanized formation located in the forward area as part of the British Army of the Rhine, to a light brigade of about 3000 troops relocated in the Lahr area of southern Germany in a reserve role. As well, 1969 saw the start of a three-year budget freeze for the Canadian forces which reduced the regular army from then 45,000 to about 25,000 men, and the militia from 24,000 down to about 13,500 . . . In many respects it was evident that mere survival would be the order of the day for the army, and to retain some vestige of a credible combat system, brigade groups were sharply reduced in scope and capability to smaller combat groups. The latter were very much ad hoc organizations, and incapable of meeting the needs of modern high intensity combat, such as would be found in Europe.

The loss of military credibility was not easily overcome despite the best efforts of the armed forces. The political credibility of Canada's commitment to Europe was also tarnished but in this area the recovery came more easily.

The Europeans took great exception to Canada's new NATO policy and let their views be known to Defence Minister Leo Cadieux at a NATO ministerial meeting in May 1969 with what the American ambassador to NATO later described as "the toughest talk I have ever heard in an international meeting."[19] Germany was concerned about Canada's reliability in times of crisis. Britain feared that it would be called upon to replace the Canadians. Others questioned the timing, coming as it did shortly after the Soviet occupation of Czechoslovakia and before talks with the Soviets on conventional force reductions. Many thought the Canadians would provide the excuse the Americans were looking for to withdraw some of their forces. British Defence Secretary Denis Healey complained that Canada "is passing the buck to the rest of us" and argued that the withdrawal of Canadian forces would lower the nuclear threshold. Canadians may have been surprised to learn that the decision was taken so seriously by the Europeans for it implied a more significant Canadian contribution to conventional defence than most Canadians were willing to believe. As John Holmes has written, however, the reaction attests to the fact that "it is only when Canada grows restless do others notice its participation at all."[20]

The complaints had little effect. European dissent was not matched by the Americans, who appeared less concerned over the Canadian decision. Perhaps this was the result of their awareness of Canadian sensitivity to complaints from the State Department on matters of Canadian defence policy, or perhaps it was that Trudeau's NATO policy in no way challenged the close bilateral military ties that had linked Canada with the United States since the late 1940s and had been the source of many of the complaints of nationalists during the 1960s. There was, for example, no expressed interest in cancelling the Defence Production Sharing Agreement which in the view of many critics had dragged Canada into complicity with the American war in Vietnam. Nor was there any move to abrogate NORAD which entrusted the RCAF to the USAF for the continental air defence of North America. Oddly, while the decision seemed designed in part to mollify those who had criticized Canada's close military ties with the United States, the aspects of Canadian defence policy which more than any others subjected Canada to American influence went untouched.

The political and economic implications of Trudeau's NATO decison became clearer two years later when the American government imposed a surcharge on imports in an effort to reduce the United States' trade imbalance with the rest of the world. The so-called Nixon Shock of 1971 made Canadians, at least those who needed the reminder, acutely aware that this country was extremely vulnerable to the whims of American policy. The Trudeau government got the message. Recognizing that there were no favours to be had among American policy makers concerned with their own national advantage and less willing to absorb the costs of pleasing allies, Trudeau returned to Europe cap in hand to find an alternative to continentalism. Canada needed to maintain contact with other power centres to avoid the full brunt of America's efforts to restore its hegemony and to shape the international order in its own interests. For the Trudeau government the immediate concern was to restore the tattered ties to Western Europe and repair the damage that had been done by its 1969 decision to reduce NATO troop commitments. While the initial and immediate interests of the Liberal government were to use Western Europe as a counterweight to American economic influence, the channel for getting access to the European Community was NATO. As one Tory MP remarked at the time "the contractual link was to be tied with a NATO knot." Through a series of policy shifts and weapons acquisitions NATO was gradually and effectively, if never officially, resurrected as the centrepiece of Canadian defence policy. As in the late 1940s, there was the explicit recognition that Canada needed a good working relationship with the states of Western Europe to withstand the pressures of continentalism and that the price of this good relationship was a firm military commitment in Europe.

## The Second Track

Canada's commitment to NATO has not been simply a matter of the commerce cart dragging the defence policy horse. NATO membership is also Canada's most effective opportunity for contributing to a moderation of the conditions that fuel conflict within the Alliance and between it and its principal adversary, the Soviet Union. Some critics contend that Canada's membership in the Alliance makes it impossible for us to play any useful role in the East-West conflict or in other areas of international politics. Such criticism overlooks the fact that members of the Alliance are not concerned solely with the military balance and view the Alliance as a vital point of political contact with the Soviet Union. War prevention has to be pursued from the playing field, not from the sidelines. Despite reducing Canadian forces in Europe, Trudeau informed the House of Commons that the "search for detente . . . is one of the compelling reasons for remaining a member of NATO." Membership alone is of course no guarantee of influence. One must have a policy to sell. While quick to condemn other allies for their lack of vision, Canadians have often been negligent in offering their own alternatives. "On a number of important issues—the neutron bomb, the nuclear modernization in Europe, or NATO's long-term defence program what has passed for Canadian policy has been nothing more than cautious, sometimes qualified, often tacit, acquiesence in multilateral decisions."[21] Membership in the Alliance is of particular significance for Canada, which might otherwise lack the geographic, let alone the political and military rationale for being directly involved in negotiations over the distribution of military power and other political settlements on the European continent. Having paid the human and material costs of fighting in two European wars in which they had little opportunity to offer opinions and retaining interests in a stable European order, Canadian policy makers have chosen to stay close to the discussions since 1945, adopting what Escott Reid referred to as the Pearson Doctrine.

> Since Canada is committed under the North Atlantic treaty to help defend the North Atlantic community if war breaks out, the Canadian government must do its best to ensure that war does not break out. This means among other things,

that the Canadian government should take advantage of every opportunity to comment on the foreign policies of its allies if it believed that those policies might increase the risks of war.[22]

Canadians have frequently been at the forefront of the Alliance in pressing for the resolution of conflicts through diplomacy and advocating a strong commitment to detente on the part of the Alliance in its relations with the Soviet bloc. Pearson was among the first ranking officials from a NATO country to travel to the Soviet Union during the 1950s. As early as 1964, then-Secretary of State for External Affairs Paul Martin proposed to the NATO Council that the Alliance pursue a two-track approach in dealing with the Soviet Union. Martin's intervention was premature but three years later in 1967 these ideas received official support when the NATO Council adopted the Harmel Report. The Harmel Report on "The Future Tasks of the Alliance" was intended not only as NATO's strategy for managing East-West relations but also as a means of revitalizing a wavering western consensus for the Alliance. The allies recognized that popular support for NATO was essential if it was to survive beyond its twentieth anniversary. In the aftermath of the French withdrawal from NATO's integrated military command in 1966 and nearing the end of its original mandate, in the Harmel Report the allies committed the Alliance to a two-track approach to East-West relations. The first track was "to deter aggression and other forms of pressure and to defend the territory of member countries if aggression should occur." The second track was "to pursue the search for progress towards a more stable relationship in which the underlying political issues can be solved." Indicative of a European conception of detente, widely shared in Canada, the report made it clear that the relaxation of tensions was not the final goal but was part of a "long-term process to better promote better relations and to foster a European settlement."[23] The ultimate political purpose of the Alliance, according to the report, was "to achieve a just and lasting peaceful order in Europe accompanied by appropriate security guarantees." If this created the impression that members of the Alliance were in agreement on the objectives of detente or the means to achieve it, then Harmel's report was illusory. The Alliance has always been an amalgam of different national interests pursued through a collective mechanism. Detente would not be any different. For Canada, as for many of the smaller European states, detente was necessary to reduce the risks of war and to allow for co-operation in areas of diplomacy including arms control. Canadian actions in pursuit of these objectives were also most likely to be influential when they were channelled through multilateral negotiations and were seen to be part of a collective effort. Having committed forces to Europe and as a member of NATO, Canada was able to participate in the Conference on Security and Co-operation in Europe, the recently concluded Conference on Confidence and Security-Building Measures and Disarmament in Europe, and the negotiations on mutual and balanced force reductions.

The Canadian commitment to detente was evident in its support for Harmel and in the government's subsequent interest in restraining the more militant western reactions to the Soviet invasion of Czechoslovakia in August 1968. In an attempt to moderate the allied response, at the meeting of the North Atlantic Council held in mid-November 1968 the Canadian delegation "urged that the communique should clearly reaffirm the Alliance's pursuit of detente, together with the achievement of arms control and disarmament measures, as its long-term objectives," then-Defence Minister Mitchell Sharp informed the House of Commons in December. In maintaining a commitment to the principles of the Harmel Report, the Alliance was able to avoid deterioration in East-West relations such as later occurred after the Soviet invasion of Afghanistan in December 1979. Beginning in 1969 and for much of the next decade, detente guided East-West relations.

Detente became a useful guide for interbloc relations during the 1970s because it was able to gloss over many of the intrabloc conflicts. Although Alliance members shared a commitment to shift East-West relations away from the military containment of the 1950s and early 1960s, they diverged widely on the more immediate objectives and on their expectations of the proper Soviet response. For many European members of the Alliance, and indeed for many Canadians, detente was viewed as a process for a normalization of relations on the European continent. It was seen as an opportunity to move beyond the confrontational politics of the postwar period to more extensive economic, cultural, and political interaction. It provided the members of the Alliance, including Canada, with room to manoeuvre as the pressures for bloc solidarity were eased. For the French it met objectives of national prestige. For the Germans it gave hope of unification. Through a process of expanded economic and political exchanges, multilateral negotiations on the political and military dimensions of the conflict and support for superpower arms control, the allies used diplomatic means to support their collective security interests; strategy was to act as the handmaiden of policy, not its mistress. Far from viewing detente pejoratively, as synonymous with appeasement (another old French term with honourable connotations before Chamberlain), the leaders of NATO saw a policy of relaxing tensions, taking measures to prevent nuclear war, and banning ballistic missile defences as advancing the security interests of the West. Detente and security were still viewed as complementary.

Both the Americans and the Soviets wanted more from detente than they actually gained. In the grand tradition of popular democracy, expectations of the victories to be won and the power that could be wielded were inflated. Perhaps its global vision was of greatest significance in determining the United States' final assessment of detente.

> We insisted that progress in superpower relations, to be real, had to be made on a broad front. Events in different parts of the world, in our view, were related to each other; even more so, Soviet conduct in different parts of the world. We proceeded from the premise that to separate issues into distinct compartments would encourage the Soviet leaders to believe that they could use co-operation in one area as a safety valve while striving for unilateral advantages elsewhere. This was unacceptable.[24]

For Americans like Kissinger, detente was merely another recipe for containment. Linkage became the centrepiece of bipolar detente between the superpowers and unlike the inter-European detente being conducted by the Germans and the French and the multilateral detente of conventional arms control and the Conference on Security and Co-operation in Europe, bipolar detente created unease within the Alliance. Linkage meant that everything was connected and that everything was vulnerable. To the Europeans it meant that improved relations between, say, the two Germanys might be sacrificed because of a superpower tempest over Angola or Central America; or that an arms control accord might be held hostage to American domestic concerns over Jewish emigration from Russia. Added to this was European anxiety that an accord between the superpowers might weaken U.S. nuclear guarantees or reinforce neoisolationist sentiments with corresponding demands for the withdrawal of American troops. These European concerns were matched by an American fear of a race to Moscow by the allies.

The differences within the Alliance were complicated further by the Soviet view that support for national liberation movements and revolutionary class struggle were totally consistent with detente. In their view Europe remained the central theatre of East-West relations and a European settlement would facilitate a more effective Soviet foreign policy throughout the Third World. Not incidentally, it would also provide them with the recognition of superpower status which had long been sought. Most importantly, the Soviets rejected the idea that detente would be used to allow the United States to dictate their foreign and domestic policies.

The conflicting objectives of detente were not easily reconciled and unlike Europe where the shared cultural, economic, and political interests had generated a solid domestic constituency in support of detente, there was very fragile support in the United States. The demise of detente between the superpowers in the mid-to-late seventies was accompanied by a sharp divergence between the United States and its allies. The comfort that detente had provided to Canada was seriously threatened by the return of cold war policies of confrontation and military containment by the Carter and Reagan administrations. By the early 1980s, the rift had deepened when the extreme-right wing of the American polity wanted to pursue a policy of calculated and gradual coercion backed by superior military strength and to "foster the seeds of destruction within the Soviet system." For the new cold warriors, the military and economic resources of the Western Alliance should be used to punish the Soviets, to destabilize the Communist bloc, to force Moscow to make far-reaching concessions. Beneath the strategy lay a deeply fixed belief that Soviet communism was "the focus of evil"—to which the only safe answers were a great buildup in military strength and a return to hegemonic control of the Western Alliance.

The demise of detente and the resurgence of the policies of containment through military pressure in the United States were the source of considerable concern in Canada. The 1970s had reminded the Trudeau government of the necessity of the Western Alliance for the exercise of Canadian foreign policy. The coming of the second cold war heralded not only the deterioration of superpower relations and the pressure for military contributions that went along with this, it also threatened Alliance unity as the Europeans tried to prevent the loss of the economic and political gains of the 1970s. The deterioration of intra-Alliance relations over the pipeline sanctions issue (see the discussion in chapter Six) was enough to encourage Canada to assist in settling American-European differences over sanctions at a special meeting of NATO foreign ministers in Montreal in the autumn of 1982. The further breakdown in superpower relations resulting from the downing of KAL 007 by the Soviet Union in September 1983 and the Soviet withdrawal from the intermediate-nuclear-force negotiations in Geneva in November of the same year were the inspiration for a more unilateralist Canadian initiative.

The utility as well as the limitations of Canada's Alliance membership for facilitating Canadian input in East-West relations were most evident at the time of the Trudeau peace initiative in 1983. In conducting what one NATO military officer referred to disparagingly as a "world walkabout," Trudeau rejected the niceties of formal, discreet consultation with NATO allies and pursued a highly publicized independent course. Trudeau emphasized five major objectives during his initiative— a five-power conference of the nuclear powers under the auspices of the UN; an extension of the Non-Proliferation Treaty to countries such as India and Pakistan; the attendance of foreign ministers at the inaugural meeting of the Conference on Disarmament in Europe scheduled to convene in Stockholm in January 1984; to devise new NATO proposals for the negotiations on conventional forces; and specific arms control proposals in the areas of verification and antisatellite weapons. While Trudeau was careful to keep his proposals in line with Alliance policies, the unilateralist style of the initiative was the cause of some concern within the Alliance even among those governments who were sympathetic to the substance of Trudeau's proposals. What support there was for the initiative was based on the shared interests of many NATO members and especially France and West Germany, who were moving in a similar direction, with the former proposing that foreign ministers attend the Stockholm meetings in January 1984 and the latter pressing to get an Alliance commitment to renew contacts with the Soviet Union despite the Soviet walkout from the Geneva arms control negotiations in November 1983. In addition, earlier in the year Belgian Foreign Minister Leo Tindemanns had received approval from NATO ministers to produce an update to the Harmel Report of 1967. It was thus evident that while acting unilaterally Trudeau was not acting in isolation.

Part of the difficulty that Trudeau encountered within the Alliance was the result of his own past lack of attention to transatlantic relations. Canada had suffered a loss of credibility within the Alliance as a result of its unilateral withdrawal of forces in 1969. Trudeau's belated recognition of NATO's significance for the conduct of Canadian foreign policy in East-West relations and his purchase of Leopard tanks from West Germany in 1975, were of some help in getting a positive response from Germany for his initiative. Trudeau had realized that "Bonn's support in Brussels, which was counted on, could not be secured with a merely nominal Canadian presence in Germany."[25] Being a paid-up member of the club was also of some probable value in opening doors in Eastern Europe and the Soviet Union.

NATO connections had helped to give the peace initiative much-needed political support from western powers. Many Europeans had previously noted the need for Canada to commit itself to NATO if it hoped to derive any influence in intra-Alliance or East-West relations. It was also evident that active Canadian involvement was welcomed, especially by some of the smaller members of the Alliance, such as the Dutch who "looked to Canada to strengthen what were seen as weakened transatlantic ties" and "saw Canada's position as a middle power like the European nations, but possessing a special relationship with the

U.S. as ideal for restoring the alliance's cohesion."[26] The success of the peace initiative was evidence of the constructive role that Canada could play in East-West relations, but its success in stemming the further deterioration in superpower relations and reviving a failing process of detente resulted from the collaboration and support of Canada's NATO allies, which had only been secured through a solid commitment to collective defence.


## An Uneasy Ally

Many Canadians have grown uncomfortable with the security arrangements that have dominated Canada's defence policy since the late 1940s. Among both Conservatives and the New Democrats there are calls for a reorientation of Canadian defence policy, a shift away from Western Europe to the Arctic and Pacific with the priority on defence of the homeland. They echo in some important respects the demands for neutrality that are again becoming more vocal in this country. The arguments used by Trudeau in the late 1960s are once again finding their way into debates about Canadian defence policy. There are many sources to this recent discontent. The ongoing stalemate between the Soviet bloc and the Western Alliance in Europe, the seemingly futile military role of Canadian forces in Europe, growing concerns about Soviet and American threats in Canada's Arctic waters, the return to 1950s-style cold war politics in American foreign policy in the early 1980s, and the everlooming threat of nuclear war have all influenced Canadians across the political spectrum to reconsider the nature of and even the need for continued participation in the Atlantic Alliance.

Much of the opposition to Canada's continued participation in the Alliance reflects a growing popular concern about the threat of nuclear war and renewed opposition to American foreign policy. NATO's decision to deploy cruise and Pershing II missiles in Europe, the testing of the cruise at home, and the return to cold war rhetoric with defence budgets to match in the United States inspired a new wave of antinuclear movements throughout Europe and North America. After years of indifference nuclear weapons were once again a *cause célèbre* and, in

Canada, the Alliance became a part of the controversy. The link with the Alliance was made by, among others, writer and broadcaster Gwynne Dyer who in his 1985 television documentary *In Defence of Canada* argued that the Alliance was Canada's major security risk because "it is only the existence of those alliances that makes us a deliberate target for anybody's missiles." He proposed instead that the country should pursue a policy of nonalignment. Contemporary critics of Canada's Alliance membership such as Dyer, believe that with a declaration of neutrality this country could be a model for other NATO members to emulate and once freed from the encumbrances of Alliance solidarity, Canadians would be free to inject an alternative voice of reason into East-West negotiations.

Opponents to continued Alliance membership have been joined by a new breed of isolationists or, perhaps more appropriately, continentalists. These continentalists, whose influence was evident in the Trudeau white paper on defence in the early 1970s and more recently in some of the defence policy proposals of the Mulroney government, have emphasized the threats to the Canadian homeland. Although they part company on specifics and do not advocate withdrawal from NATO, the continentalists and the neutralists have become strange bedfellows in advocating the need for the Canadian military to devote its attention primarily, if not exclusively, to continental defence with or without official bilateral co-operation with the Americans. While maintaining a formal commitment to NATO, continentalists are skeptical about maintaining Canadian forces in Western Europe. In their view the nature of the threat has changed in recent years. The growth of the Soviet navy and its deployment in the Northern Fleet necessitates greater attention to securing the Arctic from foreign military activities, and in response to the shifting patterns of Canadian trade the Pacific coast must also be protected. "Canada needs a three-ocean navy" said Defence Minister Perrin Beatty in responding to these demands—a response that echoes Pierre Trudeau's defence of his reduction of Canada's modest contribution to European defence in 1969. Many Canadians take exception to the lack of European contribution to North American defence and question whether the Europeans are as committed to the defence of Canada as Canada has been to Europe. After all, they argue, Europeans can now afford to pay their own way for defence. These criticisms of Canadian defence policy have been influential in shaping the defence proposals of the Mulroney government. The government has made some attempts to demonstrate continued Canadian support for the Alliance through the addition of 1200 more personnel to Europe, a renewed commitment to augment Canadian forces in West Germany, and with strong rhetorical support for NATO in the 1987 white paper. Anxious to gain popular support for increased defence expenditures, however, the Tories have emphasized the role of the military in safeguarding sovereignty. In an effort to control costs to meet these sovereignty needs the government has cancelled its commitment to reinforce Norway with the Canadian Air Sea Transportable (CAST) brigade in times of crisis.

The armed forces have been concerned for some time about their ability to meet the commitment made to Norway in 1967. The first major exercise to test this capability came in the summer of 1986. The results were mixed but made clear the limitations of the commitment as Canada lacks sufficient air- and sea-lift capability to get the forces there quickly and to sustain them for any length of time, especially when another supply line to Canadian forces in Europe would have to be maintained at the same time. The cost of improving the capability of one line (let alone two) was too great. The commitment to reinforce Norway is to be replaced with a commitment to reinforce the central front and Canadian forces in southern Germany. Instead of going to Norway the 5e Groupe-brigade du Canada from Valcartier, Quebec will be dedicated to the Canadian Mechanized Brigade at Lahr bringing it up to division strength during a crisis. The forces will remain in Canada during peacetime and as a result the shift in commitment will add no new forces to those already stationed at Canadian bases at Lahr or Baden-Soellingen. It will also not completely overcome the problems of air and sea transport, and the lack of adequate medical, personnel, and other support facilities in Europe and the problems associated with sustaining the forces during a war. Such limitations must be overcome with additional resources, but there are few resources to be saved in moving the CAST commitment from Norway and thus no more effective presence in European defence will be provided unless the government is willing to redeploy some funds from other defence commitments.

The cancellation of our commitment to support Norwegian defence efforts comes at an important time in the history of the Alliance. Presented with a series of challenging arms control proposals by Soviet leader Mikhail Gorbachev, NATO governments have a good opportunity to shift the Alliance's strategy to an effective conventional deterrent. More importantly, the arms control initiative of the Gorbachev government poses a political challenge for the hearts and minds of western elites and their publics. Norway is well-placed to respond favourably to these overtures given the proximity of the Soviet threat and Norway's long-standing resistance to the stationing of NATO forces on Norwegian territory. Norway's commitment to the Alliance and its ability to resist Soviet pressure will likely best be enhanced by assured commitments from fellow NATO states. Canada is well-placed to provide such political support. John Barrett of the Canadian Centre for Arms Control and Disarmament has criticized the cancellation of the CAST commitment primarily on these political grounds in an appearance before the Senate Committee on Foreign Affairs in June 1987. "For many years, our military commitment has provided an essential underpinning for a whole range of security co-operation arrangements with the Norwegians, including co-operation in NATO and at the United Nations on arms control matters. According to official Norwegian sources, however, this kind of co-operation is likely to dry up with the cancellation of our military commitment." The white paper's technical approach to defence questions ignores such political implications but the government will not be able to do so for long.

The cancellation of CAST does not by itself remedy all of Canada's problems in Europe. As General Manson outlined in his submission to the Senate Committee on National Defence in May 1987, there are a number of serious gaps in Canada's military presence in Europe including:

The absence of approved war establishments, except for 4 Canadian Mechanized Brigade Group in Germany . . . a long list of fragmented missions . . . essential modern components for most brigades do not exist . . . regular force strength is insufficient to man the standing forces, and the reserves are not ready to fill the gaps and are unable to provide additional forces for sustainment . . . Equipment holdings are often deficient in numbers, and much equipment is obsolete . . . (and) . . . multiple tasking creates grave difficulties for commanders in trying to carry out coherent training programs.

The white paper pledges to address these and views the cancellation of the commitment to Norway as the beginning of the process. It is quite clear that the government's defence budget is going to be stretched very thin as it attempts to meet the shopping list presented in the white paper. As a result, and despite the rhetoric of the white paper that "Canadian defence policy will continue to be based on a strategy of collective security within the framework of the North Atlantic Alliance," the political debates suggest that defence policy like charity is to begin at home. The price of a military response to threats to Canadian sovereignty might very well be an effective presence in Europe.

Canadian forces in Europe have always been a subject of considerable debate. Canada's military contribution to NATO has frequently been criticized as being insignificant and many Canadians have in turn complained about spending approximately one billion dollars annually supporting these troops amidst the wealth of our European allies. But, perhaps the most widespread view is that the threat to Canadian security has changed and Canadian forces are now needed at home, in the Arctic and in the Pacific to face the ever-changing pattern of Soviet military activity and to protect Canada's commercial and sovereignty interests. Yet for Canada the major threat remains a global war. Attacks on the North American continent are not likely to occur except during such a war and despite the politics of detente that have been conducted in Europe, that region remains the central place of confrontation.

Canadian conventional forces in central Europe can assist in meeting important strategic objectives. John Halstead, a former Canadian ambassador to NATO, has argued that "since the greatest possible threat to Canadian security is nuclear war, Canada should do what it can to help raise the nuclear threshold and the best way to do that would be to strengthen the conventional forces in Europe, where the balance remains crucial."[27] But Canada's military commitment to Europe cannot be credible unless it is capable. This is the view that General Manson expressed to the Senate Committee on Defence in May 1987.

> If Canada is to contribute meaningfully to the NATO military alliance, then it must contribute militarily viable and permanently stationed land forces in Europe and must have in Canada an adequate number of augmentation, replacement and sustainment personnel who are trained on the identical equipment and to NATO standards. At present, because of the deficiencies I have noted, Canada's land forces are incapable of adhering to this concept.[28]

Canada's troop commitment to Europe is a great deal more than a simple military contribution to NATO designed to add to the physical defence along the central front. The presence of Canadian forces in Europe reminds Canadians, Europeans, and the Soviet Union of Canada's intrinsic interest in a stable European order based on western principles and of Canada's willingness to support that stability through the use of military force. The forces also help to reinforce Canada's right to participate in Alliance discussions on East-West relations and military strategy. Finally, but not incidentally the force deployments in Europe have served as a means for protecting and furthering Canadian interests in Europe. Europe still serves a vital role in Canada's foreign trade, a role that will become even more vital if we are to avoid the creeping continentalism that has permeated global trade patterns. As Trudeau discovered in the 1970s a firm military commitment to the common defence of Western Europe can help to secure political support for Canada's economic goals. In the early 1960s John Gellner wrote that "the danger, as far as Canada is concerned, is not that she vehemently opposes this or that NATO policy . . . but rather that she may turn indifferent" to NATO.[28] The neutralists and the isolationists may well lead Canada out of the Alliance in the face of an indifferent public. If they do we need to raise Pearson's question once again—where would Canada go?

## CHAPTER TWO

# Fortress North America?

*John Foster Dulles:* You Canadians are always complaining that we never consult you about our policies. If we played golf and the score is all square on the 18th green, I'll wager that you will intervene just as I am about to make the deciding putt to demand that I consult you about it first.

*Lester Pearson:* If I did, Foster, it would be merely to tell you that you were using a No. 9 iron.[1]

## Lost in Space

Two issues have dominated the foreign policy agenda of the Mulroney government—free trade and defence policy. In a curious mixture of economic and security considerations, the Mulroney government has come face-to-face with the continentalist pressures that have always strained the fabric of Canadian society. Forty years earlier, it was Prime Minister Mackenzie King who considered the possibility of seeking economic and military security through continental arrangements with the United States. Thanks in no small part to the spirits of the deceased, King rejected the temptations of continentalism and in its place sought shelter in multilateral associations. Wary of the fate of small powers in too close association with emerging (or declining) empires, King looked for extracontinental options to foster Canadian prosperity and enhance Canadian security.

The current wave of continentalism appears in many respects to be born in desperation. Frightened by the shifting trends in other parts of the world, panic has pushed the Mulroney government into seeking special relations with the United States for trade and defence. The perceptions of fear and limited options dominated the Mulroney government's first major foreign policy statement released in 1985, its green paper entitled "Competitiveness and Security." In a comment on this statement, John Kirton remarked that it was "founded throughout on a misleading view of a world dominated by an inevitably economically predominant United States, and a militarily mighty and marauding Soviet Union, locked into a hostile bipolar confrontation."[2] The same could be said of the white paper on defence published two years later.

The government's predilection for closer co-operation with the United States has received encouragement from a similar set of conditions existing south of the 49th parallel. Many Americans have also been influenced by a new wave of fear and parochialism. Escott Reid, a former undersecretary of state for external affairs, once said that "if you scratch an American long enough you will find an isolationist." For decades the United States had resisted these isolationist impulses as it carried its hegemonic mantle throughout the globe. Yet, as discussed in chapter Five, the isolationist option becomes more enticing for many Americans as the rest of the world seems to turn its back on the United States. Confronted by the military and political challenge of the Soviet Union, by the economic challenge of Japan and West Germany, and by the subversive challenge of state-sponsored terrorism, Americans have sought comfort in their own continent. The uncertainties of the international system are being replaced by the simple formulas of trade protectionism and the Strategic Defence Initiative. If the rest of the world refuses to co-operate, many Americans seem to prefer to simply reject the rest of the world. Fortress North America beckons like a safe harbour amidst the turbulence of world politics and many Canadians seem inclined to follow.

Canadians have always been susceptible to the continentalist option. Canada shares a continent with a major power, physically removed from other regions of the globe; and the pressure for close continental co-operation has been the most persistent and significant element in the history of Canadian foreign policy. For generations Canadians have embraced continentalism with a schizophrenic attitude, fearing it as they embrace it. Canadians' concerns with the United States have never been reciprocated. American interest in Canada has depended as much on the global balance of power and matters of grand strategy as on geography, amity, or the political economy of bilateral relations. The pressure for continental security co-operation that emerges from the United States has been and continues to be a reflection of shifts in American strategy in response to changes in technology and the global distribution of power. This was evident in the 1940s when, following the fall of France and the realization that Britain was in serious peril, the Americans became concerned about continental security and searched for security guarantees from Canada. It is evident again today as the Americans attempt to establish a secure North American bunker from which to pursue unilateral responses to global challenges and seek technological solutions to the threat of nuclear war.

As the end of the "Reagan Revolution" in the United States nears, right-wing Republicans and the Pentagon are intensifying pressure for the early deployment of ballistic missile defences. For years strategists and policy makers had acknowledged that it was impossible to defend civilians against incoming ballistic missiles armed with nuclear warheads. Earlier efforts to develop ballistic missile defences had been limited to the defence of military installations and even these were not foolproof. Attitudes have changed, however, and some like Edward Teller, the developer of the hydrogen bomb, believed the technology would soon be available to develop a system that would destroy ballistic missiles before they reached their targets in the continental United States. Convinced of this possibility, President Reagan launched the Strategic Defence Initiative (SDI) in March 1983. Popularly known as Star Wars, the SDI was set up to develop and subsequently deploy antiballistic missile weapons in space and on the ground that would protect the United States in the event of a nulcear war. Instead of assured destruction, Star Wars would purportedly guarantee assured survival for the citizens of the United States. Facing sustained criticism from a skeptical scientific community and fearing that they might lose a last opportunity to see their dream become a reality, the salesmen of space-based security are working overtime to convince Reagan to begin deploying ballistic missile defences before he leaves office in January 1989. Many aspiring Republican presidential candidates such as Jack Kemp are among those who are encouraging Reagan to proceed quickly with the deployment of

Star Wars, the ultimate technological fix, despite the opposition of allied governments and demands that Star Wars be traded for radical reductions in the Soviet nuclear arsenal. For many Americans Star Wars has become the near-perfect solution for dealing with the complex world of international politics. For the politicians it has been viewed, in the words of Daniel Deudney, as a way of uniting "those who hate the Soviets with those who hate the bomb."[3] For the cold warriors, it is seen as the shield behind which they will be able to intensify their ongoing struggle to eliminate the Soviet state. For some nuclear strategists, it is seen as a way of overcoming the dilemmas of deterrence based on the premise of mutually assured destruction. And it pleases the new breed of American isolationist because it can all be done unilaterally and will not require the co-operation and compromise that reality so often imposes on their messianic visions. The temptations of Star Wars are great and are not likely to be easily overcome, regardless of the outcome of the next presidential election. Technology and fear have been as important in driving the race to defensive superiority as have the dreams of Edward Teller and Ronald Reagan. Nor are these temptations limited to Americans. Many Canadians have been captured by the fantasy of new military technology that will lead us out of nuclear nightmares and into space, the last frontier.

Star Wars is not simply a diversion of the "mad scientists" of the nuclear age. It is but the most recent and one of the more elaborate of the shifts that continue to take place in American nuclear strategy. When combined with other recent shifts in American defence policy it reflects the emergence of a strong continentalist orientation in American grand strategy. During the mid-1970s there emerged among American nuclear strategists concern about the credibility of nuclear deterrence based on assumptions of mutually assured destruction (MAD). Critics of American nuclear strategy maintained that the Soviet Union was making gains in the Third World—in Africa, Southeast Asia, and Central America—because American nuclear strategy was ineffective; it had lost its deterrent effect. Some even argued that the existence of nuclear parity between the Soviet Union and the United States had given the Soviets the capability to launch a devastating attack on the United States. These arguments, ludicrous as they were, nonetheless influenced policy decisions as the United States moved into the 1980s. The politics of fear so evident during the 1950s had returned to haunt the policy debates of the late 1970s. The Committee on the Present Danger and others pressed the American government to modernize and expand the country's nuclear arsenal and to devise conventional and nuclear strategies that would adopt a more aggressive posture in this changed international environment. The arrival of Ronald Reagan in the White House and the prevalence of virulent anti-Soviet rhetoric increased the sense of fear among the populace. Hundreds of thousands took to the streets in the United States to demand a nuclear freeze. The public has not been easily reassured by the addition of nuclear weapons but the launching of the Strategic Defence Initiative in 1983 settled most of their qualms. By quelling the fires of nuclear dissent after one of the most intensive public debates about nuclear strategy in the postwar period, Star Wars has achieved its first victory.

The continuing American commitment to the development and deployment of Star Wars is of considerable importance for the future of Canadian security interests and defence policy. The Reagan administration's interest in strategic defences combines a heightened sense of insecurity and vulnerability with a desire to pursue an aggressive foreign policy. As E.P. Thompson has written, Star Wars "is the ultimate decomposition of deterrence theory, and the attempt by U.S. nuclear ideologists to return to the womb of Hiroshima."[4] The commitment to Star Wars is indicative of a reliance on both technology and unilateralism for responding to the real problems of international politics. "If a nearly foolproof defence against incoming missiles is found a number of psychological horrors disappear. It no longer becomes inconceivable to press the button, and robust anti-Communism can be adopted at the verbal and conventional military level without giving everyone the shudders."[5] American fears, based on the recognition of their country's vulnerability in the nuclear age, are not a completely new phenomenon. They do, however, lead to additional pressure on Canada.

However Star Wars is implemented, Canadian security will be affected. It is foolish to engage in long debates over whether or how the North American Aerospace Defence Command

(NORAD) might be linked to Star Wars or what aspects of ballistic missile defences might be deployed in Canada. As the United States military begins to deploy extensive ballistic missile defences and undertakes operations as part of both defensive and more explicit war-fighting strategies, the North American continent will become one of the principal staging points for conducting a nuclear war. As American strategy reverts to this more continentalist orientation Canadians will be pressed to shift their own defence policy in the same direction and become little more than an adjunct of American strategy. Faced with the economic constraints that have already stretched Canadian defence capabilities too thin to meet multiple commitments, it is imperative that Canadians assess carefully the implications of superpower behaviour before making quick adjustments in the interests of economic and political expediency. Canada will face few alternatives if Star Wars deployments are used to reinforce the dream of a secure Fortress North America, unless Canadian policy makers begin to resist such tendencies in determining this country's contribution to the future of western strategy.

Ballistic missile defences will never be able to provide a perfect defence against attack. Other defensive systems will be necessary to ensure effective protection and reassure a frightened public. As James Schlesinger, former U.S. secretary of defence has written, "If (the U.S.) were ever to deploy ballistic missile defense, it would impose upon us the corresponding costs of developing or attempting to develop comparably effective air defenses."[6] If Star Wars is rooted in American insecurity in the wake of the growth of Soviet intercontinental capabilities, it is unlikely that people will be completely reassured by ballistic missile defences alone. Instead, they will attempt to eliminate alternative threats and the most likely alternative threats come from bombers and cruise missiles. Canadian territory and Canadian co-operation become essential to the effective deterrence of this threat. This view is even more credible if one looks at the SDI as an attempt to complement a war-fighting doctrine that once again dominates American strategy. The result of these practices will be to increase pressure on Canadians. This may not take the form of the elaborate air defence systems established in the 1950s. Indeed, there may be some credibility to the commonly cited view that, largely as a result of technological shifts that have moved defensive systems into space, the Americans may be ready, willing, and, most importantly, able to look after much of continental air defence without consulting Canada. And once the United States has begun, it will be, as Douglas Ross has written, "difficult to imagine the Canadian government successfully defying a determined American administration bent on filling an air defence gap in its strategic defences, once a defensive transition was under way."[7]

The renewed interest in NORAD and forward-based active and passive defences displayed by the American and Canadian air forces in the early 1980s reflects a return to the war-fighting doctrines that prevailed in the 1950s. Colin Gray stated succinctly in 1977 that "The only strategic context wherein a far more effective anti-bomber defence would be justifiable, would be one wherein you planned to win/survive World War III. This presumes a first strike by the United States."[8] Ross has also argued that in addition to its useful surveillance role NORAD could be used to facilitate American war-fighting strategies.

Much of this recent concern about continental air defence emerged in the United States. After decades of neglect that had seen NORAD forces decline substantially in reflection of the negligible Soviet bomber threat to North America, the American and Canadian air forces launched a joint study in the late 1970s to determine the requirements for a less porous air defence. The study was designed to respond not specifically to changes in Soviet military capabilities but to shifts in American strategic thinking; shifts that placed a much greater emphasis on the forward deployment of American forces and more elaborate and extensive early-warning systems to enhance command and control centres. Supported by a report from the Canadian Senate and the House of Commons, the Canadian government began in 1985 to increase Canadian commitments to NORAD by renewing the bilateral agreement for an additional five years in 1986 and agreeing to the construction of the North Warning System, part of which became operational in 1987, and an upgrading of airfields at five sites north of the 60th parallel to serve as Forward Operating Locations for CF-18 interceptors—Yellowknife, Inuvik, Rankin Inlet, Kuujjuaq, and Iqaluit.

The government may not stop with the prudent minimum. The 1987 white paper on defence stipulates that the government will "participate in research on future air defence systems in conjunction with the United States Air Defence Initiative (ADI). Like its SDI cousin, the ADI is an attempt to secure through technology a near-perfect solution to the marginal Soviet bomber and cruise missile threat to North America. Some in the United States have been chasing after this illusory solution since the 1950s. As John Barrett, the deputy director at the Canadian Centre for Arms Control and Disarmament, informed the Senate Foreign Affairs Committee in June 1987: "the ADI is a research program running concurrently with SDI to develop an air defence system capable of detecting, tracking, identifying and destroying bombers and cruise missiles attacking North America. Like SDI itself, it envisions a layered defence which would, in fact, be meshed technically with SDI."

Even if one were to ignore the possibility of new American demands on Canadian territory, there remain cogent reasons why Star Wars would be inimical to Canadian interests. First and foremost, Star Wars suggests the near-completion of a fundamental shift to a more overt war-fighting strategy. While proponents of such a strategy defend this in terms of its lending greater credibility to MAD, opponents question its effect on crisis management between the superpowers. War-fighting strategies emphasize the integration of all aspects of one's military forces. They also place a premium on early use of force in a crisis situation. In this respect, a war-fighting doctrine without any demonstrated positive effect on security, increases tension and the temptation to preempt. Second, a deployed ballistic missile defence system will encourage the development and deployment of additional Soviet nuclear forces that will increase military threats to the North American continent. These are likely to include the development of an enhanced bomber capability, air-launched and sea-launched cruise missiles, and the forward deployment of Soviet submarines in the Arctic and off the coasts of North America. While there may be reasons why the Soviets might move in this direction regardless of American and Canadian deployments, Canadians should not actually support policies that encourage such shifts in Soviet strategy when these will only increase the military threats to Canadian territory.

A third and more immediate problem for Canadians would be the impact of ballistic missile defences, and especially space-based ones, on other Canadian interests. An extensive ballistic missile defence system is likely to put at risk the use of space for peaceful purposes. For example, recent reports of the military applications of the proposed American space station have raised concerns here and in Europe about allied participation in that venture. Satellites currently used for communications and other peaceful purposes might also be at risk in a more militarized space environment. American facilities in support of Star Wars as well as potential Russian countermeasures would also likely increase military activity in areas adjacent to Canadian territory. More significantly, Star Wars increases pressure for Canadian military efforts to be directed primarily at continental defence and in support of this unilateral American initiative. It is this unilateral aspect of the proposed SDI that presents the most fundamental problem for Canadians. If the United States decides to proceed with a full or partial deployment of ballistic missile defences, it will pose a serious threat to the cohesion of the Atlantic Alliance. Christoph Bertram, the chief political editor of West Germany's leading daily *Die Zeit*, has argued that "Western Europeans are convinced that the United States will remain vitally concerned about Europe only if its own survival is at stake and that SDI would lead the United States away from Western Europe."[9] It will also lend support to those isolationists who are always present in American policy debates. By lending support to the facade of "Fortress America," the SDI adds further legitimacy to a growing view that the U.S. does not require allies; that once protected by the shield of ballistic missile defences the United States will be able to project its force and influence around the globe without risk to its homeland. For Canadians, it encourages a belief in the illusion of a "fire-proof house."

Despite the appeal of a potential shield against nuclear weapons the possibility of achieving this objective has received very little support even among those who favour ballistic missile defences. The first concerns about the SDI were raised by two of the three panels that were established by the administration to explore the feasibility of Reagan's proposal. The Fletcher panel, which investigated the technical feasibility of the SDI while advocating a continuation of the program, noted that "it is not technically credible to provide a ballistic missile defense that is 99.9

per cent leakproof." Critics argued that anything less would still pose catastrophic results for the United States in the event of a nuclear war. The panel went on to note that the effectiveness of the defences would rest as much on Soviet co-operation as it would on technical facilities. "The ultimate effectiveness, complexity and degree of technical risk in the system will depend not only on the technology itself, but also on the extent to which the Soviet Union either agrees to mutual defense arrangements and offensive limitations, or embarks on new strategic directions in response to our initiative."[10] The Hoffman panel, which considered the strategic implications of the SDI, also proposed a continuation of the project but argued that it should be limited to ground-based interceptors and that these should be deployed around military installations and command and control centres, in essence to protect the United States' retaliatory capability.

These conclusions as well as the views of many critics of the SDI appear to have had little effect on President Reagan. During his visit to Quebec City for the Shamrock summit in March 1985, he referred to the possibility of developing and sharing with Canada the technology that could provide a security shield and some day eliminate the threat of nuclear attack. Realism also had little effect on Canadian supporters of the SDI, such as Philip Traversy of the Canadian Coalition for Peace Through Strength. Despite the sobering accounts of the President's own commissions, Traversy still thought that "the SDI program offers the world a chance to move from the mutual assured destruction doctrine to 'mutual assured survival'."[11]

Given the technical difficulties, the numerous ways that nuclear weapons can be delivered to a target, and in spite of the popular appeal of protecting the population from nuclear devastation, members of the Reagan administration have retreated from the "mutual assured survival" rationale and have admitted that ballistic missile defences are likely to be more useful in protecting missile and other military installations such as command and control centres. Increasingly, the justification for continuing the SDI has turned to guaranteeing retaliatory capabilities and thereby enhancing MAD rather than replacing it. Americans such as Vice-President George Bush and Secretary of State George Shultz have admitted that the ballistic missile defences will not allow us to escape from MAD and former Secretary of Defence Schlesinger has argued that statements to the contrary are counterproductive. "Within the Air Force, within the Administration, within society as a whole, we should not begin to talk about the immorality of deterrence in our quest for the Strategic Defence Initiative because we are going to rest on deterrence for the balance of our days . . . if cities are to be protected they will be protected by the forbearance of those on the other side or through effective deterrence."[12] From this we can see that one of the central myths of the entire debate over Star Wars bears little resemblance to the real world of strategic planning. If further evidence is required one need only look at the U.S. Air Force's commitment to the modernization of American nuclear forces currently underway. Clearly the American military does not envision a nuclear-free future and it is imperative that Canadians recognize this rather than chase after shadows.

For some supporters, Star Wars promises a nuclear-free future. Others would settle for a great deal less. "If all strategic defence did was give us back the eight hours of warning we had in the 1950s . . . it would make the world calmer and safer."[13] It is always tempting to look fondly on the past as better times but the 1950s were not seen as calm and safe by the policy makers of the time. Moreover, the "calm and safe" strategies of the 1950s created all sorts of anxieties in Canada. Remember backyard fallout shelters?

### Back to the Future

Star Wars is not Canada's first encounter with American concern about the vulnerability of the North American continent to attack. Indeed, the objective of developing a defence against nuclear weapons animated much of the debate among American strategists in the early 1950s. Anticipating the rhetoric of the Star Wars debate by thirty years, proponents of defensive systems, such as Charles Murphy, argued that "a defense system capable of a 90 per cent kill ratio could probably be built."[14] Researchers at the Massachusetts Institute of Technology's Lincoln Laboratory in the early 1950s advocated devising a network of radar installations, air bases, and ground-to-air missiles across the North American continent to defend against a nuclear attack from the Soviet Union. Extensive lobbying by supporters of continental defences eventually persuaded the Eisenhower administration to commit funds for the development of systems to defend the North American continent. A truly effective defence, however, required Canadian co-operation. It would be of little value to set up systems in the continental United States if, as one article at the time suggested, "Russian Planes Raid Canada's Skies." President Eisenhower was therefore persuaded "to bring home to the Canadian government the urgency and the character of the threat," during his visit to Ottawa in November 1953. Despite some initial skepticism, by the end of that year the Liberal government of Louis St. Laurent had agreed to participate with the United States in a joint effort to devise an effective defence against a nuclear attack on the North American continent. This decision set the course for Canadian defence policy for the ensuing decade and led inevitably to NORAD. It also made Canada one of the principal assets, hence targets, in the Strategic Air Command's plans to launch a preemptive strike on the Soviet Union. According to David Cox the "effective decision" to join NORAD "was taken in the fall of 1953; nor was it a joint decision other than in name, but rather as the sequence of events indicates, a decision taken by the Americans that required the co-operation of the Canadian government."[15]

Between 1953 and 1963, Canadian defence policy was carried along a roller coaster of shifting strategies, changing technology and political upheaval that ultimately resulted in the most serious rift ever experienced between the Canadian and American governments. It also left the Conservative Party defeated at the polls in 1963 and internally divided. Finally, this period saw a reorientation of Canadian defence policy, as the Canadian military acquired nuclear weapons for its forces in Europe and North America and committed vast funds to the defence of redundant or nonexistent threats. Without severing its links with continental Europe, under pressure from changing American strategies, Canadian security policy was focused more intently on North America. In trying to serve the strategic interests of the United States, Canada got caught investing heavily in questionable military practices.

The 1950s were an extremely busy and significant period in the development of American (and western) nuclear strategy. Policy makers and strategists in the United States were not only organizing their own and the Western Alliance's nuclear options, they were also trying to cope with the Soviet Union's limited capabilities for attacking the continental United States. For the first time Americans and Canadians saw themselves as directly threatened by the advancing technology of modern warfare. American concern for defences against nuclear weapons was soon fused with their plans for using these weapons in an offensive attack against the Soviet Union. This combination of "offensive" and "defensive" considerations made it impossible to distinguish strategies on the basis of one or the other. In effect, the United States had only one nuclear option planned: a full-scale nuclear attack on the Soviet Union. As a result, Canadians' participation in the defence of the North American continent was part and parcel of American first-strike options for attacking the Soviet Union. Canadian involvement, as a junior but necessary partner, in the American strategy of the 1950s was more elaborate and expensive than anything Canada did before or has done since in peacetime military activity. While Canada was not alone among the allies in experiencing American pressure during this period, and did have some success in limiting direct American control, the shift this created in Canadian security policy was somewhat more dramatic—including a commitment of vast military resources to the defence of the continent and the acquisition of nuclear weapons for the Canadian Armed Forces stationed in both North America and Europe.

Canada's significance in American strategy had been apparent since the Second World War. During the war, Mackenzie King had expressed concern about American designs on Canadian territory and on one occasion expressed the view that the American government's interest in the Alaskan Highway "was less intended for protection against the Japanese than as one of the fingers of the hand which America is placing more or less over the whole of the western hemisphere."[16] As the threat to North America waned during the closing years of World War II, American strategic interest in Canada also waned. By the early 1950s, however, policy makers and military planners in the United States began to refocus attention on Canada as their fears about a possible Soviet attack grew. These fears were less the result of any overt Soviet military activity than of the mere presence of nuclear weapons in the arsenal of the Soviet military and of exaggerated intelligence assessments of Soviet capabilities. In response, the American government looked to Canada for bases for the forward deployment of the bombers of the Strategic Air Command. In the words of the American minister at the embassy in Ottawa in 1951:

> [As] the United States turned to rearmament and to the formulation of global air strategy for a possible conflict . . . Requirements for planned strategic air operations have been stepped up to a point where existing facilities available to the United States are wholly inadequate . . . In the case of global conflict, taking into account the plans of the United States Strategic Air Command, northeastern Canada will be much more than a staging route from the United States to Europe. It is now rapidly becoming an operating area, with bases from which attacks on the enemy may be launched and to which enemy counter-attacks may be directed.[17]

In addition to American bases in Canada and the intermittent use of Canadian bases by American forces, Canadian territory was also desired for its use as the defence perimeter for the continental United States. Independently and in co-operation with the United States, the Canadian government oversaw the construction of a network of radar installations, beginning in 1951 with the construction of the Pinetree Line extension into Canadian territory. This was soon followed in 1954 by the Mid-Canada Line and the Distant Early Warning (DEW) Line. By 1957 and before the establishment of NORAD, Canada had become directly linked to American nuclear strategy. As Jon McLin has noted "the purpose of the radar networks was not so much the defense of Canada's populace as of the (Strategic Air Command) force upon which the policy of deterrence depended."[18] With all of the background completed, and under considerable pressure from the Canadian military, the newly elected Diefenbaker government completed the continental defence connection by agreeing to the establishment of NORAD less than two months after winning the election of June 1957. This was done without cabinet discussion or approval, and was reminiscent of the back-of-the-envelope scratchings of Mackenzie King and American President Roosevelt when they set up the Permanent Joint Board on Defence as part of the Ogdensberg Agreement of 1940. These two significant decisions, which effectively defined the continentalist orientation of Canadian defence policy, were both made without cabinet consultation or any indication of widespread popular support.

NORAD is the best-known example of bilateral defence ties between Canada and the United States. While the agreement is only one of hundreds which link Canada and the United States in the peacetime surveillance of and wartime operations on the North American continent, NORAD's notoriety results from its reference as a symbol of this vast array of bilateral links. The repeated renewals of the agreement (the agreement has been renewed every five years since 1967, most recently in 1986 for five years) have also regenerated the debate on bilateral defence links. Perhaps of primary importance, however, the central significance of NORAD is that it reflects much of what has gone wrong with Canadian defence policy; a tendency to get locked into inappropriate arrangements based on inadequate threat assessments that end up distorting this country's defence priorities while serving questionable military objectives.

NORAD was designed to simplify the combined operations of the Canadian air force (RCAF) and its American counterpart in times of crisis or actual conflict. The primary objective of these forces became the protection of the American nuclear force (concentrated at this time in the Strategic Air Command) to enable it to get off the ground and on its way to the Soviet Union before the Soviets could destroy American bombers on the ground. To proponents of nuclear deterrence the proposal made strategic sense. If Canada was best protected through the strategic arsenal of the United States then Canada would be best off if this strategic arsenal were secured against destruction by the enemy. Joint co-operation between the RCAF and the Strategic Air Command was, from their respective perspectives, viewed as the best way of doing this. There were (and remain) two flawed assumptions in this reasoning. First, that there was a serious threat to the Strategic Air Command that could be met effectively by the RCAF and USAF; and second, that protecting the air command was primarily a defensive tactic in support of deterrence.

The need for air defence implied a threat from the air. In the 1950s that threat was marginal. President Eisenhower once admitted, in a moment of candour that "the bomber gap was a fiction." The concern with the possibility of a Soviet bomber attack on the North American continent was rooted in an ethnocentric strategic assessment by the American air force and was also used to justify an expansion in the forces made available to the USAF for conducting operations against the Soviet Union. The overwhelming predisposition toward air power among postwar American strategists was assumed to apply to their Soviet counterparts as well. Yet the Soviets had little success in developing intercontinental bombers and without the access to allies close to enemy targets enjoyed by the Americans, they were unable to mount an effective bomber threat against the United States. It was only with the development of intercontinental ballistic missiles in the 1960s that the Soviets were able to present a profound threat to the North American continent. While the Soviets were able to mount a minor attack from the air it is clear that Soviet capabilities did not require the excessive concentration on territorial air defence that was mounted in North America in the 1950s. Yet this "fiction" exercised considerable influence on American strategic debates during the 1950s. These debates were the genesis of the series of bilateral agreements between Canada and the United States during the 1950s that culminated in the formation of NORAD in 1957.

Part of the problem in assessing Soviet capabilities was rooted in the fact that the Canadian and American governments lacked the capability to make a proper assessment of the potential Soviet threat to the American bomber force. Intelligence gathering was rudimentary and as a result tended to be governed more by political considerations than by strategic concerns. Hindsight, with its 20-20 vision, tells us that no such threat existed. Hindsight also tells us that the Strategic Air Command had a considerable stake in exaggerating the threat. The more pervasive the Soviet threat, the greater resources that could be demanded from the U.S. Congress. Similar tactics were useful to the RCAF.

A second consideration in assessing NORAD was its link to the strategy that guided the Strategic Air Command in the late 1950s. Its principal mission since the close of the Second World War was strategic bombardment—the use of air power in an offensive manner early in a conflict to destroy the industrial capacity and the morale of the enemy's population. The notion of retaliation that came to dominate discussions of deterrence during the 1960s had not yet been accepted by the USAF. Strategic bombardment dominated early thinking on the role of nuclear weapons in the United States. It was an important component in the doctrine of massive retaliation—the so-called "new look" espoused by John Foster Dulles, U.S. secretary of state during the early days of the Eisenhower administration.

When asked by a reporter whether the atom bomb was being considered for use during the Korean War, President Truman responded "It always has been, Smitty. It is one of our weapons."[21] The American military and specifically, the American air force embraced nuclear weapons with the passion of discovering a lost comrade. Nuclear weapons were seen as the ultimate device for strategic bombardment which was in turn viewed as the most effective strategy in an era dominated by air power. Nuclear weapons carried by the Strategic Air Command in preemptive attacks against Soviet military and industrial targets monopolized American nuclear strategy throughout the 1950s. Strategic bombardment emphasized the importance, indeed the necessity of acquiring the offensive in times of conflict. In accordance with the writings of the early twentieth century Italian military strategist Guilio Douhet on the use of air power, strategic bombardment was designed to strike first, strike massively, and strike at the source of the enemy's power. The Strategic Air Command took these lessons to heart and with the support of faulty intelligence estimates greatly expanded their capabilities in the United States and through a network of forward deployment bases abroad. As outlined in NSC-68, a 1950 American government policy document, strategic bombardment emphasized the military advantages of landing the first blow. Thus by the early 1950s the dominant American military plan for dealing with the Soviet Union in time of conflict was a major offensive air strike with nuclear weapons on targets in the Soviet Union. Shortly after coming into office in 1953, U.S. Secretary of State John Foster Dulles gave this strategy additional support by announcing the doctrine of massive retaliation.

The proclamation of massive retaliation by Dulles in February 1954 generated one of the few fissures in bilateral defence co-operation of the fifties. For perhaps the first time, Canadian policy makers seemed to have recognized the implications of American strategic planning. Earlier, the Canadian government had been critical of the alleged American proposals to use atomic weapons in Korea and emphasized the need for consultation. American officials were opposed to granting any ally the right to prior consent and thus implicit control over the American nuclear arsenal. Pearson argued in a public radio broadcast that nuclear weapons were of such a special character that they should be treated differently. Dulles either did not hear the address or decided to ignore the advice for his strategy of massive retaliation relied on the potential indiscriminate use of nuclear weapons. In response, Pearson rejected his typical preference for quiet diplomacy and in a public address before the National Press Club in Washington, D.C. criticized Dulles' "new look." His criticism questioned the unilateralist tendencies of the "new look."

> The stakes are now higher than ever, and the necessity for co-operation and consultation greater than ever. It is essential that we work together in any new defence planning and policy—as we have already been working together in NATO—if the great coalition which we have formed for peace is not to be replaced by an entrenched continentalism which, I can assure you, makes no great appeal to your northern neighbour as the best way to prevent war or defeat aggression, and which is not likely to provide a solid basis for good United States-Canadian relations.[20]

Despite these objections, the policies of the Liberal government supported this entrenched continentalism by extending the use of Canadian facilities to American bombers and through the growing links between the RCAF and their American counterparts.

The significant role of air power in post-1945 strategic debates had not escaped the RCAF, whose flyers had distinguished themselves during the Second World War. The RCAF was very receptive to the strategic assessments developed in Washington during the late 1940s and early 1950s. Facilitating these objectives would allow the RCAF to emerge from the post-1945 budget doldrums as the elite element in the Canadian armed forces. The air force, anxious to be part of the military strategy of the Western Alliance, and to be top dog at home, looked favourably on American plans for strategic bombardment and continental air defence. Canada's defence capabilities were already stretched too thin and, to the consternation of some in the RCAF, strategic bombardment had to be left to the Americans. "We were sorry to have to do (this)" reported one RCAF officer, "because we had done rather well in the bomber field."[21] Continental air defence became a second best option, but one which the RCAF embraced warmly. Working with the USAF became a way of life and during the 1950s the RCAF had come "to see the air defence of the continent more and more as a joint effort and less and less of one in which sovereignty should play a role."[22] A new fleet of fighter aircraft was to be Canada's ticket for a full partnership in defending the continent from attack.

"We have started on a program of development that gives me the shudders," was how C.D. Howe described the Arrow fighter-aircraft project during debates in the House of Commons in 1955. The Arrow, like much of Canada's continentalist-oriented defence policy of the 1950s was rooted in a jaundiced perspective of Soviet bomber capabilities. Specifically it was based on an assumption "that by 1958 the Soviets might have the capability to attack North America with turbo-jet bombers carrying atomic bombs."[23] These fears were encouraged by Soviet attempts to exaggerate their bomber capabilities during the May Day parade of 1954 and the readiness of the U.S. Strategic Air Command to fuel the myth of a "bomber gap." As these early false intelligence reports filtered through to Canadian policy debates, the RCAF pressed the government to accelerate and expand the Arrow program. There is no need here to recount the oft-repeated debates on the fate of the Arrow. It is, however, necessary to discount the nationalist fervor that often surrounds such debates. The government's short-term commitment to the Arrow was primarily the result of American assessments of the Soviet bomber threat to the North American continent. Its demise was in turn the result of shifting strategic concerns in the United States as the bomber threat failed to materialize and attention began to shift to intercontinental ballistic missiles (ICBMS). Whatever its technological prowess, the Arrow was designed as an adjunct to American air strategy. It was a reflection of Canada's willingness to defend the offensive arm of American strategy, its Strategic Air Command. As a result, the fate of the Arrow rested as much on the whims of American strategy as it did on policy decisions in Ottawa. In this respect, the fate of the Arrow shared many parallels with the ensuing debate on the acquisition of BOMARC ground-to-air missiles and the stationing of American nuclear weapons on Canadian soil.

Pretensions aside, Canada has never been independent of the nuclear strategy of the United States and the Western Alliance. Involved from the beginning in the development of nuclear weapons through the Manhattan Project that developed "the Bomb" and as regular suppliers of fissionable material for American and British nuclear weapons, the great Canadian debate of the early 1960s was not about whether to get involved with nuclear weapons but how extensive such involvement would be. Here too it is unnecessary to review in detail the particulars of this well-known period in the history of Canadian defence policy. The manner in which the issue was handled reflects both strengths and weaknesses in Canada's relationship with the United States. The Conservative government of John Diefenbaker was forced to confront the issue of equipping Canada's armed forces with nuclear weapons as a result of shifts in the strategy of the United States and other NATO allies. During the late fifties members of the American strategic community continued to pursue efforts to develop an effective defence against a Soviet attack on the North American continent. When John Kennedy became president in the early 1960s, the single integrated operational plan for American nuclear forces was still a blunt offensive attack conducted by the Strategic Air Command against hundreds of military and industrial sites in the Soviet Union. The central concern for American strategic planners thus remained the defence of the air command. Canada had already been intimately involved in this mission as a result of the series of programs which culminated in the NORAD agreement of 1957. It was thus inevitable that Canada would be called on again once the

Americans decided which weapons system would be used for continental defence. Significantly, the cancellation of the Arrow was not based on a view that in the age of intercontinental ballistic missiles air defences had become unnecessary. Instead, the Diefenbaker government justified the Arrow's cancellation by arguing that it was necessary to keep up with changing technology. Not that they believed that changing technology in the form of intercontinental ballistic missiles was making the bomber threat redundant. They felt a defence against bomber attacks would still be necessary but Arrows were to be replaced by BOMARCs—a ground-to-air missile armed with nuclear warheads that would be launched against incoming Soviet bombers in defence of Strategic Air Command forces. The Canadian government agreed to accept these missiles from the United States when the production of the Arrow was cancelled in the autumn of 1958.

The BOMARCs were an integral part of the prevailing American strategy of strategic bombardment. It was at this time, however, that American strategic thinking was undergoing an evolution, despite the resistance of the United States Air Force. Once the Soviet Union displayed its ability to produce ICBMs many American policy makers and strategists realized that the bomber would no longer be able to dominate American nuclear strategy. The advanced technology of rocketry not only made the air power of the USAF more vulnerable to a preemptive strike; it also brought into question the utility of the counterforce options that had been pursued by the Strategic Air Command and had governed much of the western world's strategic planning to that date. In its place American strategists began to accept the view that deterrence would now be dependent on a retaliatory or second strike capability. With the rather rapid deployment of land-based missiles of intercontinental range and the development of submarine-launched missiles, the bomber was no longer the carrier of choice. More significantly, the U.S. Navy moved in and, using the rationale of deterrence based on secure retaliatory forces, assumed the primary responsibility for implementing this revised American nuclear strategy.

While Canadians were embroiled in debate about the BOMARCs, these strategic shifts meant that the BOMARC was no longer at the cutting edge of strategic policy in the U.S. As a result, one of the more prolonged and intense debates on military issues that this country had experienced during the cold war ended up having little military significance. By 1960 the American Congress had begun to reduce its commitment to continental defences and the BOMARC specifically. The issue at stake was no longer the immediate necessity for a Canadian contribution to continental defence but Canada's willingness to serve on the front lines of continental defence when the need arose. Having pressed the Canadians into assuming commitments for continental defence the American government was reluctant to see this willingness to support American strategy go unrewarded and thus retained a marginal commitment to BOMARCs even as the Congress acknowledged that they were ineffective and unnecessary. Continental commitments had caused this country to drift into a defence posture that saw us purchase systems of no real military value to defend us against threats that were marginal. The events of this period also fostered among policy makers and the public a degree of distrust of the military that is only now beginning to disappear.

## The Ruse of Sovereignty

In May 1986, three nuclear-powered attack submarines from the American navy broke through the ice and surfaced at the North Pole. Some crew members left the vessel to snap photographs while others guarded against polar bears. A similar exercise was completed in May 1987 when two U.S. Navy subs were joined by one from the British fleet. These manouevres were intended, according to one American military spokesperson "to show the Soviet Union that we are not ceding that area to them."[25] The events, however, appear to have created more consternation in Ottawa than they did in Moscow. Many Canadians were surprised to learn that the American government thought it their territory to cede, and when combined with the concern generated by the passage of the Polar Sea icebreaker in August 1985 the Mulroney government was pressed to enhance its surveillance capabilities in the Arctic. Sovereignty protection in the Arctic thus emerged as the centrepiece of the new debate on Canadian defence policy and the acquisition of a fleet of ten to twelve nuclear-powered submarines has become the flagship of the policy.

The use of the military to protect Canadian sovereignty echoes the concerns expressed in the last white paper on defence policy produced in the early 1970s. Unlike the Trudeau government's white paper which used sovereignty protection as a way to reduce military spending, the Mulroney government has moved in the opposite direction and decided to emphasize sovereignty to generate popular support for higher levels of military spending. The preoccupation with Arctic sovereignty is also a politically useful approach for framing a debate on Canadian defence policy. It creates the potential for uniting those who are worried about possible encroachments by Soviet Typhoon class submarines equipped with ballistic missiles with those who have condemned American commercial and military pressure in Canada's territorial waters. Minister of Defence Perrin Beatty has, of course, led the refrain by repeatedly asserting that "if there is going to be somebody's navy in the north it should be ours."[26] Chauvinistic nationalism is somewhat untypical of Canadians but the government may very well have found the right tone for selling its new defence priorities. The rallying cry of sovereignty may ensure the political success of the government's decision to acquire nuclear-powered submarines. It is unlikely, however, to ensure either security or sovereignty. Instead, the strategic realities of today are likely to translate the government's plans to purchase under-ice-capable submarines into a politically and economically costly reorientation of Canadian defence policy that was neither intended nor desired, and which does little to protect and serve Canadian interests.

The Arctic has once again become prime strategic territory for the superpowers. It has always been this way for the Soviet Union but the Americans lost interest in the region except as a surveillance outpost once intercontinental ballistic missiles arrived on the scene in the late 1950s. During the 1970s, the Soviet Union slowly but steadily expanded the size and quality of its navy; including a fleet of nuclear-powered attack submarines and Delta and Typhoon class submarines loaded with ballistic missiles; much of which was deployed in its northern fleet based at Murmansk on the Kola penninsula. Encouraged in part by the renewed competition in strategic defences, in part by American pressure to alter its nuclear force structure, and no doubt in part to rival the Americans' long-standing supremacy at sea, the Soviet fleet has been expanded further during the 1980s. While it would be wrong to suggest that a country that needs to keep more than half its fleet in dry dock because of lack of crews and equipment is a maritime power equivalent to that of the United States, it is important to recognize the growth of Soviet naval capabilities and the concentration of vessels in the northern and Pacific fleets.

The United States, for its part, has continually sought to maintain its mastery at sea and has since the mid-1960s relied on submarine-launched ballistic missiles as its primary retaliatory force to deter a potential attack from nuclear weapons. Control of the seas has thus always been central to American strategic planning. Until quite recently, however, the Arctic has not been an integral part of these plans. The renewed concern with the Arctic, as evident in the voyage of three attack submarines to the North Pole in May 1986 is partly a reflection of the growing Soviet and American capability to move through the Arctic; the importance of the Northern Fleet to the Soviet navy; and the increased concern with the commercial potential of the area. A more significant development affecting Arctic waters and the superpower rivalry at sea is the Maritime Strategy of the United States Navy (USN).

The USN's Maritime Strategy has thus far avoided much of the attention that has been devoted to the SDI but its implications for East-West relations and the prospects for nuclear escalation are as profound. While the SDI has captured media attention and that of peace groups, the USN has been revolutionizing its operations and has invested itself with the mandate of leading the offensive against the Soviet Union in times of crisis. In the 1950s it was the Strategic Air Command that held sway over American plans for preempting the Soviet Union's war-fighting capacity through a massive air strike on Soviet military and industrial targets. In recent years the USN has devised its own plan to strike at the jugular by moving quickly and assertively to choke off the Soviet navy as close to its home base as possible and then destroy it before it has a chance to use its weapons to support Soviet actions in central Europe. The Maritime Strategy is a recipe for a preemptive strike on the Soviet

Union's conventional and nuclear naval forces. As such, it runs a high risk of precipitating a shooting war during periods of crisis and lowering the nuclear threshold at a time when the Western Alliance appears willing to move in the opposite direction. A former American secretary of war, Henry Stimson, once lamented "the peculiar psychology of the Navy Department, which frequently seemed to retire from the realm of logic into a dim religious world in which Neptune was God, Mahan his prophet and the United States Navy the only true church."[27] The successors of Mahan are alive and well at the Naval War College in the United States and the Maritime Strategy is their sacred text.

The crusade for the Maritime Strategy was conducted by former American Secretary of the Navy John Lehman and the Chief of Naval Operations James Watkins. The strategy founded on the proposed 600-ship navy with its fifteen aircraft carrier groups was put forward by Admiral Thomas Hayward in a May 1979 issue of the *U.S. Naval Institute Proceedings*. Under the Reagan administration the strategy was proclaimed in 1983 and has as its primary objective the task of "carrying the fight to the enemy." The strategy is divided into three stages, the first of which is designed to maintain deterrence as it readies American naval forces for war through the forward deployment of these forces. Once in position these forces would be prepared to move to the second phase which would involve seizing the initiative "as far forward as possible." At this stage the strategy envisions a full-scale attack on Soviet naval assets around the globe, including base support facilities. Watkins explains that in practice this would include "classic Navy tasks of antisubmarine warfare, antisurface warfare, counter command and control, strike operations, antiair warfare, mine warfare, special operations, amphibious operations, and sealift."[28] The objective would be to strike at Soviet forces around the globe and through this tactic of horizontal escalation force the Soviets to divert their attention away from the central European front. The principal concentration of American naval activity, however, would be on the home bases of the Soviet northern and Pacific fleets in the Barents and Bering seas in and near the Arctic Ocean. It is at this stage of the strategy that the USN would also target and destroy Soviet ballistic missile submarines or in the words of Watkins, "shoot the archer before he releases his arrows." In its third and final phase the objective of the strategy would be to "complete the destruction of all the Soviet fleets." The task would be formidable and the prospects for a quick victory unlikely because American naval forces would have to operate in areas well-defended by the Soviet Union. Moreover, it is doubtful the Soviets would accept significant losses to their submarine fleet before they decided to escalate the conflict and use their nuclear weapons rather than see them destroyed by the U.S Navy. The strategy thus involves substantial risks with little benefit for deterrence.

The Arctic is of considerable importance to the planners of the Maritime Strategy. Because of the concentration of Soviet forces in the region, naval strategists consider it essential to confine the Soviet navy to their own northern waters. The growing concern in the United States for the strategic significance of the Arctic as part and parcel of this Maritime Strategy is evident in the commitment to construct a new fleet of attack submarines with enhanced capabilities for handling the Arctic terrain and a series of exercises designed to assess existing capabilities in this area.

The Maritime Strategy poses problems for Canadian policy makers not only because of its potential for turning the Arctic into the primary battlefield for the next war, but also because of its potential for actually creating the conditions that will ensure that such a war takes place. To date Canadian policy makers have tended to ignore the impact of the Maritime Strategy on strategic deterrence (as of June 1987 the Department of Defence, according to John Lamb of the Canadian Centre for Arms Control and Disarmament, had not yet undertaken an in-house study of the strategy) and have instead viewed American military activities in the Arctic primarily as a challenge to Canadian sovereignty. The concerns for sovereignty, while not insignificant, are overshadowed by the strategic issues involved.

The Maritime Strategy is not a recipe for stable deterrence. Instead, it seems likely that it could be fuel to feed the next world war. The strategy emphasizes the theme of "horizontal escalation" (shifting the conflict to other areas by launching attacks against Soviet interests away from the main battlefield) as a means for deterring Soviet aggression in central Europe. It is based on the faulty premise that by challenging Soviet interests in the Third World and especially on the northern and eastern approaches to the Soviet homeland, the Soviets will be dissuaded from attacking central Europe or forced to shift their military resources to these areas, losing their alleged advantage in the central front. By challenging Soviet interests before a conflict the strategists hope to deter war. Failing that the strategy envisions destroying Soviet assets including Soviet submarines carrying ballistic missiles early in a conflict. The fact that the strategy rests on the early use of massive military force renders it unlikely to be useful in controlling either crises or armed conflict. Indeed in most respects the Maritime Strategy harks back to John Foster Dulles' doctrine of "massive retaliation." Even the language being used to describe the strategy is reminiscent of terms used in the mid-1950s in debates on massive retaliation. As with the doctrine of massive retaliation, the Maritime Strategy attempts to blur the distinction between nuclear and conventional weapons. It also suggests a revival of the spirit of the offensive and that the "best defence is a good offence." But now under conditions of nuclear parity between the superpowers the rhetoric echoes of madness.

The Maritime Strategy undermines the Western Alliance's commitment to strategic stability and the Canadian government's priority of strategic deterrence. It also undermines crisis stability by placing an emphasis on the early first use of massive destructive power. Finally, but no less important to the extent that the strategy identifies Soviet submarines as a primary target, the strategy adopts a counterforce posture toward Soviet nuclear forces. When combined with the enhancement of American land- and air-based nuclear weapons, the Maritime Strategy will give the American military a first-strike posture that threatens the stability of deterrence. The United States, with good cause, has been encouraging the Soviet Union to shift its nuclear retaliatory forces to reflect those of the United States and to be deployed in submarines as the Americans have been for the past twenty years. The Maritime Strategy threatens these retaliatory forces and thus contradicts what had apparently been American strategic objectives. By destabilizing the strategic balance on the high seas the Maritime Strategy increases the prospect that future East-West crises will escalate to war and that future wars will be fought with nuclear weapons.

The Maritime Strategy is also partly responsible for the new-found interest in this country for patrolling under the polar ice cap. The 1987 white paper on national defence makes clear the government's intent to replenish Canada's maritime forces which have been in a sorry state. After decades of neglect the Canadian navy is being justifiably readied for a revival. It is not enough, however, simply to commit resources to the maritime forces. As the American naval strategist Alfred Mayer Mahan once queried "all the world knows, gentlemen, that we are building a new navy. Well, when we get our navy what are we going to do with it?"[29] With a government-estimated cost of between 4-6 billion current-year dollars the Mulroney government's proposal to purchase nuclear-powered submarines and deploy them in the Canadian Arctic has become the first priority of the capital equipment program for the Canadian armed forces. The rationale for the decision is, however, as obscure as the subs will be once they dive below the polar icecap.

Under the ruse of sovereignty, the government's excessive concern for security threats in the Canadian Arctic has not only led it to propose expensive solutions to suspect problems but has also left it poorly equipped to deal with the threats that are likely to materialize in that region. Actions in the interest of sovereignty are of course politically useful. It is difficult to fault a policy that is ceremoniously wrapped in the maple leaf. But John Honderich admits in *The Arctic Imperative*, "It is hard to justify spending the hundreds of millions of dollars required for military hardware in the North solely on the basis of hyped-up national pride."[30]

Far from enhancing Canadian sovereignty, the proposals of the Mulroney government are likely to undermine it by linking Canada's Arctic and maritime forces ever more closely with the American navy's interest in turning the Arctic into the next theatre of strategic operations through its Maritime Strategy. Once again Canadians are faced with the persistent dilemma of attempting to respond to shifting American strategies in a manner that will best serve Canadian interests. The Canadian government's attempt to join the ranks of the world's naval powers appears destined to lead the country into yet another misguided affiliation with a wrongheaded American military strategy; it runs the risk of distorting Canadian defence policy for yet another generation.

In the late 1940s as the United States worried about the threats that loomed in the land of the midnight sun, Mackenzie King was of the view that such threats were remote and should be kept that way. In his words, "our best defence in the Arctic was the Arctic itself."[31] It is no longer possible for the Canadian government to ignore the Arctic. Canada's maritime interests now encompass the Arctic to an extent unmatched in the past. These interests are likely to expand considerably over the next generation as the commercial development of the North intensifies. Threats to these interests must, however, be assessed carefully so that this country makes the most appropriate response.

Canada's former defence minister, Barney Danson, has recently argued that the possibility of a Soviet attack over the polar icecap "except by air, still seems so remote that any diversion of Canada's limited military resources is unjustified."[32] Nevertheless the view persists that the Soviet Union poses a significant threat to Canada's interests in the Arctic. One often-cited concern about Soviet activity in the Arctic is that Soviet missile-carrying submarines would be able to hide under the polar ice cap and with little warning break through the ice and fire their missiles on targets in North America. Obviously this possibility is a matter of concern but it is not fundamentally different from the threat already posed by Soviet intercontinental ballistic missiles deployed on Soviet territory which also have the ability to reach targets in North America. Moreover, as Harriet Critchley of the University of Calgary and other observers have noted, the Soviet submarine capability has improved to the point where the Soviets do not need to move outside their own territorial waters to reach targets in North America with their submarine-based nuclear forces. If Canadian submarines designated for Arctic patrol are there to chase away Soviet submarines they are likely to have to move into Soviet waters to find them.

A second concern is that the Soviet Union will use the polar ice cap to hide submarines equipped with cruise missiles or attack submarines armed with conventional weapons which would then be deployed in the North Atlantic or the North Pacific destined either to launch their cruise missiles against North American targets or to attack the sea lanes of communication that link North America to Europe and Japan. It is perhaps the latter fear that deserves the most attention because of the concern that if Europe is to shift to a conventional defence the supply routes between North America and Europe will take on additional significance and because of a view that the Soviet submarine fleet is so large and the Western Alliance's merchant fleet so small that the former would be able to wreak havoc on the latter. Such concerns are, however, overstated. Not only are they of questionable validity but there is also room to doubt that submarines are the best means for meeting these threats. Despite frequent assertions by American military planners about the potential devastation that Soviet submarines could wreak on transatlantic shipping, other analysts including Kurt Lautenschalger and John Mearsheimer have recently demonstrated that such assertions are quite doubtful, given the limited number of Soviet submarines available for such a task, the relative success historically of antisubmarine warfare techniques, and the likely duration of any future war.[33]

In summary, the Soviet submarine threat from Canadian waters is not sufficient to warrant an excessive commitment of nuclear-powered submarines. The forward deployment of Soviet submarines in Canada's waters does not provide the Soviet fleet with any significant strategic advantage that could not as easily be acquired from its own territory or from open water on the high seas. One possible exception to this conclusion has been noted by retired Rear Admiral Frederick Crickard who recently wrote that "the probability of the Soviets using the Canadian Arctic as a patrol area for nuclear submarines that fire ballistic or cruise missiles is very remote, unless vigorous anti-submarine warfare efforts by the U.S. Navy makes the situation untenable for the Soviet Navy in the Russian Arctic."[34] In short, threats to Canadian security in the Arctic are as likely to arise from American strategies as they are from Soviet designs. Even if one is unwilling to accept this view of the limited utility of the high Arctic to Soviet naval vessels it is still questionable whether a Canadian response is likely to be effective.

It is not at all clear how a relatively small fleet of Canadian submarines will be able to play traffic cop for Soviet and American submarines under the polar icecap. Intercepting submarines is not an easy task under the best of conditions and is extremely complicated under the polar ice because of the uneven terrain and the excessive noise of the shifting ice. It is evident that submarines have some capability to track other submarines and that "under polar ice, submarines are essentially the only effective anti-submarine weapon and sensor platform."[35] Despite the potential utility of submarines for antisubmarine warfare and the lack of real alternatives for this task under the ice, Lautenschlager concludes that "without significant advances in detection technology" the prospect of an effective antisubmarine warfare capability using submarines is remote. Tom Stefanick of the Federation of American Scientists is more blunt in asserting that changes in submarine technology that are making these weapons carriers even quieter will make the "whole notion of going up near the Soviet Union and hunting for their subs very doubtful."[36] And Captain John Moore, the editor of *Jane's Fighting Ships* has been cited as stating that "he doubted whether Canadian nuclear submarines would actually be able to find either Soviet or U.S. submarines in Canadian waters." [37]

Despite these criticisms, Defence Minister Beatty and other supporters of the government's proposals argue that the mere presence of nuclear submarines under the ice would discourage the Soviets from deploying submarines in this area and contain them in the Soviet Arctic and would also provide the government with information on the activities of allies. Foreign Minister Joe Clark acknowledged to a House Committee on National Defence that this "sounds a little like science fiction" but despite Clark's skepticism the government is pressing ahead. The questionable need for and utility of a Canadian submarine patrol under the ice in peacetime is not the only criterion for assessing this option. It must also be challenged on its role in a crisis. If implemented effectively the Maritime Strategy would restrict the Soviet fleet to their home ports, prevent submarines and surface vessels from reaching the high seas, and make them easy prey if the crisis were to escalate to a shooting war. If it were to succeed this tactic would not radically alter the strategic balance to favour the West and may actually undermine the Canadian government's stated objective of maintaining strategic deterrence because its likely effect may be to reduce the opportunity for alleviating tensions during crises and make the Soviets more likely to use their weapons in a preemptive manner when faced with the threat of war.

In summary, the likelihood that the deployment of nuclear-powered submarines in the Arctic would contribute to Canadian security even in a crisis, let alone in peacetime, is so remote that it cannot justify the investment.

The lack of a sound security rationale for nuclear-powered submarines is one reason why the government has presented the policy as one that will serve Canada's sovereignty interests in the region. As the Minister of Defence has so often remarked "Our sovereignty in the Arctic cannot be complete if we remain dependent on allies for knowledge of possible hostile activities in our waters, under our ice and for preventing such activities."[38] The Minister's contention that Canadian sovereignty can only be assured if the Canadian military is capable of identifying and responding to all military threats on or near Canadian territory is absurd. The country has never independently attempted to ensure its own security. Its defence policy has always been tied to those of imperial states—initially Great Britain and more recently the United States. The idea that Canada could or should attempt to unilaterally counter the strategic designs of the superpowers is as dangerous as the notion that Canada has no strategic interests of its own.

Canadians have long realized that the country cannot pursue a unilateralist path toward security. The establishment of a navy was one of the earliest acts of nationhood undertaken by a Canadian government. Yet Laurier's "local navy" policy was not designed to provide complete protection for Canada's maritime interests. Instead, as Cuthbertson notes, "its strategic realism lay in the planned development of a navy in close co-operation with the Royal Navy and acceptance that British navy supremacy was essential to Canadian security and hence a vital national interest."[39] A great deal has changed in the intervening years and despite the retention of many maritime interests and the expansion of many others, Canada's local navy policy has yielded to a no-navy policy. The government's proposal to adopt a unilateralist response to perceived security threats in the Arctic will not, however, solve the problem. Inevitably it will lead this country into bilateral arrangements with the United States in which we contribute to their strategic plans in exchange for some recognized presence in our own territory. This is likely to be a very costly exchange when the American strategy with which we will be linked is one that is likely to complicate arms control negotiations and return the world to the brinkmanship advocated by John Foster Dulles. Lester Pearson opposed the doctrine of "massive retaliation" because it would undermine the Western Alliance and lead Canada into an entrenched continentalist defence posture. The current proposals of the Mulroney government, when combined with the Maritime Strategy of the U.S. Navy, bring with them a similar risk.

A local navy policy tied primarily to the American navy is an unacceptable option given the latter's operational strategy. The dilemma for Canadian policy makers is one of responding effectively to challenges to Canadian jurisdiction in the Arctic and making a worthy contribution to international stability without increasing the prospects that crises will trigger shooting wars or that shooting wars will quickly degenerate into total war. The answer lies in a wider multilateral approach. As Nicholas Tracy has argued "the essential means to the end of protecting Canada's Arctic jurisdiction is the preservation of a secure alliance of Western Europe and North America."[40] The current long awaited white paper of 1987 fails to meet these requirements and the country must look for other options.

## CHAPTER THREE

# The Alliance and the Bomb

The military authorities may argue that the atomic bomb is just another weapon. But, in the minds of ordinary people everywhere in the world, it is far more than that and has acquired an immeasurably greater intrinsic significance. The anxiety with which the possibility of the use of the bomb, by either side, is regarded has been strikingly and increasingly evident of late among our friends in Europe and in Asia. This is the main reason for the appeal, even in free countries, of the cynical Communist "peace" campaign.

The psychological and political consequences of the employment of the bomb, or the threat of its employment, in the present critical situation would be incalculably great. The risk of retaliation, to which our allies in Europe feel themselves to be exposed, would affect materially their will to resist, and the imminent prospect of atomic war over Korea, when our defences elsewhere are still weak, cannot fail to stimulate the tendencies toward "neutralism" which the development of strength and unity on our side is beginning to overcome.

L.B. Pearson, "Korea and the Atomic Bomb",
December 3, 1950.[1]

At the heart of many of NATO's dilemmas and debates lies, not the Soviet Union, but the absolute nature of nuclear weapons. Such is the unearthly power, the unimaginable destructiveness of these weapons of mass destruction, the unbelievable horror that would follow their use in a military conflict, that they have changed beyond human recognition the traditional meanings of words such as "war," "strategy," "alliance." Students in university classrooms are asked to consider the meaning of Clausewitz's dictum that war is an act of policy, a continuation of politics by other means; yet neither the students nor their professors have the faintest idea how this could be applied to a nuclear war. Nor do traditional meanings of strategy—the employment of armed force for political ends—have much relevance for nuclear weapons, except for their role in deterrence. The weapon of mass destruction, as a great American diplomat once put it, is simply not something with which one readily springs to the defence of one's friends: it demoralizes allies rather than reassures them; it concentrates power and centralizes decision making within an alliance; it weakens self-reliance; it prompts doubts about the credibility of nuclear guarantees; it tends to undermine co-operation rather than promote it.

In this chapter we want to explain the historical origins of NATO's long-standing dependence on the Bomb; to show how their reliance on American nuclear weapons discouraged the Europeans (and Canada) from building up their own conventional forces; and to present in broad outline the thesis that NATO is in fact capable of defending itself with conventional forces against a Soviet attack on Europe, and that the costs to the Alliance of providing for such a strategy are not prohibitive. There are complex political as well as strategic problems associated with a shift to an all-conventional defence, and it is difficult to see how the risk of an escalation to the use of nuclear weapons can be eliminated entirely while the superpowers, Britain and France, insist for security reasons on having their own nuclear arsenals. But the risk can be greatly reduced, along with the politically divisive and corrosive impact of the Bomb on the Alliance. We think Canada's interests would be served by supporting an all-conventional strategy, even if it means higher defence spending or a reallocation of resources within the existing defence budget in favour of the European commitment.

## NATO's Nuclear Habit

The ruling assumptions and military plans of NATO's member states were, as we noted in the previous chapter, transformed by the outbreak of the Korean War in June 1950. Until that moment in the cold war, it was accepted by most policy makers in

Ottawa, Washington, and the capitals of NATO Europe that America's ability to strike at the Soviet Union with atomic bombs would deter Stalin from using overt military force to pursue his goals; and it was generally agreed, too, that the principal threat to Western Europe was to be found less in the likelihood of a Soviet military aggression than in Europe's own weakness in the face of what Canada's secretary of state for external affairs called the forces of apathy, despair, doubt, and fear. "The feeling of insecurity is not always due to a defined threat, a visibly prepared aggression," the French foreign minister, Robert Schuman, remarked during the ratification debate on the Atlantic Pact in 1949. "The mere imbalance of forces that is maintained by the stronger and not compensated for by serious international guarantees in favor of the weaker suffices to create insecurity."[2] At this point Schuman sought guarantees against the European Left, particularly the Communists who were tightly controlled by Moscow through the Cominform; but he was also a man without a Maginot Line looking for a new defence against the Teutonic hordes. In the aftermath of the coup in Czechoslovakia in February 1948, British Foreign Secretary Ernest Bevin, not a man given to visions of the apocalypse, warned his cabinet colleagues of an imminent "threat to civilization" arising from the Soviet Politburo's aim to acquire "physical control of the Eurasian land mass and eventual control of the whole world's Island." Yet even at the height of Europe's great fear in the summer of 1948, few expected military aggression from Russia. The fear was of a general collapse of society in Western Europe that would let the Left and its allies in Moscow take power.[3]

So far as Canadian and U.S. policy makers were concerned, NATO was conceived as a traditional military guarantee pact committing North American power to the defence of Europe to bolster West European resolution. It was intended to act as a form of military reassurance, something to stiffen European resolve and self-confidence. Neither Canada nor the United States, each of which retained suspicions of European designs, intended more than the guarantee. NATO was not created to marshal military power, either in being or in potential, to deter an imminent attack on Europe. Like Russia's huge army, it was intended to provide political and psychological reinforcement in the continuing political warfare of the cold war. There was no significant fear of a massive Russian invasion.[4]

In the absence of such fear, Canadian policy makers fought off any suggestion that Canada fulfill its obligations under Article III of the North Atlantic Treaty by increasing military spending, sending military equipment to Europe or, worse still, stationing Canadian troops in Europe. This attitude was fully consistent with the initial strategic concept of the Alliance, as set out by General Omar Bradley, chairman of the U.S. Joint Chiefs of Staff, to Congress: the concept (which bears a close resemblance to the ideas of present-day Canadian and American isolationists) saw the North Americans protecting naval supply routes and providing the strategic bomber deterrent while the Europeans were to bear the burden of the "hard core of the ground power in being."[5] This simple division of labour minimized any U.S. continental commitments; as such, it was well-suited to a traditional guarantee pact and to the realities of American domestic politics. But it was based on the crucial assumption that the United States would continue to enjoy a monopoly over atomic weapons and would not be deterred by a Soviet capacity to hit back. The corollary—that U.S. strategic air power could defeat the Soviets in Europe without large-scale land operations and that, accordingly, there was no reason to build up North American armies in Europe—was popular among isolationists in the American Congress, exceedingly unpopular with the military and the European allies. Even before the Soviets exploded their first atom bomb in September 1949, General Bradley himself had drawn the link between the victory-through-airpower strategy and the politics of alliance cohesion:

It must be perfectly apparent to the people of the United States that we cannot count on friends in Western Europe if our strategy in the event of war dictates that we shall first abandon them to the enemy with a promise of later liberation. Yet that is the only strategy that can prevail if the military balance of power in Europe is to be carried on the wings of our bombers and deposited in reserves this side of the ocean. It is a strategy that would produce nothing better than impotent and disillusioned allies in the event of war.[6]

In effect, this was a call unwelcome to isolationists—to support containment with a visible U.S. military presence in Europe. It was heeded, but only after the Russian bomb, the fall of China, and the invasion of South Korea had thoroughly traumatized the American people. Driven along by these events and by the rise of McCarthyism, Truman ordered a complete reappraisal of American security policies. The report called NSC-68 of a joint State and Defence Department effort submitted to Truman in April 1950 painted a grim view of future Soviet intentions and of the growing military threat from Russia: once Soviet atomic weapons were sufficient to cancel out the U.S. deterrent, Europe would be vulnerable to conventional aggression. NSC-68 called for both "a much larger scale" of European rearmament and "deeper participation by the United States than has been contemplated" to restore Europe to a position of influence and strength. "Considering the Soviet Union military capability," the report turgidly argued, "The long-range allied military objective in Western Europe must envisage an increased military strength in that area sufficient possibly to deter the Soviet Union from a major war or, in any event, to delay materially the overrunning of Western Europe and, if feasible, to hold a bridgehead on the Continent against Soviet Union offensives."[7] Rearm, rearm, rearm.

The NSC-68 report's pessimistic view of the Kremlin's methods and intentions seemed to be borne out by events, particularly by North Korea's invasion of the South in June 1950. The threat to Western Europe was no longer thought to be a political one of subversion or disintegration; now Europe was deemed to be in danger of imminent military invasion. American military planners, who had badly underestimated Russia's technical capability to produce an atomic bomb, now had to reckon on dealing with the Soviets from a position of eroding superiority. Politically, however, the crisis was an opportunity to be seized—"Korea came along and saved us," Truman's secretary of state, Dean Acheson, subsequently recalled; saved America from isolationism, he meant. Truman acted swiftly and without prior congressional debate to commit four divisions of U.S. ground forces to Europe (two other divisions were still in Germany, part of the postwar allied occupation of that defeated power), though not before securing a commitment from France to promote an integrated European army under the proposed European Defence Community. The United States launched a full rearmament program, which quadrupled U.S. defence expenditures within three years, and announced that henceforth aid to Europe would be directed to military rather than economic ends. The North Atlantic Council decided that a "forward strategy" would be adopted in Europe—meaning that NATO would embrace West Germany and resist any aggression "as far to the East as possible." It was at this point, as we saw in chapter One, that the decision was made to integrate NATO's forces under a centralized command headed by a Supreme Allied Commander, Europe. NATO's first Supreme Commander, General Dwight Eisenhower, was appointed in December 1950.

Truman's troops-to-Europe decision posed the issue of allied "burden-sharing"—the distribution of costs and benefits of alliance membership among NATO's members. Who should bear the costs of collective security? During the 1951 "great debate" on the Alliance in the Senate and House, Truman's Republican critics worried that the cost of building up land armies in Korea and Europe would cause ruinous inflation, a bloated federal budget, and the creation of a garrison state. Senator Robert Taft, who led the attack on Truman's policy, feared an open-ended commitment to the Europeans and the permanent costs of a conventional buildup on the continent. Like former President Herbert Hoover, Taft wanted to leave European defence to the Europeans and concentrate on control of the seas and air; a much enlarged air force equipped with atomic bombs would better deter Soviet expansionism than would U.S. troops based overseas.

Taft also sought to restrict the authority of the President, whom he accused of overreaching his constitutional powers in dispatching troops to Korea and Europe in 1950; a good fiscal conservative, he wanted to limit the growth of big government and its defence budget.[8] What he objected to was committing the United States to fight the worldwide battle with communism "primarily on the vast land areas of the continent of Europe or the continent of Asia, where we are at the greatest disadvantage in a war with Russia."[9] Truman's decision was upheld, but only after Congress had impressed on the executive its fear of excessive commitments and its intention to limit America's share of the economic burdens of collective defence. Congress required the Joint Chiefs of Staff to certify that the European allies were making their contribution to the defence of Europe, and it also wanted provision made to use the military resources of Italy, Spain, and West Germany. Had Congress known that American, British, and Canadian ground forces were going to Europe as hostages, to play the role of "trip-wire" to activate the U.S. nuclear guarantee, and not as part of a multilateral conventional army capable of defending Western Europe against Soviet military actions, it seems probable that Truman's decision would have been overturned.

These were some of the trends and forces that foreshadowed the American nuclear strategy of the "new look," or massive retaliation, adopted by President Eisenhower shortly after assuming office and given public expression by Secretary of State Dulles in his famous speech of January 1954. As in the burden-sharing debate, economics and security were closely linked in the Republican view of national strategy: the empire would be defended but, where feasible, on the cheap. Hereafter, Asians should fight Asia's battles, and (with less emphasis) Europeans Europe's.

Though he had been NATO's first Supreme Commander, Eisenhower subordinated the European commitment to the larger interest of keeping America solvent. Better than most postwar presidents, he grasped the material limits of American power. Security was more than armaments; strategy was more than troops and firepower in the right place. The lesson of Korea was that neither the American public nor the U.S. economy would tolerate a succession of limited, conventional wars. The public opposed the dispatch of troops overseas for anything less than total victory; the deficits and inflation incurred in drawn-out conflicts and rearmament would destroy America's economic and financial stability. That stability and America's superior industrial power were factors of no less moment than the state of U.S. armaments in deterring a would-be aggressor, and therefore the formulation of military strategy must begin with a consideration of the real costs of defence requirements. Recalled to Washington in 1951 to testify in behalf of Truman's policy, Supreme Commander Eisenhower seemed to align himself with Taft's position. American troops had gone to Europe to build confidence and morale, he told Congress, not as part of a continental land army. The U.S. must continue to produce and equip, but not supply troops around the periphery of the Sino-Soviet empire: "We cannot concentrate all our forces in any one section," Eisenhower warned, "even one as important as Western Europe. We must largely sit here with great mobile, powerful reserves ready to support our policies, our rights, our interests wherever they may be in danger in the world."[10]

It was the deadlocked conventional war in Korea and the erosion of public support for defence spending that gave the American air force's Strategic Air Command, under General Curtis LeMay, its opportunity to sell strategic deterrence through airpower as North America's first line of defence. As the air command's size and mission dramatically expanded during the Korean War, the limited range of its bombers and the requirements for a sustained nuclear offensive against Russia led the United States into a series of bilateral agreements with friendly countries for construction of and access to overseas bases. The U.S. had one base (Puerto Rico) outside the continental United States in 1950, and fourteen in 1955: the Strategic Air Command acquired landing rights at many other overseas bases, and rights to additional bases in Newfoundland, Labrador, Libya, and Turkey. The exigencies of airpower doctrine and technology also underlay, as we showed in chapter Two, the growing military integration of North America in the early 1950s.

Returning from a preinauguration trip to Korea on board the USS *Helena*, Eisenhower was pressed by Admiral Arthur Radford, commander in chief of the Pacific fleet, and by Dulles to retrench, to reduce U.S. garrisons overseas, and to develop American nuclear striking power as a deterrent to Soviet-backed aggression.[11] The military would accept deep cuts in conventional ground forces, but only on condition that the Joint Chiefs received a commitment from the President that he would authorize the use of tactical and strategic nuclear weapons wherever this was militarily advantageous. The opportunity to achieve security with solvency, to bring military necessities and economic limitations into line, was at hand. By October 1953 Eisenhower had accepted the strategy, as outlined in NSC 162/2 on "Basic National Security Policy,"[12] to maintain "a strong military posture, with emphasis on the capability of inflicting massive retaliatory damage by offensive striking power." In Europe, both allies and adversaries had to be persuaded of the "manifest determination" of the U.S. to use its massive retaliatory capacity in the event of aggression. If hostilities broke out, the United States "will consider nuclear weapons to be as available for use as other munitions." As President Truman had remarked during the Korean War, the Bomb was merely another weapon. On that dubious proposition the United States substantially reduced its defence budget, cutting back the army from its post-Korean War strength of twenty divisions to a 1957 target of fourteen, a drop of nearly half a million men. On the other hand, the air force would increase from 115 to 137 wings and add 30,000 men.[13]

Eisenhower was curiously untroubled by the fact that the buildup of Soviet nuclear capabilities was producing an atomic stalemate, and that the coercive power of America's Strategic Air Command was fast diminishing (something which the Truman administration had admitted in defence of the troops-to-Europe decision). The implications of this stalemate for the strategy of massive retaliation had not been grasped in the West: Robert Osgood notes in his seminal study of NATO that "well after 1955 the West's strategic outlook remained under the dominant influence of nostalgic memories of the period of America's atomic monopoly."[14] In another sense, the new strategy was part of a U.S. military tradition of substituting technology for manpower, one that found great support among the civilians in the Eisenhower White House. The "new look" represented the ascendancy of domestic economic requirements over strategy; the substitution of nuclear weaponry for conventional manpower offered "a bigger bang for the buck." Because of this strong economic point in its favour, the heavy emphasis on nuclear weapons was to become a permanent feature of NATO's strategy.

But NATO did not promptly accept the new strategy. There was serious political opposition to atomic weapons throughout Europe. There was a great fear that Europe, not Russia and not the U.S., would be the site of any atomic war. Undaunted, Dulles urged the merits of getting in the first blow when the NATO Council met in December 1953. "All would prefer I sup-pose not [to] be first to use A weapons—certainly of mass type. *But first to use gains tremendous advantage."* But, with the exception of Churchill's Britain, the Europeans remained skeptical. Dulles told the National Security Council how he had made "every effort to get the other NATO Ministers to thinking in something like our terms of atomic weapons and of the atomic age. This had not been wholly successful, and the other Ministers were still very frightened at the atomic prospect."

When Dulles told the Council on Foreign Relations on January 12, 1954 that the U.S. was abandoning the strategy of preparing to fight in any theatre and substituting a new approach— "to depend primarily upon a great capacity to retaliate, instantly, by means and at places of our choosing"—dovecoats fluttered all across the Alliance, as James Eayrs has put it.[15] Canada had not been consulted about the Dulles speech or about the far-reaching shift in U.S. strategy; nor apparently had any other ally. Lester Pearson, the Canadian minister for external affairs, publicly criticized Dulles's unilateralism but expressed much more substantive reservations about the drift of U.S. strategy to Prime Minister St. Laurent. The prefatory quote to this chapter, taken from a Pearson memorandum on the proposed use of atomic weapons by the Americans in Korea, amply illustrates his rejection of the military thesis that the Bomb was just another weapon: it was universally viewed as the *ultimate* weapon, and that was the basis of its use as a deterrent. If used in Asia, the threat of retaliation would be felt across Europe and NATO; employed indiscriminately in whatever theatre, it had the potential to destroy the alliance and to automatically engulf all in a general war. Canadian military planners warned that the U.S. was relaxing its restrictions on the use of atomic weapons and was planning their use in any type of military action. "Therefore, because of our close association in the military field we may find ourselves involved in an atomic war without much consultation."[16] Here an old Canadian fear of automatic involvements in great power conflicts coexisted with the new insecurities of the atomic age.

On massive retaliation, Pearson warned St. Laurent three weeks after the Dulles speech that the Americans might abandon their continental commitments in an "Operation Disengagement" and adopt a peripheral (or maritime) strategy:

The Americans may now argue that as Europe will not unite to defend itself, they are relieved of certain responsibilities for that defence which can, in any event, now be left predominantly to the Germans! This being the case, United States strategy should now become peripheral, holding a sea and air line running roughly from Norway to the United Kingdom through Spain and the Mediterranean to Greece and Turkey—and Pakistan? From this line, in case of war, victory by atomic retaliation can be assured.[17]

Anticipating many academic criticisms of the new U.S. strategy, Pearson argued that "local aggressions cannot be answered by atomic weapons," and that the threat of retaliation was likely to prove hollow. "The new strategy may result, therefore, in greater rigidity, rather than greater flexibility, of policy. If it becomes a question of the atomic bomb and all-out war, or nothing, it may be, too often, nothing." Well short of the test of war, however, America's depreciation of local defence was certain to generate fear and uneasiness among Europeans, a sense that the U.S. was planning to let Europe defend itself, assisted by overseas weapons, rather than by overseas troops. Europe's likely military response was accurately predicted by Canada's deputy to the North Atlantic Council, Dana Wilgress. On grounds of economy, the Europeans would themselves opt for nuclear dependence and for greater participation in the making of allied nuclear strategy:

The French and a number of European countries will not accept an arrangement whereby they will be expected to contribute largely manpower while the United States will concentrate on a small highly mobile reserve force supplemented by scientific weapons of mass destruction. They will wish to be supplied themselves with these weapons, they will also try to effect such economies as may be compatible with the agreed requirements of effective defence and they will press to have a voice in the shaping of the strategy which will determine the use of such weapons.[18]

In the last analysis, America's allies were no more willing to forego the domestic economies afforded by the substitution of nuclear firepower for costly standing armies than was the White

House. Virtually by default, the American concept of allied strategy controlled the debate. It was as much a technological as a military solution. The U.S. was still expected to enjoy overwhelming superiority in most aspects of its nuclear arms competition with Soviet Russia, notably in the production and deployment of small fission bombs for tactical use. The first generation of so-called tactical nuclear weapons, developed for use on the battlefield, offered NATO the cheapest firepower available to offset the imbalance in conventional forces in central Europe. "An army equipped with tactical nuclear weapons should be able to hold up an enemy many times its own size," argued Denis Healey, the British Labour Party strategist.

In December 1954, the Alliance officially adopted its strategy of tactical nuclear response to Soviet conventional aggression and the door quietly closed on the original division of allied labour and responsibilities, in which the creation of a large standing army was to devolve upon the Europeans. Now their security would rely increasingly on complex weapons of mass destruction that were American-controlled and whose early introduction into a military conflict with the Soviets was ensured by the existing imbalance in conventional forces. Thereby, the Europeans got their defence on the cheap by delegating the crucial questions of war and peace to their protectors in Washington. Such were the false economies of an age of atomic plenty.

**Europe in Arms**

The logic of American and NATO strategic doctrine in the mid-fifties was that conventional rearmament was pointless. Conventional war had been superannuated by the Pentagon. Therefore, the limited ground forces available to the West were not expected to fight a local resistance against an aggressor; their role would be to hold the enemy until the nuclear deterrent was activated—to be a "trip-wire" that could not itself deny gains to the Soviets but would provoke all-out nuclear retaliation. Conventional armies had become auxiliary to the principal purpose of force, the deterrence and waging of war with weapons of mass destruction. The divisions of U.S. troops dispatched to the continent by Truman in 1950 were viewed by the Europeans as hostages, who ensured that the president of the United States would not retreat into a peripheral strategy but would fight for Europe.[19] American forces on the continent were also seen as part of an unspoken pledge by the U.S. to limit and contain any revival of German militarism. Thus, to keep the U.S. troops in Europe and the commitment of America's military power intact became the true *raison d'etre* of much of Europe's security policy.

In October 1953 the first massive 85-ton, 280-millimetre atomic artillery piece arrived in Europe from America, a down payment on the Dulles plan. It was followed in the next year by hundreds of the latest tactical nuclear weapons, missiles, and rockets such as the Honest John, Matador, Davy Crockett, and the Lance. The following features were important: first, their yield or destructive power, calculated in equivalent weights of conventional high explosive TNT, ranged from several hundred tons to well over one million tons (a megaton); many U.S. weapons designated tactical were far too destructive to permit any real discrimination between civilian and military targets in the highly urbanized and industrialized areas of central Europe. The Pershing I missiles deployed a bit later in West Germany (and which became the focus of a near-collapse in arms control negotiations between Russia and America in the 1980s) carried warheads capable of dwarfing the power of the Hiroshima bomb and surpassing the destructiveness of most American "strategic" weapons systems. Second, none of these ground-launched tactical weapons had the range to hit the Soviet Union itself from Western Europe, although nuclear-capable American F-111 and F-4 aircraft based in Britain and the continent did have such range. Most of the new tactical weapons had a range of a couple of hundred kilometres or less, which made their likeliest target somewhere in West Germany; a grisly phrase was coined in the 1980s to describe this situation—"The shorter the range, the more German the effect." Finally, the new weapons were immobile, poorly protected and highly vulnerable to early, preemptive attack: in a serious crisis they could well induce a "use it or lose it" psychology and even precipitate a war. As the Soviets moved quickly to develop a preemptive capacity to neutralize NATO's tactical nuclear forces in Europe, these instabilities grew.[20]

Nevertheless, NATO's nuclear strategy did offer allied governments relief from the domestic political difficulties of imposing burdensome new defence programs, of raising taxes, of increasing conscription requirements. Atomic weapons were a technological fix, a solution to the heavy costs posed by rearmament on European recovery. Canadian diplomats noted in 1954 that the allies were no longer subject to American pressure over burden-sharing and conventional defence spending. No longer was there talk of meeting the Lisbon force goals of ninety-six ground force divisions and 9000 aircraft. On the contrary, Admiral Radford, chairman of the U.S. Joint Chiefs of Staff, was attempting to cut the American armed services by 800,000 men, limiting the ground forces to civil defence and token overseas missions on the assumption that local wars on the Korean scale would be deterred or fought with atomic weapons. What then was the purpose of building a 500,000-man West German army? asked the parliamentary opposition during debate on the German draft law, particularly since Chancellor Konrad Adenauer's own conception had been that NATO's conventional forces should be increased until they could defend the Federal Republic *without* resorting to nuclear weapons.

It was a perfectly reasonable question and the answers did not become clearer when NATO carried out a large-scale wargame, "Carte Blanche", in May 1955 in West Germany, the Netherlands, and France. This first simulated test of NATO's tactical nuclear strategy revealed that in a 48-hour period, (hypothetically) 335 nuclear weapons had been used against military targets, 268 on German territory, and that 1.7 million Germans had been killed and 3.5 million wounded—not counting those affected by radioactivity. During the entire Second World War allied bombers had killed 305,000 German civilians and wounded 780,000. Later studies and wargames conducted at the Pentagon suggested that the initiation of a tactical nuclear war in Europe could leave 100 million dead if it escalated to attacks on cities. Such weapons, Helmut Schmidt stated in his 1962 book *Defense or Retaliation*, "will not save Europe, but destroy it." That was also the premise of the first antinuclear protest movements which sprang up in Britain and elsewhere in Europe in the late 1950s. Unilateralism, the demand for unilateral nuclear disarmament by the West, had roots of course in Europe's earlier peace movements, but there was something new as well. The unilateralists were less worried by the prospect that the United States might shrink from using nuclear weapons in defence of Europe than by the possibility that she *would* use them and thereby destroy her allies as well as her foes.

If only because of their divisive impact on the politics of NATO Europe, it seems plain that the Alliance would have been better off had it never attempted to use nuclear weapons to redress its weaknesses in the conventional area. Overreliance on weapons of mass destruction brought unexpected political complications: deployed to reassure, instead they discouraged and frightened the peoples of Western Europe. Nuclear weapons created anxiety and feelings of powerlessness and dependence. Fear of the Bomb engendered in many European countries a volatile mix of nationalism, neutralism, and defeatism. The technology of these new weapons was terrifying and impenetrable. They were under remote foreign control, as was NATO itself. To the lay civilian, the language of nuclear strategy was arcane and, like the weapons, accessible only to specialists. Whether nuclear weapons were being introduced to Europe or being taken out was possibly less important than the fact that the final decisions on deployment and use would not be made by the Europeans. Europe's own armed forces, representative since Machiavelli's day of the people's part in war and of a state's capacity to protect its independence, had been reduced to the status of a "tripwire" to the nuclear deterrent.[21]

The risks in this strategy of overreliance on the Bomb revealed themselves later in the fifties when it became plain that the Soviets were capable of waging a two-way nuclear war in Europe and also of firing intercontinental ballistic missiles at the United States. Russian doctrine for the European theatre emphasized the necessity for preemptive strikes against NATO, initially with conventional forces to prevent a swift escalation to intercontinental nuclear war and with the hope of knocking European NATO out of the war and presenting Washington with a *fait accompli*. Russia's capacity to strike the U.S. with nuclear weapons made it much less likely that NATO would resort quickly to its atomic arsenal; but if it did not, Western Europe would be in the utmost peril.[22]

The threat to use tactical nuclear weapons now implied a willingness to be blown up in reply—in other words, a threat without credibility. In the event of some local aggression, the U.S. would have to choose between passivity or all-out war. Critics of the "new look," such as Captain B.H. Liddell Hart, the British strategist, denied that any responsible government would ever dare use the H-bomb as a response to local and limited aggression in Europe. In a book on total war published in 1955, France's preeminent strategist and social thinker, Raymond Aron, argued that the United States had "lost rather than gained by its famous atomic monopoly," and that American military strategy—i.e., massive retaliation—was demoralizing its allies in Europe.

> The strategy of intercontinental atomic war, which the Joint Chiefs of Staff in the Pentagon seemed to have adopted, is partly responsible for European defeatism. How could the nations of the Continent have failed to be discouraged in advance when their transatlantic ally and protector relied on a weapon against which they themselves would be defenseless . . . Every European would be a hostage in a total war—until and unless there are enough divisions to ward off Soviet invasion at the frontier.[23]

But there was little incentive to raise those divisions. As noted, the Dulles policy of using tactical nuclear weapons to close the gap between existing capabilities and the objective of defending Europe against an all-out attack had the effect of discouraging the allies from spending money and manpower to build up their conventional forces. In later years when the Americans raised the burden-sharing issue, threatening to withdraw forces from Europe unless the Europeans spent more on defence, the historical context was seldom recalled. As the Europeans then saw it, if the role of NATO's armies was only to activate a nuclear war, why should the allies expand them? Indeed, why not begin to dismantle their conventional forces and take the nuclear road themselves? If American commitments to use tactical nuclear weapons to defend the Europeans lacked credibility in light of Soviet capabilities, all the more reason for some Europeans to develop their own nuclear weapons. France shifted much of its conventional military force to Algeria, Britain cut its German-based forces by two divisions, and the Federal Republic fell well short of its force goals. By 1960, NATO had fewer than twenty poorly equipped divisions ready for combat on the central front, while it was estimated that the Soviets deployed 126 (smaller) divisions west of the Urals, two-thirds of which were at seventy per cent or more of war strength.[24] As we shall see, such estimates rested upon some debatable assumptions and calculations, and because they reinforced the consensus that Europe could never defend itself they were seldom challenged. The Bomb bred dependency. The trouble was that a widespread belief in Russia's great preponderance in conventional arms and the fact of its growing nuclear striking power were bound to weaken allied cohesion and promote a psychology of neutralism in Europe once the Soviets began to reactivate the tensions over, say, Berlin (as First Secretary Khrushchev did in November 1958).

Was there a workable alternative to a dependence on the Bomb? It was probably inevitable that nuclear weapons would play some role in NATO, especially in the formative years, but an overreliance on them—a policy of using them where they could not work, as substitutes for conventional forces—could (and should) have been avoided. This would have required a strategic concept of collective North Atlantic security and European defence based on robust conventional armed forces, with the atomic deterrent kept well in the background. In turn, this partially depended on the emergence of a much stronger European identity in security matters, a pattern of European defence co-operation within the framework of the Alliance that would submerge ancient national rivalries and mistrust—particularly those between the French and Germans.

## Keeping the Germans Down

West European defence co-operation since World War Two has had two separate and distinct phases. In the first phase, lasting roughly from 1950 to 1954, the push for such collaboration grew out of the perceived need of the U.S. to encourage West Germany's rearmament while ensuring that it was contained and limited within an integrated European structure. France's attempt to reduce Germany to perpetual military inferiority through a proposed European Defence Community (EDC) foundered in a sea of interallied troubles; West Germany was then anchored firmly to NATO after Britain and the United States had more deeply entangled themselves in European defence. An Atlantic axis based on German-American dominance of NATO emerged as the alternative to a French-dominated European defence system.

The second phase lasted from the early 1980s to the present. Its centre of gravity is a Franco-German *entente* based on security interests: France's concern over pacifism and neutralism in the Federal Republic; German insecurities over the credibility of American commitments in the face of Soviet military power and the unpredictability of U.S. policies; and a shared fear of super-power deals concerning the strategic balance in Europe. An assertive, self-confident France, strengthened by President de Gaulle's creation of a domestic consensus in the sixties, has assumed the leadership of a movement toward a more self-reliant Europe within the NATO coalition. How far European military co-operation proceeds, and the impact it has on broader international stability, depends in large part on the Alliance and the steadfastness of other western states, especially the U.S. and Canada.

To return once more to that postwar watershed, the outbreak of the Korean War in June 1950; this event had a major impact on NATO, transforming it into a full-scale military alliance and prompting the U.S., Britain, and Canada to send troops to the European continent to back up their treaty commitments. The war also forced the allies to face up to an issue that had the potential to tear NATO apart—the rearmament of West Germany and its incorporation in the Alliance. For the dominant western power, the United States, this was a logical extension of the policy of setting up a separate West German state, aiding the revival of its capitalist economy, and consolidating America's embryonic alliance with Konrad Adenauer's right-wing, pro-American Christian Democrats. On strategic grounds, the American Joint Chiefs had contended before the Korean crisis that it would be impossible to defend Western Europe without West Germany's rearmament and participation in NATO. Her geographical situation made her participation a necessary condition in military plans to defend Western Europe as far to the east as possible: Europe must be defended at the Elbe instead of the Rhine. But France was fiercely opposed to the buildup of any German army, especially one under national control, and her policy was to postpone, to hem Germany in with restraints, and to subordinate her to French military superiority. French officials informed the Americans in 1949 that they considered the Atlantic Treaty to be a security guarantee against Germany as well as Russia. The basis of all French ideas about European defence co-operation was fear of German preponderance.

After the North Korean attack, the U.S. military insisted that Germany's rearmament be made an explicit condition of an enlarged American military commitment in Europe. The Joint Chiefs presented President Truman with a package in three parts: additional U.S. forces to Europe; creation of a unified NATO command with an American Supreme Commander; and the establishment of a European defence force including German units up to division strength. In September 1950, Secretary of State Acheson proposed to the NATO Council the creation of a large integrated NATO force consisting of units contributed by each state, including Germany. "There is no question of raising a *Wehrmacht*," Acheson told the French; he merely wanted ten German divisions placed under American control. Canada's Lester Pearson, falling in step behind the Americans, pleaded for support for the principle "of using in some way German manpower for the defence of freedom in Europe."[27] But the French —more fearful of the Germans than the Russians—rejected this out of hand and subsequently put forward their own counterproposal (the Pleven Plan) for the creation of a European defence force, a military counterpart to the new European coal and steel community. There was to be an integrated European army, a European minister of defence, and German participation in the EDC would be strictly limited to small combat units within a tightly integrated military framework. The high-minded concept of a European army operating under supranational political institutions could but thinly disguise French ambitions to tame the spectre of a revived German chauvinism by reducing the German military to subservience and near-impotence. France's project to keep Germany weak, dependent, and outside the Atlantic Alliance eventually emerged as the European Defence Community Treaty, signed in May 1952 and buried on August

30, 1954, when for a variety of motives (including Britain's unwillingness to support the EDC) France's own National Assembly refused to ratify it.

This *denouement* marked the failure of the "European" solution to the problem of West Germany's revival as a military power, and the beginning of France's diminishing influence and growing isolation in the Alliance. West Germany was finally admitted to NATO in 1955 in an "Atlantic" solution worked out on British initiative and strongly backed by the United States.[28] To win France over to the participation of a German national army, the dormant Western European Union (established under the 1948 Brussels Treaty as a European defence forum) was revived, linked to NATO, and expanded to embrace Germany and Italy. The U.S. and Britain agreed to strengthen their existing commitments on the continent if Germany was firmly anchored to the Alliance. It was, but not before France succeeded in imposing a number of restrictions and restraints on West German sovereignty and military potential, including Konrad Adenauer's commitment for Germany "not to manufacture on its territory any atomic weapons, chemical weapons or biological weapons," along with provisions requiring Germany to accept foreign troops on her soil and stipulating strict limitations on the size and deployment of her army.

In the circumstances, these were not unreasonable constraints; there undoubtedly was (and still is) a risk of a resurgence of German militarism; since 1955 that risk has been a strong reason for countries such as Canada to support NATO and West Germany's participation in the Alliance. It is worth noting however that there was tremendous opposition within Germany itself to the concept of rearmament and the buildup of a new army; any revival of German militarism would be fiercely opposed. The fact is that France saw the restrictions solely from the perspective of maintaining her own military superiority over the Federal Republic. If atomic weapons were now essential to security and great power status, then France alone would have the right to make them. It was a policy born in fear. Isolated, intransigent, unreconciled to her changed status in Europe and the world, France had fought the inevitable reemergence of Germany as a power and now had to live with the consequences. A new Bonn-Washington axis formed the core of the

Alliance after 1955, and it was this Atlanticism that would control NATO's politics and strategy for the next three decades:

> Thus it came about that the effort to obtain West Germany's active participation in a forward strategy led to a further integration of NATO's forces and the further entanglement of the United States and Great Britain in Continental defense, while the proposal for a European army, which had gained much of its impetus from the sentiment for a purely European integration, ended by binding Europe more tightly to a trans-Atlantic framework.[29]

The push for European self-reliance in defence had stalled almost as soon as it began. It was not to be renewed for almost thirty years. An idea well before its time, European military cooperation could not proceed in the fifties parallel to the steady movement toward European economic integration because of France's profound insecurities about Germany, because of the Federal Republic's dependence on the United States, and because of Europe's own weakness and collective memory of itself in a permanent Hobbesian state of war, driven by fear and mutual mistrust in (as Hobbes said in Leviathan) "continual jealousies, and in the state and posture of gladiators; having their weapons pointing, and their eyes fixed on one another; that is, their forts, garrisons, and guns, upon the frontiers of their kingdoms; and continual spies upon their neighbours; which is a posture of war."

The Western Alliance has restrained some of the worst features of this posture of war by providing Europe with a wider security framework involving external guarantees. Provided Canada and the U.S. do not retreat into a North American Maginot Line, the Alliance should continue to support Europe's security and stability. But in the early years, this also entailed an American hegemony over the entire Atlantic and European system; so long as this "Atlanticist" dominance of the U.S. persisted, Europe's dependence on American decisions and weapons systems continued to grow. Particularly did the Europeans— the formidable exception was General de Gaulle—come to see the advantages in assuming the hopelessness of defending themselves in the face of Russia's alleged massive superiority in conventional forces. Only nuclear weapons under U.S. control kept

Europe from being dominated by the Red Army; nothing therefore should be done that would give the Kremlin any reason to doubt that war in Europe would mean an intercontinental nuclear war. Nothing therefore *was* done until the Americans themselves began to challenge the assumptions and myths that underpinned the Alliance's suicide-or-surrender approach to military strategy.

## Kicking the Habit

We have argued that NATO's reliance on nuclear weapons for the purpose of deterrence or to offset conventional force weaknesses has deep historical roots. Like Dean Acheson, U.S. secretary of state under Truman, this dependence on the Bomb was "present at the creation" of the Alliance. It has persisted. Why?

The forces of inertia and the political difficulties involved in making changes in Alliance strategy—e.g., West Germany's opposition to the adoption of a "no-first-use" policy on nuclear weapons—go part of the way to explain NATO's failure to kick the nuclear habit. There has always been a self-defeating (but also self-serving) conviction in the Alliance that it is and will remain hopelessly outmatched by Warsaw Pact conventional arms. Long accustomed to relying on weapons of mass destruction to fill in the holes, to postpone spending, to patch up disagreements among the allies, to test the political loyalty of the sixteen member states, and of course to keep the Russians guessing, NATO clings to the Bomb less from a faith in its own military strategy than from fear of the political and budgetary consequences of attempting to overhaul it. In particular there has been a fear on the part of many influential Germans and other Europeans that any weakening of NATO's resolve to use nuclear weapons would lead to American "decoupling" from the continent. This fear stems from a situation familiar to every Canadian—an unhealthy dependence on the United States that produces almost as much anxiety about being abandoned as about becoming a potential battleground in another great power conflict. The fear is understandable and needs to be assuaged. It is not, however, a sound basis for a rational allied strategy.

NATO's nuclear dependence is powerfully supported by one great myth. This is the myth of an overwhelming Soviet conventional superiority in central Europe—a superiority alleged to be so great that if NATO substantially cut its nuclear arsenals in Europe and adopted a no-first-use strategy, it would be akin to surrender, to another Munich. This is rubbish, but unlike most rubbish it serves some useful ends. The assumption of Soviet conventional preponderance and of the hopelessness of NATO's own conventional position plays an important role in interallied consensus politics, and for that reason it is stated and restated *ad nauseam* in NATO's own briefings and publications and in the white papers and official defence statements of all of its sixteen members. Canada's 1987 white paper, for instance, paints a most depressing picture of the Alliance's conventional forces in the face of the Soviet threat. It alleges that ninety Warsaw Pact divisions confront just thirty-eight NATO divisions (2.7 million men vs 1.9 million), that the Pact has a three to one superiority in artillery and armed helicopters, and a two to one ratio in main battle tanks and tactical aircraft. Worse:

> While the Warsaw Pact would be able to select the time and place of attack and concentrate its forces accordingly, NATO, as the defender, would be obliged to thin out its divisions across the entire front. Under these circumstances, NATO maintains forces barely sufficient to cover the ground. (p. 12)

These then are the "facts," the gloomy conventional wisdom that every parliamentarian, journalist, or academic interested in security issues is expected to accept at face value (many do). To suggest that the true balance of forces in Europe is not this way at all, that NATO's prospects for a vigorous conventional defence are not at all hopeless, in fact have not been hopeless for decades, and that the Warsaw Pact's weaknesses have been grossly understated because the NATO allies have a powerful interest in stressing the current untenability of conventional defence—these are unpatriotic heresies. So deeply pessimistic are the assumptions that underlie the Alliance's orthodoxy that one is left to wonder just what it is that keeps the Russians from walking to the English Channel. Whatever else it is, it can hardly be NATO.

To exaggerate a threat can be just as dangerous as to understate it. "In the case of NATO, overstatement has led to strategies of desperation, particularly with respect to the threatened prompt use of nuclear weapons. The effect of overstating the strength of the Soviet army has been not only to get a smaller NATO force but also to reduce the incentives for the NATO countries to make the NATO armies fully combat-ready. Overstatement also undermines public credibility, encouraging the feeling that we are getting nothing useful for our public spending."[30] There is of course a threat in central Europe from the Warsaw Pact's conventional ground and air forces, but the threat is not unmanageable in spite of NATO's existing deficiencies and scarce resources. This has been understood since the sixties.

### The Whiz Kids Search for the Soviet Threat

To have one's deepest assumptions subjected to outside scrutiny can be an unwelcome experience. Those assumptions that allow us to stay inert and to postpone unpleasant action are also those we prefer not to question. If they are revealed to be irredeemably wrong, we may become even more resolute in defending them.

Robert McNamara, secretary of defence under presidents Kennedy and Johnson, took up his post in early 1961 with a simple but radical idea—that military requirements cannot be determined without a systematic analysis of costs, an explicit consideration of alternatives, and a long-range plan of both forces and costs based on an overall concept of the national interest. McNamara was attempting to impose a rational, cost-effective discipline on U.S. defence policy, and this involved relentless interrogation and debate on fundamental issues as well as on specifics. His favourite question (unspoken since his day) was: "How much is enough?" To pose the hard questions and find alternatives, he set up an Office of Systems Analysis staffed by independent civilian analysts, the arrogant, young "Whiz Kids" whom the military detested and dubbed "pipe-smoking, tree-full-of-owls defense intellectuals," lacking "the worldliness or motivation to stand up to the kind of enemy we face." Long used to a process in which defence requirements were sacrosanct and decided outside the civilian budget, in which conflicts between, say, bombers and aircraft carriers were resolved by building *both* bombers and carriers, the military inhabited an unreal world. Even for a power such as the U.S., the incredible costs of new and rapidly obsolescing weapons systems and the spiralling requirements of all of the services were bound to produce a McNamara-type intervention. Had President Eisenhower himself not warned in his farewell address of the dangers of the expanding "military-industrial complex"?

Kennedy and McNamara were critics of massive retaliation and of NATO's heavy reliance on nuclear weapons for deterrence and defence. They came to power in 1961 at a time when many American strategists were pushing for a strengthening of NATO's conventional defences and for increased European spending on nonnuclear forces. The idea was to give the Alliance (and the U.S. president) more options, to make the early resort to nuclear weapons in a European conflict less likely (McNamara reportedly wanted to make NATO's capabilities consistent with a no-first-use doctrine, but this met intense European opposition). Of course, the Americans were acutely conscious of the vulnerability of the United States itself to intercontinental nuclear attack, and like the Russians, had a strong interest in keeping any military conflict in Europe a) confined to Europe and b) conventional. Beyond this, the Americans were hoping to show the feasibility of conventional defence in order to forestall further moves by the Europeans to build their own nuclear weapons; and after the test of the 1961 Berlin crisis, both Kennedy and McNamara wanted strong conventional forces in Europe to support their cold war diplomacy with Russia.

When the Whiz Kids set out to challenge NATO's prevailing strategy, they immediately ran into the deeply rooted assumption that the Alliance was hopelessly outmatched in the conventional forces balance. "On both sides of the Atlantic," recalled Enthoven and Smith, two of McNamara's senior analysts, "the key 'fact' was the overwhelming Soviet conventional superiority. Any discussion of conventional defenses soon became stuck on this 'fact' and the enormous expense and effort that would be required to offset it."[31] As the Whiz Kids discovered, the belief in Soviet conventional superiority had become a self-fulfilling prophecy: one of them asked a European official why his country's army had only a three-day supply of ammunition. "Because we don't expect to hold for more than three days," was the reply. But as the American retorted, if one stocks only a three-day supply of ammunition, it is self-evident that one can't hold any longer.

How was it that the much poorer economies of the Warsaw Pact nations were able to support such a vastly larger conventional force in Europe—according to the standard view, 175 well-equipped and combat-ready divisions against NATO's ill-equipped and unready twenty-five divisions? Reviewing population, economic, and technological variables, the Whiz Kids concluded that it should be far harder for the Soviets than for NATO to support a large army. They also learned that the 175 Soviet "divisions" totalled about two million men, whereas the U.S. had nearly one million men on active duty in the army, organized into just sixteen combat divisions! It became clear that NATO and U.S. intelligence were including many combat-unready units—paper aggregrations of manpower—in their estimates of Soviet strength. It emerged that the Soviets might have eighty combat-ready divisions, but the Whiz Kids were able to show that these were organized very differently than NATO's: "if we organized along Soviet lines, we could have about three divisions for the cost of one of our present divisions (without reducing the American soldier's standard of living); but it was not at all clear that such a reorganization would produce a more effective U.S. Army."[32]

> Thus, by 1965, we knew that a Soviet division force cost only about a third that of a U.S. division force, had only about a third as many men, and (we have strong reason to believe) was only about one-third as effective. Moreover, in terms of men per division deployed in the centre region of NATO at the time, the U.S. division forces had about 40,000 soldiers per division in Germany compared with about 13,000 for the Soviets. In short, eliminating paper divisions, using cost and firepower indexes, counts of combat personnel in available divisions, and numbers of artillery pieces, trucks, tanks, and the like, we ended up with the same conclusion: NATO and the Warsaw Pact had approximate equality on the ground.[33]

The capacity of the Soviets to mobilize rapidly and deploy large numbers of their undermanned divisions as well-supported, combat-ready units has likewise been overstated for decades, while NATO's reinforcement and sustainment problems have typically been emphasized as part of an argument for early use of nuclear weapons. Only by assuming that everything went magically right for the Pact and disastrously wrong for NATO could the Alliance's worst case scenarios about short warning times and rapid mobilization and deployment of the Pact's forces be realized. The Whiz Kids demonstrated that the myth of Warsaw Pact superiority in tactical air forces could not stand up under serious analysis, and they argued that what NATO really required was not large increases in divisions but better training, larger ammunition stocks, aircraft shelters, etc. Given such unglamorous improvements in the use of existing forces, a nonnuclear defence capability was well within NATO's means.

Now, all of this was profoundly unsettling to NATO and most of its member states. Not surprisingly, the findings of the Whiz Kids were rejected or rationalized away. "The initial reaction of the Services and the NATO commanders to these studies was not to reexamine their estimates, but to explain away the differences on other grounds. A whole new set of arguments was raised to account for the overwhelming Soviet conventional superiority. The arguments came in various forms, but they all made essentially the same point: these differences could be accounted for by the higher standard of living and better treatment of the individual soldier in a Western army . . . At one briefing it was explained at great length that the Army had to have a fancy mobile kitchen to give each of our soldiers a hot meal every day, while the Russian soldiers were accustomed to eating soup out of one huge kettle. Apparently, we were going to lose a war in Europe because U.S. soldiers didn't eat soup."[34]

To challenge a powerful orthodoxy is to be reminded of Keynes's remark that the world is ruled by little else than ideas. For NATO, the idea that seems most entrenched is that Western Europe cannot be defended: the memory of May 1940, when the Germans broke through at Sedan and shattered France's armies, may be too strong. Certainly the heavy costs of fighting a conventional defence against a well-armed adversary are better known to Europeans than to North Americans. Still, the orthodoxy of the Alliance is self-fulfilling and defeatist: it insists that NATO has always faced an insurmountable imbalance in conventional forces, and that the attempt to redress it would be well beyond the means of the allies. Gloomy demographic forecasts have been used to "prove" that a conventional defence is impossible because of manpower constraints; using the right assumptions, it can be shown that the economies of NATO Europe are not strong enough to sustain a larger share of the burdens of a conventional strategy. The truth seems to be that it is comforting to be outnumbered, for then there is little point in spending money to make sure one's forces are well-trained and properly deployed or that the aircraft shelters are built. A conventional wisdom or consensus—even if it is profoundly pessimistic—at least has the advantage that it spares one from taxing thought and unwelcome "facts," such as the proposition that NATO does not need the Bomb. What could be more disturbing than that?

## Use It or Lose It

It was one thing for the American government to decide that a renewed push for the conventional defence option was desirable and that more flexibility in strategic nuclear planning was needed, quite another to sell these ideas to skeptical allies. At a meeting of NATO ministers in Athens in 1962, McNamara laid out the whole U.S. approach—an early version of "flexible response"—stressing the need for flexibility, the centralization of control over nuclear weapons, the dangers of a proliferation of independent nuclear forces within the Alliance, and the high risks of using tactical nuclear weapons as a substitute for a strong conventional posture. Excessive reliance on tactical weapons entailed a grave risk of escalation to all-out war, and conventional strength was indispensable in crisis diplomacy. The burden of escalation should be put on the aggressor—i.e., NATO should base its strategy on no-first-use of nuclear weapons. The Alliance should not "depend solely on our nuclear power to deter the Soviet Union from actions not involving a massive commitment of Soviet force. Surely an Alliance with the wealth, talent, and experience that we possess can find a better way than this to meet our common threat."[35]

It took more than five years to persuade the Europeans to buy a watered-down version of flexible response. France, already committed to its own *force de frappe*, rejected McNamara's arguments against other centres of nuclear decision; other suspected the U.S. of trying to back out of its nuclear guarantee to Europe and some contended that a reemphasis of conventional defence options would undermine the deterrent and make war thinkable. Denis Healey, perhaps the leading defence intellectual in European Social Democracy in this period, strongly supported the retention of the option of a rapid escalation to nuclear weapons as part of flexible response. As David Schwartz notes of the European opposition: "Rarely expressed but never far from the surface was a belief that the escalatory potential in the tactical nuclear arsenal was beneficial to Europe, in that its use would quickly lead to an intercontinental nuclear exchange involving the territory of the United States."[36]

The compromise worked out in 1967—and which remains the Alliance's declared strategy—involved a tradeoff between the need to be able to respond directly to aggression at whatever level (direct defence) and the retention of the option of deliberately escalating to the nuclear level if necessary. Flexible response was more of a political compromise than a military strategy—it was designed to appeal to both nuclear and conventional advocates—but its implementation represented another victory for the forces of inertia: tactical nuclear forces in Europe increased to 7000 weapons; the allies continued to integrate conventional and tactical nuclear weapons in NATO's force posture; and NATO rejected McNamara's no-first-use concept. As McNamara later recalled in a celebrated *Foreign Affairs* article, the essential element of flexible response—building up conventional capabilities in Europe to reduce the threat of early preemptive use of nuclear weapons—did not go forward.[37] Canada helped matters along by withdrawing half its land forces from Germany.

To adopt no-first-use of nuclear weapons as more than a pious declaration of intent would require some large structural changes in NATO's forces and strategy. The Whiz Kid critique of NATO overlooked the inconvenient fact that even if it were true that the Alliance was capable of mounting a good conventional defence, it was most unlikely to do so because of the close integration of nuclear and conventional forces. As NATO's forces developed, many dual systems capable of firing or carrying either nuclear or nonnuclear ordinance were introduced into its structure. Though these weapons are usually called deterrents, many are short-range (e.g., artillery shells), vulnerable to preemptive Soviet strike, and thoroughly commingled with purely conventional forces. The complex political controls on the nuclear forces and the problems of getting allies to agree to a first-use policy would complicate NATO's capacity to exploit its conventional strength; far from supplementing NATO's conventional posture, much of NATO's nuclear force detracts from it.[38] The deployment of nuclear systems in forward units, together with their vulnerability to preemption, introduces a strong incentive toward their early use in combat: use it or lose it. Dare NATO use it?

War, Clausewitz wrote, is the realm of uncertainty, chance, and unpredictability. This is part of its nature that we cannot control. There is enormous uncertainty about what might happen in the opening stages of a war in central Europe; the conventional balance is even enough that the consequences of an attack would be unpredictable and the risks of a nuclear escalation incalculable.[39] However, we can say that the growth of Soviet nuclear capabilities since the sixties has eroded a good deal of the credibility of the NATO doctrine of flexible response, especially the threat of first-use of the Alliance's tactical or theatre nuclear forces. The passing of western nuclear superiority means the Alliance's 1967 compromise has had its day: the threat of moving from conventional to nuclear war at a moment chosen by NATO has become an empty one, as British strategist Michael Howard (among many others) has noted:

A guarantee by the United States to its partners in Western Europe that it would be prepared to counter a Soviet attack on Western Europe on any level by initiating the use of nuclear weapons may have been effective when the West enjoyed a virtual nuclear monopoly, but it looks very different when the Soviet Union has attained nuclear parity. For either side to initiate the use of battlefield nuclear weapons would now make a desert of Central Europe . . . It is not simply a question of whether the President of the United States would or should be willing, in an emergency, to do such things. It is more profoundly a question of whether his proclaimed readiness to do so is any longer credible to an adversary, or can be made so by any new deployment of forces. And there are a growing number of people, both in Western Europe and in the United States, who see little advantage in being defended by such means.[40]

We stress once more the uncertainties that attend the concept of a war waged in central Europe solely with conventional forces. There are far too many intangibles and "moral factors," by which Clausewitz meant military leadership, courage, morale, discipline, etc. for anyone to be sure of the outcome; and this uncertainty would exist with or without nuclear weapons. However, many of the studies that we have reviewed are persuasive that, as in the sixties, the prospects are very good that NATO could have more conventional forces deployed with greater firepower and mobility than is generally supposed. Soviet opportunities for a rapid conventional victory are badly overstated in NATO's orthodox estimates (why is it that the same persons who are quick to point out the inefficiencies and failures in the Soviet domestic system also assume that Soviet military forces are somehow spared the problems that plague everyone else's armies?).

Using methodology not unlike that employed in the Whiz Kids' studies, William Kaufmann, one of the earliest critics of U.S. nuclear deterrence, has argued that "considering the investment the alliance has already made, a vigorous conventional defense is well within NATO's grasp and . . . the costs are well within its means."[41] Posen and Van Evera have demonstrated that by relaxing some of the unreal worst-case assumptions that give the Warsaw Pact every advantage, NATO's forces appear adequate to prevent the Pact from making an armoured breakthrough; and they argue for investments to repair the areas of greatest uncertainty.[42] And John Mearshimer makes a plausible case that although NATO conventional forces cannot actually *win* a war in central Europe, they are certainly sufficient to deny the Soviets a *blitzkreig*-type victory.[43]

These studies are well known, yet they have barely made a dent in NATO's worst-case orthodoxy. Most analyses continue to adopt the most pessimistic assumptions about NATO's capacity to act promptly, while assuming at the same time that the Warsaw Pact will use magical powers to get everything right in the shortest possible time. Static rather than dynamic analyses are used in comparisons; little account is taken of the unreliability of East European forces, and so on. The effect of this is to create a sense of inevitability about NATO's prospects that weakens public support for defence, demoralizes the Alliance's armies and sets up a 1940 scenario in which politicians, long conditioned to believe in the hopelessness of the situation, act in a defeatist, panicky manner and lose the war.

The Warsaw Pact has some important advantages, while NATO has others; but the Pact does not enjoy the superiority it would require to guarantee a victory. Conventional defence, then, is possible; but under present-day conditions there also remains an incalculable risk of any conflict expanding very rapidly to a nuclear war. Those who wish to keep that risk to support deterrence have yet to convince many people that they or anyone else knows what allied leaders would or should do next, if deterrence broke down. Walk over the abyss? "Win" a nuclear war? A sensible strategy is first to try to deny the opponent any gains without running risks so appalling—i.e., a strictly conventional defence is worth the effort and cost. A shift from nuclear deterrence to conventional defence would also mean shifting the primary responsibility to the Europeans for the defence of their own continent, which is where it should be. A more self-reliant Europe would benefit all of NATO's states.

The trouble is that although there are good reasons for moving away from a nuclear-oriented NATO strategy and for improving conventional defence capabilities, someone must pay. NATO's ex-Supreme Commander, General Bernard Rogers, estimated in 1982 that the allies would have to increase their defence spending in real terms by four per cent annually for the 1983-88 period to acquire a robust conventional defence. But in the recessionary years of the early eighties the non-U.S. NATO allies were well below the target of three per cent real annual growth agreed to by NATO ministers in 1978. European economic and social problems and public resistance to rising military spending in the face of cutbacks in social services made it difficult for all governments to persuade their legislatures to vote more funds. Many allies, such as Britain and Canada, were facing very large capital outlays to modernize or replace aging military equipment, and the economic constraints bit deeply into governments' resolve to increase military spending beyond levels of public acceptability. Between 1983 and 1985, in the midst of the new cold war, NATO Europe's average GDP/GNP growth was 2.5 per cent, and its defence expenditures showed an increase of just below two per cent in real terms for the period. This in spite of dramatic threats from the U.S. Congress, especially the 1984 Nunn-Roth Amendment, to place a ceiling on U.S. troops in NATO and to cut them by 30,000 a year unless the states of NATO Europe strengthened their nonnuclear defences. Without savage cuts in health, education, and social security spending beyond those already implemented by conservative governments across the NATO bloc, military spending simply could not continue to increase. Congress began to scale back the deficit-bloating defence budgets of Defence Secretary Weinberger in 1985-86, and the allies stiffened their resistance to U.S. pressure to spend more. The prospect of better East-West relations rightly induces politicians to think of more popular things to spend the people's money on than new weapons. But the net effect is a weakening of the chance to reduce NATO's reliance on nuclear weapons—an option which in any event is unpopular with many conservative Europeans. Thatcher's Britain and Mitterand's France remain totally wedded to nuclear deterrence and deeply skeptical of superpower efforts to "denuclearize" Europe.

In these circumstances, the Mulroney government's commitment to increase defence spending over fifteen years by a minimum of two per cent in real terms annually—a figure regarded by the Canadian military as well below what it needs to replace its existing equipment—is probably flim-flam. The capital costs of the proposed fleet of ten to twelve nuclear-powered submarines have, according to respected naval critics, been vastly understated; if so, cost escalations in the SSNs will force reductions in spending on other major equipment, such as new tanks for NATO. *Jane's Defence Weekly* quoted the senior Canadian officer in charge of Force Development thus:

> If we don't solve the navy's problems pretty soon, then the army who's waiting in line you might say, is going to find that everything is falling apart on it . . . And around the turn of the century, the air force [will be] starting to get terribly desperate. Its training aircraft, its helicopters, its trans-

port aircraft, and even the CF-18, will require additional aircraft to replace those that we've lost by the end of the century.[44]

Defence policy is about "how much is enough?" It is about budgets and the allocation of scarce resources. It involves trade-offs between competing priorities. Equipment decisions involve multibillion dollar capital expenditures over decades; they foreclose other options; they tie the hands of future governments. As we argued earlier, equipment and budget decisions tend to drive strategic doctrine—not the reverse. White papers are nothing more than declarations of intentions promising far more than they can deliver; the proof lies in the implementation, in what gets shelved and what gets built. And they are, moreover, declarations of present-day governments. Their successors will have new ideas. A future NDP administration, for instance, may find it convenient to go ahead with the naval building program on sovereignty grounds while abandoning plans to reequip land and air forces committed to NATO. Thereby, Canada could simply "rust out" its last days in the Alliance through equipment deterioration and obsolescence.

The exigencies of technology and economics and the forces of inertia therefore seem likely to prevail. As will be shown in later chapters, unilateralist tendencies have been straining the Alliance on both sides of the Atlantic throughout the 1980s and it remains to be seen if a new consensus on strategy can emerge amidst so much mistrust. We are not optimistic. Meanwhile, the fundamental dilemmas of NATO's continued reliance upon the Bomb persist: while nuclear deterrence of Soviet ambitions seems durable in that Moscow is most unlikely to risk a war by invading Western Europe, an unexpected and unintended crisis could bring us yet to the brink. At that point the dead hand of past decisions would grip NATO by the neck, for it would have the awful choice of deciding whether to try to resist conventionally or to use its nuclear weapons quickly before they can be disabled during the conventional phase of the conflict. In the final analysis, NATO would come up hard against the illogic of its own strategy. Whichever way it decided, it could be the final decision it would make.

## CHAPTER FOUR

# The Myth of Arms Control

> Even in the fifteenth century, professional diplomatists re-
> garded with grave doubts the method now known as 'Diplo-
> macy by Conference', which in those days took the form of
> personal interviews between sovereigns. There was always
> the danger that one monarch might kidnap the other mon-
> arch and for this reason the interviews generally took place
> in the centre of a bridge, when the two sovereigns could ex-
> change compliments through a stout oaken lattice erected
> between them . . . They were enormously expensive, since
> each side competed with the other in ostentation; they
> aroused exaggerated expectations at home and deep suspi-
> cion abroad; they raised a wild covey of disturbing rumours;
> and, since such agreement as might be reached was verbal
> and not written, opportunities were open for subsequent mis-
> understanding and prevarication. It is not surprising that Phi-
> lippe de Comines, an experienced if corrupt diplomatist of
> the [15th century], should have recorded the following opin-
> ion of Diplomacy by Conference: "Two great Princes, who
> wish to establish good personal relations should never meet
> each other face to face . . .
>
> Harold Nicolson, 1954[1]

The prominence of nuclear weapons in Alliance strategy has
been met with persistent pressure from some domestic groups to
disarm. As the liberal democracies of Western Europe and
North America entered their fourth decade of uninterrupted
peace this pressure intensified. Fearful of the devastating consequences of a nuclear war and worried by the excessive cold war
rhetoric in the early days of the Reagan administration, people
took to the streets in the hundreds of thousands throughout
Northern Europe, Britain, the United States, and Canada. The
specific target of the protests varied from the nuclear freeze in

the United States to cruise missile testing in this country or the deployment of intermediate nuclear forces (INF) in Europe. The sentiment of a nuclear-free world was, however, shared. A similar wave of antinuclear discontent had swept through the Alliance in the late 1950s. At that time, in an attempt to secure the hearts and minds of the discontented, the Soviets and the Americans traded proposals for complete disarmament: the reduction and eventual elimination of weapons. Removed from the reality of the superpower confrontation, the proposals only encouraged cynicism. After the mid-1960s, arms control became the favoured approach of strategists and disarmers alike. Arms control does not require that weapons be reduced or eliminated, merely that any expansion of weapons be done in a managed framework. Today the popularity of arms control has begun to fade. Along with it there has been a persistent effort to deny the military and political utility of nuclear weapons. People from both the Left and the Right have condemned nuclear deterrence on both moral and practical grounds. The result for NATO members has been to lay bare the nuclear dependence of the Alliance and to question the credibility of its military strategy. In abandoning both arms control and deterrence many western elites are reaching back for proposals for complete and total disarmament. Nowhere were these more evident than at the Soviet-American summit in Reykjavik in October 1986.

**Rendezvous in Reykjavik**

On Saturday, October 18, 1986, Icelanders peddled summit sweaters and ash trays as Miss Iceland posed for photos and told visiting journalists that "it's the best publicity we could ever get." By Monday morning residents worried that their island country might forever be equated with failure. Not since the American Bobby Fischer met the Russian Boris Spassky in the world chess championship of 1972 had Reykjavik been host to delegations from the world's two superpowers. Unlike the earlier match, "Ron—Gorby II" ended in a draw. Nevertheless, it is destined to be remembered as one of the most bizarre Soviet-American summits of the postwar period. As if touched by the elfin magic believed to inhabit the island, Ronald Reagan and Mikhail Gorbachev nearly turned the nuclear generation on its collective head. In an attempt to outdo one another in their quest for a world rid of nuclear weapons, "the two chiefs found themselves lifted from the harsh realities and complexities of nuclear negotiations to competitive visions of utopia."[2] The two leaders jumped quickly from a drastic cut in intermediate-range nuclear weapons stationed in Europe, to a halving of ballistic missiles, and then to the ultimate elimination of "offensive" nuclear weapons within the next decade. The frenzied negotiations ended as quickly as they had progressed and the dream of a nuclear-free future vanished as the two leaders refused to compromise on the meaning of two words— laboratory testing—which reflected the profound differences between Soviet and American views of the Anti-Ballistic Missile (ABM) Treaty and its compatibility with research on ballistic missile defences. Potentially historic agreements had been sacrificed in deference to the promise of assured survival through the Strategic Defence Initiative. The unexpected and revolutionary proposals exchanged at the Reykjavik summit generated as many worries as any superpower summit in recent memory. The worst fears of many, however, were not that the summit had ended in failure but that it had come so very close to succeeding. "My reflection on all of this," concluded one French official, "is that you should not allow two men to negotiate on a Saturday night in a haunted house."[3] They have hallucinations!

Summit diplomacy between heads of state has always been problematic. Without the technical expertise required for complex negotiations, pressed for time to reach an agreement, lacking the opportunity to ponder proposals, and always conscious of their public image, political leaders are not well-equipped to settle disputes with their adversaries during a weekend of talks. This is why summits are usually reserved for signing agreements concluded elsewhere by others. However, few leaders can resist the temptation of the drama that summitry presents. The world waits with bated breath as they negotiate behind closed doors, talking earnestly late into the night as they deliberate on the fate of the planet. The imagery exaggerates the significance of the event, as do the media and our own tendency to overestimate the ability of two individuals to control our collective fate.

In practice, superpower summits have rarely yielded substantive results. More often they have been of symbolic significance, either pointing the way to improved relations in the future (as did the Nixon-Brezhnev detente summits of the early 1970s) or souring the relationship for some time (as did the Kennedy-Khrushchev summit in 1961). The Reykjavik summit had its own symbolic significance even if the symbols were not easily interpreted. Indeed the amount of confusion generated by the meeting was so great that both the Americans and the Russians sent delegates to meet with political leaders and the media throughout Europe and Canada. Like other summits, the allies had been left at home and except for a telephone call each to British Prime Minister Margaret Thatcher and West German Chancellor Helmut Kohl, Reagan put forward unilateral proposals leaving the rest of the Alliance to wait for the morning paper to learn how their interests had been treated.

Unlike previous summits, including the Washington summit of December 1987, where leaders sat and smiled as they signed agreements negotiated beforehand and offered banal toasts to massage each other's egos, the Reagan-Gorbachev exchange at Reykjavik was exceptional and dangerous for the intensive negotiations on such far-reaching proposals. From the time Gorbachev unloaded his briefcase and Reagan realized that "he had more papers than I did," until late Sunday evening the two leaders conducted an extensive review of their respective arms control agendas. With a well-prepared script in hand, Gorbachev outlined a sweeping proposal to reduce the superpowers' nuclear arsenals. The Russian proposals centred on a fifty per cent reduction in strategic (intercontinental) nuclear weapons within five years. Despite his feeling that "we aren't supposed to be in these negotiations," Reagan responded and spent nearly twelve hours from mid-day Saturday until late Sunday evening trading nuclear weapons with his Soviet counterpart like so many pawns on a chessboard. After more than two decades of an arms control facade that had actually supported ever more powerful and technically sophisticated weapons, the superpowers were seriously considering reversing the tide. By late Sunday the two had reached agreements in principle. These agreements included the removal of INF missiles from Europe, limiting to 100 the number of these missiles that could be deployed on one's own territory, a phased-in ban on weapons testing, the reduction of nuclear warheads on strategic missiles and bombers to 6000 and a limit of 1600 on the bombers and missiles that would carry them, and provisions for the on-site verification of some aspects of these agreements. Observers such as former American Secretary of Defence James Schlesinger, found the prospects of this agreement unsettling. "Reykjavik had the potential for upsetting the military balance, for suddenly vitiating Western military strategy, and for destroying the cohesion of the Western alliance."[4] Others disagreed, including American Congressman Edward Markey who thought the package was "the best deal the Russians have offered us since they sold us Alaska."[5]

The agreements failed to survive the weekend. Eventually the arms reduction proposals fell victim to Reagan's Star Wars project and opposing interpretations of the Anti-Ballistic Missile Treaty of 1972. Unwilling to separate these far-reaching arms reductions from restrictions on ballistic missile defences, the Soviets proposed that both parties commit themselves to a strict interpretation of the ABM Treaty for a ten-year period. This would limit the testing of ballistic missile defences outside the laboratory. On this issue, President Reagan was unwilling to yield. Ever-vigilant in defence of the SDI Reagan proposed a less restrictive interpretation of the treaty that would allow more extensive testing of Star Wars components. Reagan defended his commitment to ballistic missile defences on the grounds that they would be essential even in a world without nuclear weapons because they would protect the United States in case other states were to acquire nuclear weapons. While most opponents of the SDI were quick to blame it for the summit's failure, many military and political elites in Europe thought Star Wars had saved the West from a fate worse than a world with nuclear weapons—a world *without* nuclear weapons. Star Wars had destroyed its first target, at least temporarily. The relief of these European opponents was shortlived, however. In one surprise move after another, the Soviet Union began to drop its condition that an agreement to withdraw INFs from Europe be linked to an American compromise on the SDI. A nuclear-free world remained a distant dream but a nuclear-free Europe now loomed on the horizon. Could Europe do without the Bomb?

The events in Reykjavik were a clear departure from the more common superpower summitry of the postwar period, and they suggested a sharp break with the arms control practices of the past twenty years. Left on their own, Reagan and Gorbachev spoke freely about their different visions of a world with fewer nuclear weapons. Arms control had given way to disarmament and real reductions in nuclear arsenals had become the main objective of Soviet-American negotiations. The two leaders seemed lost in time as their proposals reached back to the ideas for complete and total disarmament that prevailed in the late 1950s and early 1960s. These earlier proposals for a nuclear-free world never moved beyond the rhetorical, and disarmament soon yielded to arms control, a less utopian but no more successful approach to managing the arms race.

### Arms Control: Do We Want It?

It has become a matter of faith on both the Left and Right that the main problems confronting East-West relations today are nuclear weapons and the balance of terror called MAD (mutual assured destruction) that they have produced. President Reagan has spent much of his eight years in office decrying nuclear deterrence as he modernizes American nuclear forces and drums up support for the SDI, allegedly to eliminate nuclear weapons. The antinuclear angst has also spread to many elites in Europe, and in Christoph Bertram's view "most NATO leaders now present nuclear weapons as a burden that everybody would like to see disappear if possible."[6] In Canada, "negotiated radical reductions in nuclear forces and the enhancement of strategic stability" have been the main arms control priority of the Mulroney government. Even the Soviet Union, as we shall see, has displayed a very active arms control policy in recent years. It goes without saying that antinuclear activists have been ardent supporters of reducing, if not eliminating, nuclear weapons for decades and the leaders of the two superpowers now seem to be speaking their language; the language of nuclear disarmament. With all this support for reducing nuclear weapons it is surprising that arms control negotiations between the superpowers remain a matter of the highest priority for many NATO governments and their citizens alike. The substantial popular support for arms control is one of the great imponderables of the nuclear age. Why is it that a method that has proven so consistently unsuccessful in achieving any real reductions in weapons has been valued so highly throughout the West? Why is it that we look to arms control as a method for ending the arms race when it has more often encouraged it through qualitative improvements in weapons systems and greater spending in areas not covered by formal agreements.

Left unchanged, arms control has as much chance of undermining security and postponing a successful East-West detente as do the weapons it seeks to control. American commentator Theodore Draper has written, "the lesson I draw from the entire course of Soviet-American nuclear negotiations is that they have done more harm than good; they increase tensions and mistrust; at best they end up letting both sides keep what they really want to keep and give up what they really do not want."[7] Arms control emerged in the early 1960s, and was adopted by western strategists in response to a concern for strategic stability in the wake of the Cuban missile crisis. It was also viewed as a necessary corrective to the proposals for nuclear disarmament that had dominated debates on nuclear weapons in the late 1950s and early 1960s. As the United States and its NATO allies, including Canada, increased their reliance on nuclear weapons and accepted the necessity of deterrence, nuclear disarmament became a danger to be avoided. Arms control, alternatively, was considered necessary for strategic stability.

Arms control was able to serve many different tasks, but most importantly it could manage both disgruntled publics and the expansion of the Soviet nuclear arsenal while attempting to maintain the credibility of nuclear deterrence. Arms control was consistent with the need to deter the Soviets by retaining one's nuclear weapons. It could be used to limit the size of one's own nuclear forces, but this was not essential to the American view of arms control. Arms control was primarily intended to reassure both the Russians and the domestic public that nuclear weapons would not be used to achieve a superior position or launch a first strike. The utility of arms control, as opposed to disarmament, was that given its objective of stability and not arms reduction, it could as easily be used to justify new weapons as to dismantle old ones. Arms control could thus drive the arms race and make it seem legitimate at the same time by reducing the risks of instability. Indeed, as it has been practised for the past two decades, arms control must be viewed as an integral and important part of American (and by implication the Alliance's) nuclear strategy. The dilemmas of arms control are tied to the dilemmas of this strategy.

Churchill thought that "jaw jaw was better than war war." He was right. It would be absurd to pretend that negotiations are not better than war; unless negotiations make war likelier. Why then should we worry if Soviet and American leaders get together to talk about arms control? Oddly, the popularity of the negotiations contributes to their failure. Throughout the Alliance, citizens and their governments are constantly putting pressure on the superpowers to be actively involved in arms control negotiations. Largely as a result of their popularity, negotiations are viewed as the barometer by which the Soviet-American relationship is measured. When talks are in progress the relationship must be in good condition. When talks are suspended it must be stormy. The all-too-prevalent tendency to see arms control as the centrepiece of East-West relations has, in Lawrence Freedman's view, created "an anxiety for visible signs of progress (that) has resulted in uncritical enthusiasm for any negotiating activity regardless of its content."[8] The waiting media and their worldwide audience expressed great disappointment in the wake of the Reykjavik Summit's failure to reach substantive agreements and the signs for superpower co-operation appeared doomed until a few days of effective public relations allowed the Reagan administration to claim a success. That propaganda has become the main focus of arms control is evident in the fact that among the first people that Reagan wished to consult on his trip back to Washington from Reykjavik was his White House pollster. The Russians understand this as well, which accounts for the attention they devoted to the western media and to western publics after the summit. When viewed as the principal symbol of the superpower relationship, arms control negotiations encourage us to neglect other aspects of the relationship and to ignore the underlying political interests that ultimately decide the prospects of crisis and conflict or stability and co-operation. More worrisome is Freedman's concern that "the consequence of high-level negotiations on matters that touch on each side's most vital security interests is to ensure that the subject matter increases, not decreases, in salience."[9] Thus arms control agreements become more difficult to conclude and when they fail the situation seems much worse than it really is.

The elite and popular consensus that has supported arms control in the West for the past twenty years showed signs of weakening until Reykjavik. Many had begun to question the utility of an approach that not only made possible but actually seemed to encourage the rapid expansion of the superpower's nuclear arsenals during the 1970s. More than two decades of arms control negotiations had not brought about the destruction of a single nuclear warhead, and after countless rounds of negotiations and numerous agreements, both the Americans and the Soviets had deployed more than four times the number of nuclear warheads they possessed when the process started. This was all consistent with the fundamental objective of arms control as seen by western strategists: to reduce the risk of nuclear war by creating and sustaining strategic stability, by controlling the size and disposition of nuclear forces to reduce the temptation for a preemptive or surprise nuclear attack. Ever fearful of quantitative and qualitative changes, the requirements of stability demanded that technological developments be accommodated, not prevented, and that the size of stockpiles be kept in balance, not lowered. Support for arms control was based on a view that radical moves toward disarmament in the nuclear age were likely to be destabilizing and might encourage one side or the other to strike first with its ever-diminishing nuclear arsenal.

> The problem was that arms control grew out of deterrence dogma. It accepted the deterrers' definition of credibility, which assumed a malevolent enemy who would seize any chance, however adverse the odds, to neutralize U.S. deterrent forces by surprise attack . . . To make matters worse, the requirements of stability implied that the already high level of capability needed to ensure a credible deterrent had to be increased even further to meet the requirements of an assured second strike capability.[10]

Arms control would eliminate any first-strike temptations by accepting as legitimate the need to maintain large quantities of weapons. In effect, arms control was used as a rationale for building more and better weapons systems.

Why have arms control negotiations failed to cut the stockpiles of weapons possessed by the superpowers? One reason has been the negotiating process itself. First, it is accepted wisdom that one way of bringing the other party to the negotiating table is to undertake the development, construction, or deployment of new weapons systems which pose a threat to that other party. NATO's two-track decision of December 1979 to deploy 464 ground-launched cruise missiles and 108 Pershing II missiles in Western Europe has been seen as the primary motivation for the Soviet Union's decision to begin negotiations with the Americans on Euromissiles in 1981. The subsequent deployment of these weapons and NATO's determination to follow through on deployment confirmed the belief in some quarters that new weapons are needed to force the Soviets to the table. It is difficult to counter these perceptions. Indeed, they are probably correct. The net effect, however, has been to increase the number of weapons or their quality and thereby undermine the overriding objectives of controlling expenditures and preserving stability even before the negotiations commence. There is something perverse about an arms control process that requires an expansion of arsenals before it can even start.

A second, and related, problem with these negotiations is the belief that weapons must be held as bargaining chips to secure concessions. This generates strong pressure to deploy more weapons than are required for purposes of security in order to seize a bargaining advantage. Alternatively, weapons that should be dismantled are retained so that you have something to give up. The Soviets apparently delayed dismantling their intermediate-range ss-4 and ss-5 missiles (which were being replaced by the ss-20s) so that they could be traded off against American weapons in the negotiations. Assuming the successful implementation of a Soviet-American INF accord it is probable that many battlefield or tactical nuclear weapons will be difficult to remove from Europe, because they might serve as bargaining chips in a future round of negotiations. This is hardly innovative or surprising as a bargaining technique. But it does make clear how the negotiating process has fostered more rather than fewer weapons, with the effect of negating the long-term objective of controlling the size of the respective stockpiles. The negotiated route to arms control also discourages unilateral initiatives because any reduction in one's own stockpile of weapons must be met by some reciprocal action on the part of the other party. Thus even when arms reductions may be in your own interest for economic or security reasons or both, they are delayed until they can be used in the bargaining process.

Arms control as practised to date has also encouraged an expansion of weaponry because of the tendency, readily apparent in the United States, to buy political support for arms control agreements by increasing military expenditures. Evidence of this can be found as long ago as 1963 at the time of the Limited Test Ban Treaty when the late Senator Henry Jackson, a consistent opponent of arms control, made his approval of the treaty conditional on a presidential commitment to intensify weapons research and development through underground testing. The treaty was approved and atmospheric testing did cease, but the overall rate of testing actually increased. It was simply moved underground. This practice of buying support has continued and was evident most recently in the futile efforts of President Carter to gain political support for SALT II by giving his commitment to such contentious programs as the MX, among others. One observer compared this to stuffing a sausage . . . restraints in one area force bulges in others. Historical experience suggests that the political environment in the United States and especially the treaty ratification process almost demand a further expansion in military spending and hardware for an arms control agreement to be accepted, thus undermining the objectives of arms reductions.

Many conservatives opposed to arms control condemn the practice for failing to stem the expansion of Soviet military spending and the deployment of more and better nuclear weapons. The accuracy of these charges overlooks a similar pattern evident in the United States. Evidence indicates that both parties underwent a sizeable expansion in their nuclear forces during the 1970s with the Soviets adding nearly 4000 strategic warheads while the Americans have added over 6000. Even if one accepts the need to maintain strategic stability, both sides have been adept in undermining the arms control objectives of damage limitation and reduced expenditures. Many of these practices have created conditions that are not fundamentally different from those that would have existed without arms control negotiations, and guided by the requirements of deterrence alone. It may even be argued that the practice of arms control to date has yielded larger arsenals and has made these more politically acceptable than would have been possible otherwise. George Kennan considers that arms control negotiations "are not a way of escape from the weapons race, they are an integral part of it."[11] Agreements to date may have prevented the superpowers from doing more but it is difficult to identify areas into which they would have moved if it were not for these agreements. Instead it is possible that the agreements have channelled activity into areas that might have been left alone (multiple warheads and cruise missiles are examples) or have compelled activity simply because existing agreements did not cover it and there existed a fear that the other party might take advantage of this.

While arms control negotiations have generally failed to reduce nuclear weapons or, arguably, to secure strategic stability, they have been relatively successful in quelling dissent within the Alliance and among domestic publics. The arms control process has thus far been dominated by the superpowers. Other states, such as Canada, have been involved only indirectly in negotiations on nuclear weapons. (The more active Canadian presence in the field of arms control has been in multilateral forums such as the Committee on Disarmament in Geneva, the discussions on conventional forces in Vienna, and the Conference on Disarmament in Europe in Stockholm.) On strategic issues Canada and other allies have sought to influence American negotiating strategies through consultations on a bilateral basis or through NATO. There were for example considerable, although ultimately unsuccessful, attempts on the part of the allies, including letters from Clark to Shultz, to secure an American commitment to the arms limits set by the unratified SALT II agreement and to the Reagan administration's interpretation of the Anti-Ballistic Missile Treaty of 1972. The allies also put pressure on the Americans at the NATO foreign ministers meeting held in Halifax in the fall of 1986 during which one delegate said that if a vote had been taken on adhering to the SALT II limits it would have been fifteen to one in favour. Unfortunately the sole opposing vote was the United States which shortly thereafter with much fanfare and the clear rejection of the allies' advice exceeded the limits set by SALT II.

As evident in the INF negotiations discussed below, the United States has not always been anxious to consult with the allies even when it is the allies' interests that are most directly effected. Despite this, in the interest of Alliance solidarity many NATO member governments including Canada have been reluctant to criticize American negotiating positions or have agreed to support other ventures such as cruise missile testing or, as in Britain's case, support the SDI as long as arms control negotiations were in progress. As Secretary of State for External Affairs Joe Clark told the House of Commons Standing Committee on National Defence in April 1987 to explain why the government had not pressed the Americans to include cruise missiles in their negotiations with the Russians, "our view has been that there is not much utility, that it does not work, for countries not at the table to try to insert items that are not on the table if the people who make the decisions are going to regard that as being another agenda or potentially counter-productive to the agenda they are pursuing."[12]

Alliance management has become an important aspect of the superpowers' arms control relationship. Despite this the allies remain strong supporters of the arms control process. Limited opportunities for injecting their interests into bilateral negotiations have not deterred them from making such efforts and while their chances for success are often slim they may have some effect. For example, as part of the NATO foreign ministers' agreement to adopt the two-track decision of 1979, there was also an agreement to remove 1000 battlefield nuclear warheads from Europe. At a subsequent meeting at Montebello in October 1983 it was decided to withdraw an additional 1400 weapons. Jane Sharp writes that these decisions were "in reaction to widespread protest against the double-track INF decision . . . (and were devised) . . . in the NATO Shift Study undertaken at the instigation of the Dutch government."[13] On balance, however, the allies do find their efforts to influence arms control constrained when so much of the discussion on arms control in the area of nuclear weapons takes place between the superpowers. This has created particular difficulties in the INF negotiations.

Arms control, which had been the creation of the liberals, has become the adopted child of the cold warriors who, despite their criticisms, have used the process quite well. Not only has this led to bad arms control, it has also undermined an appropriate Alliance security policy. This is best exemplified in the practice of defining security as weapons parity and exacerbated by attempts to mimic the size, type, and disposition of forces deployed by the Soviet bloc. Commenting on the INF deployments of new medium-range missiles in Europe in the early 1980s, Michael Howard wrote that "the belief of some strategic analysts that the Russians can only be deterred from attacking us by the installation of precisely matching systems— ground-launched missiles must be matched by ground-launched missiles—is politically naive to the point of absurdity."[14] Arms control negotiations encouraged this tendency and both opponents and proponents alike have emphasized the significance of parity. Parity has now been integrated in strategic doctrine. This leads to bad security policy. All weapons are not equal and equal levels are not always necessary to ensure security. American strategist Thomas Schelling has written that "nothing about the concept of ballistic missiles . . . should lump them all together for disarmament planning or . . . should treat them all as generically alike in their attractiveness as deterrent forces." In considering the Reykjavik proposals to eliminate ballistic missiles Schelling argues that the United States and its allies would be much better off if they unilaterally destroyed their land-based ballistic missiles while retaining their sea-based systems as their protected retaliatory force. Schelling maintains that this would obviate the Soviets' need for land-based ballistic missiles (ICBM) or as Schelling states "if we cannot dismantle their land-based missiles by negotiation, we may gain a lot by dismantling their targets instead."[15]

The opportunities for unilateral action that will enhance both security and arms limitations are evident in other areas. Battlefield nuclear weapons introduced into Western Europe in the 1950s when there was an illusion that one could fight limited nuclear wars pose another serious risk to nuclear escalation in Europe because of their potential for early use in times of conflict.

These weapons have yet to fall under an arms control regime yet their questionable utility and limited deterrent credibility have encouraged the allies to reduce these weapons. This successful venture in arms reduction was made with little fanfare and without securing compensatory measures from the Soviet Union. Instead it was rooted in an independent assessment of the Alliance's requirements. Its success was as much in spite of arms control as it was because of it.

> Indeed, if arms control negotiations had been underway in the past, they would probably have been used as an excuse for not undertaking the modest measures of reduction that have been set in train by NATO. Why, it would have been asked, reduce unilaterally when you might bring down the Warsaw Pact numbers in multilateral negotiation? The difficulty in bringing any such negotiation to a conclusion would have kept both NATO and Warsaw Pact numbers up. Here, then, is a case in which hard questions of sufficiency are more useful, and the idea of parity is a diversion.[16]

By allowing the arms control process to shape security policy in this way, security becomes so much arithmetic and the numerical balance is allowed to define the political interests at stake. Nuclear strategy has over the years become increasingly apolitical. Arms control has unfortunately tended to follow the same course. Because of the concentration on numerical balances to the neglect of these wider political interests, arms control and the nuclear strategy it supports are destined to remain isolated from these interests.

The Reykjavik summit and the INF accord which followed seemingly challenged many of these critical views of arms control. Reagan and Gorbachev have apparently broken the deadlock that has impeded effective disarmament for the past twenty years. While these events have encouraged many arms control supporters they have also (somewhat ironically) pleased many of the most fervent critics of arms control. Some credit the success of recent arms control ventures to the seven years of unrelenting expansion in American military spending, or to the actual deployment of medium-range missiles by NATO or as proof positive that Star Wars and arms control were not incompatible as so many critics of Reagan's space-based program had alleged. If these practices are to be continued, the new variety of arms control will not differ fundamentally from the same set of assumptions that have guided past practice. The summit in Iceland may indicate the start of a shift away from the superpower animosities of the early 1980s. It does not signify the last days of nuclear weapons. Nor does it offer a way out of the problems that have been experienced with arms control to date. The events at Reykjavik clearly demonstrate that the superpowers remain committed to a quantitative assessment of the utility of their respective arsenals, a commitment to parity, and the need for reciprocity before weapons are removed.

## A Nuclear Munich?

The first victims of the post-Reykjavik fallout are likely to be the intermediate nuclear forces deployed by the Americans and the Soviets in Europe. Anxious to have at least one good arms control agreement in hand with which to face their domestic constituencies, both Reagan and Gorbachev have proceeded first to settle the matter of INF missiles in Europe. (There remain a number of issues that might prevent the implementation of an agreement, including opposition from conservative senators in the United States, problems with verification, or differences over dismantling procedures.) Negotiations on the INF had been underway since 1981 but the frenzied activity after Reykjavik reflected the mutually shared interest in an arms control agreement that would remove the stigma of failure that surrounded the Iceland summit. An INF agreement was the likeliest candidate, in that it would have little direct effect on the security interests of the United States and only a slight effect on the Soviet Union. The agreement if and when implemented eliminates a mere three per cent of their respective (and growing) stockpiles of nuclear warheads. The elimination of these missiles also does nothing to impinge on their respective abilities to deliver an effective retaliatory attack on each other's homeland. Instead the agreement essentially involves the security of European states and the strategy of the Western Alliance. Perhaps it was as Francois Heisbourg, incoming president of the London-based International Institute of Strategic Studies noted, "easier to reduce one's problems by dealing with the interests of others."[17]

The INF agreement signed in Washington in December 1987 by American President Ronald Reagan and Soviet General Secretary Mikhail Gorbachev provides for the elimination of all intermediate- and short-range (between 500 and 1500 kilometres) American and Soviet nuclear weapons. As a result of the agreement the United States will withdraw and destroy 859 ground-launched cruise missiles and Pershing IIs that have been deployed as a result of NATO's two-track decision of 1979. The Soviet Union will destroy 1752 missiles including the modern ss-20 intermediate-range missiles, each of which carried three nuclear warheads, and the older ss-4s and ss-5s and shorter-range missiles. After years of negotiations, the Soviet Union in its eagerness to secure an arms control agreement, made a number of concessions to the United States and its allies and eventually accepted the "zero option," whereby all medium-range missiles would be removed from Europe, first proposed by the American government in 1981. The zero option had originally been proposed for its propaganda value and as a means of quelling opposition within the Alliance to the INF deployments and the American approach to arms control rather than as a sincere bargaining position. The ploy eventually rebounded as the Soviets finally said *da*. The co-operative Soviets caught many in the West off guard. Some, such as American Republican Congressmen Jack Kemp who once thought that the zero option was "the most historic contribution to strengthening the free world alliance that has been made by any president in many years" referred to the agreement that confirmed the zero option as "a nuclear Munich (that would) imperil the NATO alliance."[18]

Many in Europe and especially NATO generals at Alliance headquarters were also concerned about the effect of an INF agreement on the military balance in Europe. They worried too about President Reagan's born-again commitment to arms control. For most Canadians and Americans the European anxiety was difficult to comprehend. When faced with European concerns about the INF accord, Canada's External Affairs Minister Joe Clark said: "We can't allow a process which has involved this much movement by the superpowers to be frustrated at the beginning by some understandable but surmountable differences within the alliance."[19] Why were the Europeans being so stubborn about removing weapons that they seemingly never wanted in the first place? Why did Henry Kissinger and Richard Nixon among others react to the first significant arms control accord in nearly a decade, saying it might create "the most profound crisis of the NATO alliance in its forty-year history"?[20]

American nuclear weapons in Europe carry a heavy political burden. Like Canadian and American conventional forces, their primary role is to reassure the Europeans that the United States would be willing to risk its own security in defence of the West. More so than conventional forces, however, nuclear weapons are seen to guarantee that the United States would not allow a conventional or nuclear war to be limited to the European continent. As argued in the previous chapter the American nuclear guarantee to Europe was strongest when the United States seemed invulnerable to a Soviet nuclear attack. As North America came within range of Soviet intercontinental ballistic missiles the credibility of the American nuclear deterrent was reduced as many questioned the likelihood that the United States would be willing to risk a Soviet nuclear attack in defence of Western Europe. The deployment of American nuclear weapons in Europe had been intended to reassure the Europeans that the United States would come to Europe's defence in time of war. It had instead left them hostage to American nuclear strategy. Many within Europe believed the American nuclear guarantee would not survive once American interests were directly threatened. Others feared that the United States was only too willing and able to fight a limited nuclear war on the European continent. Ironically, arms control reinforced these fears, both of which were instrumental in shaping the INF debate in Europe.

The INF missiles were the offspring of SALT II. Suggestive of the tendency of arms control in one area to intensify pressure for expansion in others, the deployment of American nuclear weapons in Europe was a direct response to the restrictions on American and Soviet strategic forces under the SALT II accord. Discussions on the need for additional nuclear weapons for the Alliance had begun as early as the mid-1970s in the wake of American Secretary of Defence James Schlesinger's call for flexible nuclear options. The so-called Schlesinger Doctrine was yet another attempt to devise a "credible" nuclear response to conventional aggression short of total war. Parity between American and Soviet nuclear forces as a result of successive rounds of arms control negotiations and the steady expansion of Soviet strategic forces had allegedly inhibited the United States from using nuclear weapons during a conflict and thus reduced the credibility of the American nuclear deterrent. Schlesinger attempted to reassure the Europeans of the credibility of this posture by changing American targetting policy; changes made possible by the improved accuracy of nuclear weapons and the development of multiple warheads on American ICBMs. Such efforts were only partially successful in responding to European concerns about the strength of the American commitment and further assurances became necessary.

Once again the Alliance looked to a military response for what was and remains a political problem. In December 1979 in Brussels, NATO member governments agreed to the deployment of American intermediate-range nuclear weapons in Europe. The deployment of these Euromissiles would mark the return of American INF weapons to Europe after an absence of nearly two decades. NATO's decision to deploy them, like so many collective decisions, reflected a grand political compromise. The decision was designed to appeal to those who supported arms control, those who believed the Soviet missiles had to be countered, and to meet a number of military and political objectives. The lack of unity of purpose created considerable difficulties for member governments and their constituents, some of which have only now become clear as the INF missiles are prepared for the return voyage across the Atlantic.

One of the early proponents favouring the INF deployments was West German Chancellor Helmut Schmidt, who in 1977 called attention to the deteriorating imbalance of nuclear and conventional forces in central Europe, an imbalance that had been encouraged by the strategic arms limitation talks between the two superpowers. Schmidt believed that the superpowers' acceptance of parity at the level of intercontinental weapons required adjustments at other levels. "No one can deny that the principle of parity is a sensible one. However, its fulfilment must be the aim of all arms-limitation and arms-control negotiations and it must apply to all categories of weapons."[21] The significance of parity was in its effect on the American nuclear guarantee to Western Europe. In almost all respects this guarantee was more a function of political relations than military ones. Yet the prerequisites of parity for strategic stability as defined by the practice of arms control demanded that NATO respond to any Soviet military actions that touched Europe. The Soviet Union had begun to modernize their intermediate-range forces in Europe in the mid-1970s, replacing their outdated, stationary, single-warhead ss-4s and ss-5s with the mobile multiple warhead ss-20s. Europeans like Schmidt, as well as some Americans, argued that new weapons for NATO were needed to counter these Soviet deployments. For others like Zbigniew Brzezinski, then national security advisor to President Carter, there were no compelling military reasons for an INF deployment. Amidst growing uncertainty in Europe about the reliability of the Carter administration, the decision to deploy INF missiles was made by the Alliance.

The immediate catalyst for the Alliance was the neutron bomb fiasco of 1978, when the United States first offered and then subsequently withdrew the offer to deploy the neutron bomb in Europe. The withdrawal of the offer came only after Schmidt had committed his government to accept the weapon and was, as a result, the source of considerable political embarassment. Affronted by this politically inept move on the part of the Carter adminstration NATO ministers sought even closer co-operation in defining the Alliance's nuclear needs. The leaders of the United States, France, Britain, and West Germany met in Guadaloupe in January 1979 where they agreed to deploy INF missiles with Schmidt's condition that West Germany not be the only continental state to host the weapons. In December of the same year at a meeting of NATO foreign and defence ministers, the two-track decision received unanimous approval. The first track of the decision was to deploy 464 ground-launched cruise missiles and 108 Pershing II missiles in five NATO countries, including West Germany, Great Britain, Italy, Belgium, and the Netherlands. The second track, implemented primarily to reassure those who feared an arms race on the continent, was a commitment to negotiate an arms control agreement with the Soviet Union covering these weapons. Unlike previous deployments of American nuclear weapons to NATO members, which had been done on a bilateral basis, this decision required and received the support of all member states, including those like Canada who would not receive any weapons. This reflected a concern for the political risks that might be encountered in implementing the deployment decision. It was this notion of risk sharing that the Trudeau government used to defend its decision to test the air-launched cruise missile.

The need to respond to new Soviet weapons was for policy makers a useful, if only partial, explanation for INF deployments. By tying the deployments to Soviet actions western governments could lay the blame for the escalation of armaments in central Europe to Soviet modernization and rearmament policies. The explanation was far from complete, however, and left NATO with a credibility problem. The problem stemmed from the fact that the Soviet Union had since the early 1960s deployed short- and intermediate-range nuclear weapons in Europe. Many opponents to NATO deployments argued that it was the Alliance and not the Russians that was fuelling the escalation of the arms race in the European theatre. Moreover, opponents to the deployments could also point to the fact that NATO's INF would not redress the imbalance but would still leave the Alliance in a quantitatively inferior position as evidence of their view that the alleged link with the ss-20s was fallacious. If the only concern was to respond to Soviet missile deployments then sea-based systems could have been deployed with the same, if not an enhanced, deterrent effect. The military rationale for NATO's INF deployment was based not on Soviet actions alone but on the perception that the credibility of NATO's strategy of flexible response, which since 1967 was the link between the conventional defence of Western Europe and the strategic nuclear forces of the United States, had to be reinforced. Yet if such reinforcements were necessary, then the zero option would not be acceptable because NATO would still be missing a link between conventional defences and the American strategic arsenal. An acceptance of this military rationale for nuclear weapons in Europe still left room to oppose the cruise and Pershing deployments because of their extreme vulnerability. Like the Thor and Jupiter missiles that were deployed in the late 1950s, the more recent INF missiles would also have to be used early in a war. As a result they would provide a natural preemptive target for an adversary and as such increase the temptation to attack first in times of crisis.

For most observers the decision to deploy American theatre nuclear weapons in Europe was made for political not military reasons. The deployment of Euromissiles would reinforce the linkage between the defence of Western Europe and the strategic forces of the American nuclear arsenal. This is evident in the final number of medium-range missiles deployed in Europe.

> Deliberation over the number of missiles to be deployed indicated the extent to which NATO needed to create a symbol of American involvement. NATO's High Level Group, which studies military needs, concluded that between 200 and 600 missiles should be deployed. Fewer than 200 missiles, it reasoned, would not provide a visible American commitment to Europe; more than 600 would suggest the existence of a separate European balance of nuclear forces, thus decoupling American from European forces and increasing the probability that a conflict could be confined to Europe.[22]

A further political consideration in the decision to deploy Pershing IIs and ground-launched cruise missiles instead of relying on sea-based systems was that weapons systems deployed in various European states would be more visible than sea-based systems, presumably both to the allies and to the Soviets, and would therefore convey the message that the Western European states were willing to accept some of the responsibility for maintaining the deterrence.

The INF debate began as a test of American loyalty by a small number of European elites. As the demonstrations against deployment grew, it became instead a test of European loyalty for some members of the Reagan administration. The Europeans eventually displayed their loyalty but only after considerable anxiety as they wavered between schizophrenic fears of being entrapped in an American-Soviet confrontation or abandoned to their own defence as the Americans and the Soviets looked after their own interests.[23] The European fear of American abandonment in the face of a Soviet attack has been around since the founding of the Alliance and has been influenced more recently by a number of developments. The expanded range of superpower arms control in the 1970s and the apparent tendency in

American arms control practices to emphasize intercontinental weapons to the neglect of those weapons that were intended for use in Europe led some in Europe to think that American policy makers were primarily interested in securing the American homeland. The problems with the neutron bomb and the concern over apparent vacillation in American foreign policy added to this uncertainty. More recently, the unqualified commitment to the SDI has further encouraged this belief. For some European policy makers, the approach to all of these issues at Reykjavik confirmed it. What was lost amidst this debate was the fact that the American commitment to Europe has always been more a function of American interests than of American weapons.

Given the political sensitivity of the missiles' mission it is not surprising that in withdrawing the missiles as the result of a unilateral action the United States runs the risk of exacerbating the very conditions the missiles were designed to subvert; the fear of abandonment that had led to the demands for their deployment in the late 1970s. If the Euromissile deployment was necessary to reassure the Europeans of the permanence of the American commitment to their defence, then an arms control agreement with the Soviet Union that would withdraw Pershing IIs and cruise missiles from Europe was unacceptable. This became evident in the European reaction to the Reykjavik summit.

European opposition to an INF accord appeared immediately after the Reykjavik summit. Allied governments were annoyed that the Americans were not consulting them on arms control proposals such as the 1982 "walk in the woods" agreement between American and Soviet negotiators which was subsequently abandoned by the Americans without consulting the allies. Even President Reagan's staunchest European allies, Mrs. Thatcher and Herr Kohl, were quick to travel to Washington after the summit to seek American reassurances that their interests would be protected in future arms control negotiations. Untouched by Reagan's long distance feeling during his Icelandic weekend, both leaders wanted more than telephone notices before their security blankets were traded away. The concerns of Thatcher, Mitterand, and Kohl were echoed by NATO officials in Belgium and NATO Supreme Commander General Bernard Rogers who publicly questioned the wisdom of eliminating a significant part of NATO's seamless web of nuclear deterrence. Rogers' opposition was rewarded with early retirement and his replacement, General John Galvin, has been more discreet. The opposition, while posing some problems for Reagan's arms control plans, has not prevented him from pressing ahead. In the midst of all this dissent the NATO foreign ministers returned to the scene of the original crime in Reykjavik in June 1987 where they were persuaded to give their approval in principle to an INF accord. Support for an accord that would remove what fewer than ten years earlier had been considered militarily necessary for a credible nuclear deterrent, had only been secured with a number of conditions attached. Most important among these was to exclude from the agreement seventy-two Pershing I missiles controlled by West Germany and available for use with American-controlled nuclear weapons and to limit future talks on banning shorter-range nuclear weapons in Europe. The first condition was out of deference to West Germany's "independence" and the latter because of lingering concern over the feasibility of the conventional deterrent and the independent French and British nuclear forces. In subsequent negotiations with the Soviets and as a result of some gentle persuasion from the United States, West Germany indicated that it would not modernize the Pershing Is when they become obsolete in the early 1990s. Despite these qualifications and to the surprise of many, the Russians, who had their own arms control agenda to look after, set aside NATO's objections and indicated their willingness to conclude the agreement. In the face of such readiness and the pressures of domestic politics, both Thatcher and Kohl were forced to yield and give their support to the agreement.

An INF agreement will not sit well with the European powers. It is too early to discern clearly their longer-term response to what is being read in some quarters as the beginning of the end of the American nuclear commitment to the defence of the continent. European fears of a post-INF environment are most pronounced in France but are also evident in Britain and West Germany. These fears result, in part, from the unilateralist approach to arms control being pursued in Washington. It is also influenced by the unpredictability of American policy toward the

Soviet Union which has moved from hostility to camaraderie with reckless abandon in the eyes of Europeans. Remembering the quick and complete American rejection of detente, Europeans can only wonder how long this latest euphoria will last before it degenerates into another cold war. The Europeans, and especially the French, also worry about the American commitment to nuclear deterrence. Nuclear deterrence is viewed by the French as essential for preserving the peace on the European continent. The rhetoric and now the arms control policy of the Reagan administration seems to have rejected this view. Such concerns are no doubt premature and alarmist given the thousands of "tactical nuclear weapons" scattered throughout Europe and the continued presence of well-stocked American nuclear forces on bombers in Britain and in submarines in the Mediterranean Sea and Atlantic Ocean, all within easy reach of targets in central and Eastern Europe and the Soviet Union. The visible coupling of American nuclear weapons with the European continent may disappear but some American strategic forces will remain nearby. Nevertheless, some Europeans exhibit continuing anxiety. This is especially evident in the case of the French government which has recently embarked on a sizeable nuclear modernization program. In fact, assuming existing plans only, the French and British nuclear forces will undergo a six-fold increase by the year 2000. France has also been actively engaged in soliciting British and German support for intensified military co-operation. Thus while a successful INF accord may eliminate some Soviet and American nuclear weapons from central Europe, the denuclearization of the continent remains a distant dream. That is unless Mikhail Gorbachev has his way.

## "A Revolution—Without Bullets"

Soviet General Secretary Mikhail Gorbachev is upsetting the West. His pacificist tendencies appear boundless. Indeed the only thing he has seemed interested in launching in recent years has been peace initiatives. Since assuming power in 1985, Gorbachev has pursued an arms control agenda without precedent in the history of Soviet foreign policy. In a speech in January 1986, he outlined plans for the total elimination of nuclear weapons by the end of the century. Forty years after the Hiroshima bomb he began a unilateral moratorium on nuclear weapons testing that only ceased eighteen months later after repeated extensions and the failure of the western powers to co-operate. More recently he has paid off the Soviet Union's long-standing debt at the United Nations; proposed a treaty on Arctic co-operation with Canada (to which the Canadian government has not responded); complained that the "growing militarization of (the Arctic) is assuming a frightening character" and needs to be controlled with demilitarized zones; adopted the rhetoric of the European disarmament movement by advocating nuclear, conventional, and chemical weapons reductions "from the Atlantic to the Urals"; and reiterated his view that an arms control accord with the United States "might start a peaceful chain reaction in the sphere of strategic offensive arms, the non-placement of arms in space and many other items on a possible agenda of international dialogue."[24] The man has been busy!

This impressive array of proposals has been the source of much consternation in the West. Yet the responses have been tentative at best. Gorbachev has clearly seized the initiative and to a western audience starved for arms control after a hiatus of nearly a decade, the proposals are falling on receptive ears.

> One can hardly overestimate the significance of the Soviet disarmament proposals. They mark a dramatic break with the cautious approach of the Brezhnev generation. Such initiatives as the unilateral test moratorium and the acceptance of extensive on-site verification, including the presence of American scientists near Soviet test facilities, are particularly striking indications of how far the Soviets have been willing to come.[25]

The only exception to Gorbachev's enthusiasm for arms control is his entrenched opposition to the Strategic Defence Initiative. The continued American commitment to the SDI may prevent many of the aforementioned proposals from reaching fruition. From a Soviet perspective real reductions in nuclear weapons are untenable if there exists the possibility that the United States could deploy even partially effective ballistic missile defences. Alternatively a willingness on the part of the Americans to abandon the SDI could bring about a radically different balance of conventional and nuclear forces, a balance as much in favour of western interests as such a balance is ever likely to be. The current Soviet interest in arms control is indeed unprecedented but as with western approaches to arms control it is a reflection of evolving Soviet military strategy. Unlike western strategy that has since the 1950s placed a priority on stability with nuclear weapons consistent with the need for deterrence, the Soviets have shown signs of changing their military doctrine in response to shifting domestic and foreign policy priorities.

Leonid Brezhnev, in a widely noted speech in Tula in 1977 said that "the purpose of (Soviet) military power is directed to avoid not only a first strike but also a second strike, and to prevent nuclear war itself."[26] The speech marked the public announcement of a significant shift in Soviet strategy (which had been initiated as early as 1966, by one account). Before this the Soviet view of military power and particularly nuclear weapons was simply that more was better than less. Based on an assumption that any future war would quickly become a nuclear war and involve direct attacks on the Soviet homeland, the purpose of Soviet military forces was to outshoot the West. This necessitated an ever-increasing nuclear stockpile because nothing less than clear superiority would allow the Soviets to emerge on top after the cataclysm. Arms control had little relevance unless it was used to limit the nuclear arsenals of the United States and its NATO allies. By the late 1960s the strategic priorities had been revised and with it Soviet military doctrine. The shift in strategy changed Soviet military planning in many important respects but especially in the area of arms control. At the 26th Party Congress in 1981, Brezhnev said bluntly that "to try to prevail over the other in the arms race is dangerous madness."[27] Since the early 1970s there has been a persistent interest on the part of Soviet leaders in the arms control process for more than merely its propaganda utility. By the early 1980s, for the first time Brezhnev proposed eliminating weapons already deployed. This radical adjustment in Soviet arms control policy has been traced to a change in its military doctrine.

Unlike their American counterparts, the Soviet military did not adjust readily to the appearance of nuclear weapons. Lacking easy access to targets in the United States, in the early years of the cold war the Soviets concentrated their military efforts on maintaining a conventional threat to Western Europe to discourage American nuclear attacks on the Soviet Union. The successful launch of Sputnik in 1957 encouraged the Soviet military to develop a strategic rocket force and thereby present a credible nuclear threat to North America. Lacking a sizeable force, however, Soviet strategy emphasized the need for preemption, for the first and early use of nuclear weapons during periods of crisis. The deployment of Soviet nuclear weapons to Cuba in 1962 was most likely an unsuccessful attempt to overcome this gap in delivery capability. During this early period the Soviet leadership was inclined to conclude that the West had an interest in a premeditated attack on the Soviet Union and that any future war with the United States or its NATO allies would be nuclear. As mentioned in the previous chapter, NATO's strategy had been especially designed to encourage this latter belief, beginning with the adoption of a "first-use" policy in 1954, continuing with the deployment of tactical and short-range nuclear weapons in Europe in the late 1950s and ending with an expansion of nuclear stockpiles in Europe in the early 1960s. To overcome the gap between their own nuclear forces and those of the United States, the Soviets undertook a sizeable expansion of their ICBMs during the 1960s. The nuclear arms race was on in earnest. By the end of the decade, however, developments on a number of fronts combined to shift the focus from arms racing to arms control.

Michael MccGwire in an important study of Soviet military objectives has noted two important areas in which NATO played a significant role in shaping the reforms that took place in Soviet strategy.[28] In a third vitally important area NATO had little say. By the late 1960s, the Soviet Union had in place an existing and planned structure of nuclear weapons able to destroy the United States in a nuclear war. Through the expansion of their strategic rocket forces and by recognizing that American ICBM could be as effectively destroyed by targetting their control centres as the missiles themselves, the Soviets had overcome the gap in strategic weapons. As they moved ever closer to parity in strategic weapons it became possible to consider alternatives to their highly unstable strategy of preemption. The abandonment of preemption was also encouraged by NATO's release of the Harmel Report which maintained that the allies were not committed solely to a military confrontation. The withdrawal of France from NATO's integrated military command and the Alliance's formal decision to adopt a strategy of "flexible response" encouraged the Soviets to rethink their views on the inevitability of nuclear war and the utility of arms control. In Jane Sharp's view, "having reduced their long-standing vulnerability to the West by achieving parity, and reassured by NATO's adoption of a less belligerent doctrine and by the recent advances in satellite technology, the Soviets by the late 1960s viewed arms control as a much less risky prospect."[29]

MccGwire has shown how Soviet military objectives and the strategies that supported them changed dramatically in the late 1960s. No longer were the Soviets convinced that a future war would involve nuclear weapons; they began to plan for the possibility of fighting a war that would leave the Soviet homeland untouched by nuclear devastation. Arms control became a central part of this process and NATO's flexible response strategy supported the change in thinking. As MccGwire writes:

2. First, the policy indicated that if NATO had a choice, the early stages of a war in Europe would be conventional. Second, the debate within NATO that preceded the policy's adoption had certain implications about the U.S. nuclear guarantee of Europe (which) . . . could also be read as reflecting a reluctance to make good on the nuclear guarantee of Europe, now that the United States was vulnerable to nuclear attack.[30]

The Soviet interest in arms control has persisted throughout the 1970s and into the 1980s. At the strategic level the interest was motivated by a concern for limiting the size of the American offensive arsenal to prevent the possible return of American strategic superiority. A central objective of Soviet arms control strategy has been to assure parity and a Soviet retaliatory capability in the face of an American attack. This explains the Soviet concerns with the SDI which, if effective or perceived to be effective, could encourage Americans to believe that the North American continent was once again secure from a Soviet nuclear attack. This in turn might encourage the United States to initiate the use of nuclear weapons in some future conflict.

Revisions to NATO's nuclear force posture and the deployment of medium-range missiles in Europe in the early 1980s renewed fears among the Soviet leadership about limiting a European war to conventional weapons. Concerns within NATO about the commitment of the United States to Western Europe's defence in the early 1970s encouraged the Alliance and the United States to adopt a targetting plan in wartime that would commit nuclear weapons for use in Europe, and thus decrease the prospects that a war in Europe would be limited to conventional weapons. As mentioned earlier the so-called Schlesinger Doctrine that was formalized by Presidential Directive 59 in 1979 emphasized the need for flexible and credible nuclear options at all levels and stages of warfare. This encouraged a firm commitment to "first-use" and support for short- and medium-range missiles in Western Europe. The Soviets used propaganda successfully to counter the American proposal to deploy neutron bombs in Europe but were unable to stop NATO from agreeing to and subsequently deploying medium-range missiles in the early 1980s. Their opposition to the deployment was evident as early as 1978 when Brezhnev first made proposals for restricting intermediate-range weapons in Europe. Between then and November 1983 when the first cruise missiles and Pershing IIs were deployed by NATO, the Soviets presented a series of offers to limit and even reduce their ss-20 deployments. By the end of 1985 the Soviets were withdrawing ss-20s from Europe as an incentive for an agreement.

There has been a tendency to conclude that the agreement to eliminate medium-range missiles was only possible as a result of displays of military strength and political resolve on the part of the Alliance. In a more general vein it is repeatedly argued that the West must convince the Soviets to come to the bargaining table. Whatever truth there may be to such views, they overlook the possibility of an intrinsic interest of the Soviets in arms control. A close examination of the Soviet negotiating record between 1978 and 1983 suggests that the Soviets were willing not only to stop, but actually to reduce, their ss-20 deployments in exchange for a halt to similar deployments by NATO. This indicates that the Soviet Union has an intrinsic interest in arms control negotiations that is not solely a result of displays of strength on the part of the West.

> The most direct diplomatic effort to forestall new long-range NATO missiles . . . took the form of a series of Soviet offers, through 1978 and 1979, to include Soviet medium-range missiles in SALT III limits. In October and November 1979, Brezhnev upgraded this offer by proposing actual *reductions* in Soviet medium-range missiles if no new NATO missiles were deployed, and he offered—even urged—immediate negotiations on medium-range nuclear systems without waiting for the ratification of SALT II which at the time was still being considered by the Senate.[31]

The strength of the Soviet commitment to the recent INF agreement is perhaps best demonstrated by the fact that they were willing to accept an agreement that even the most hardline anti-Soviet elements in the United States admitted was a nonstarter and put forward for its propaganda content and little more—the so-called zero option. This despite the fact that the Soviet leadership recognized that they were leaving the door open for western hawks to argue that strength was the only language the Soviets understood.

How much longer will Gorbachev be able to maintain his initiatives? How much longer will the West be able to resist without responding in kind? Is any of this likely to lead us out of the dead end of arms control? Proposals for complete and total disarmament are not possible. Nor are we likely to be rid of nuclear weapons.

> The nuclear genie is out. To destroy all stocks could be naive and suicidal. We need to break the arms spiral, and halt the move to forward deployments, minimal warning, and computer dependence. We need to cut redundant arsenals, arsenals that exceed deterrence requirements, and spawn fear, and jitteriness. We cannot disarm, or at least not without a radical change in mindsets, East and West. In today's world, Gorbachev's dream, like the siren songs of Greek mythology, promise danger not relief.[32]

These views from Carl Jacobsen of the Stockholm International Peace Research Institute make clear the limits to Gorbachev's arms control initiatives and suggest a measured response on the part of western states. Gorbachev has, however, broken with the past and the West cannot ignore this. As many observers have noted, Gorbachev's objectives for domestic reform cannot be achieved with a foreign policy or international environment caught in a cold war. Gorbachev is not a liberal democrat and the Soviet Union will remain a great power for some time to come. A state of permanent seige is not, however, a necessity for western security. The evolving Soviet strategy has been designed to reduce the potential for nuclear war through a posture of minimum deterrence. More recently, with an emphasis given to defensive strategies in the Warsaw Pact's Budapest statement of June 1986, the Russians appear to be interested in altering their approach to conventional forces in Europe. These developments are particularly attractive to Canadians because they may result in declining threats to the North American continent without an increased threat in Europe. They also provide significant opportunites for the Alliance. The West must reappraise its orthodox assumptions about the nature of the Soviet threat and the requirements for security. The Alliance remains an important conduit for a constructive approach to future talks with the Soviets. Indeed, as the Soviets shift their attention to conventional arms, NATO takes on even greater significance.

## Building Confidence in Place of Arms

As the superpowers implement their agreement on medium-range weapons and make noises about an agreement on ballistic missiles, the attention of others turns toward conventional weaponry. The common refrain in the wake of the INF agreement was that the Americans had now made Europe safe for conventional war, that the Warsaw Pact possessed a clear superiority of conventional forces, and that without nuclear weapons these forces could not be deterred. As the previous chapter indicates, this is a far too simplistic appraisal of the conventional balance of forces in central Europe. It is an equally facile perspective on the factors that encourage states to choose war in pursuit of their interests. Despite the overwhelming amount of attention that has been given to nuclear arms control in recent years there have also been developments in other areas such as conventional forces, chemical weapons, and confidence-building measures designed to reassure the adversary that the threat of war is not imminent, that while less popular hold out more hope for getting at the more likely causes of war. Discussions in these other areas also open opportunities for Canada and other NATO allies to have direct input in efforts to ease East-West confrontation through arms control. Oddly, these areas have ranked low on the Canadian government's list of arms control priorities. Fortunately, they do not rank so low in the area of Canadian activity.

When he came to power in the fall of 1985, Prime Minister Mulroney identified six objectives of Canada's arms control policy. These were and remain: negotiated radical reductions in nuclear forces and the enhancement of strategic stability; support for a comprehensive test ban treaty; prevention of an arms race in outer space; maintenance and strengthening of the nonproliferation regime; negotiation of a global chemical weapons ban; and confidence-building measures to facilitate the reduction of military forces in Europe and elsewhere. In a statement to the House early in 1986 Joe Clark indicated that the government would emphasize "encouraging compliance with existing treaties, developing verification mechanisms; and building confidence between East and West."[33] The government has been severely disappointed in its efforts to influence American compliance with SALT II and the ABM Treaty. It has also been criticized for undermining its own arms control objectives by John Lamb, of the Canadian Arms Control and Disarmament Agency, who has argued that the government's decision to acquire nuclear submarines will both contradict and make less credible its efforts to enhance the nonproliferation regime.[34] Despite these serious shortcomings the government has intensified its efforts in the areas of verification, chemical weapons, and confidence-building measures. While success in these areas depends ultimately on the co-operation of others and especially the superpowers, the Canadian government can increase its potential for influencing events by emphasizing the areas where it can play a more direct role.

As most of the world's attention focused on the preliminaries of the Reagan-Gorbachev Iceland summit, Canada, the United

States, and thirty-three European states signed the final document of the Stockholm Conference on Confidence and Security-Building Measures and Disarmament in Europe. The signing after two and one-half years of negotiations provides for extensive advance notice of military activities such as troop deployments and military exercises on the European continent. The Warsaw Pact and NATO are now required, as a result of this agreement, to provide six weeks notice of exercises involving more than 13,000 troops and must invite observers to any exercise involving more than 17,000 troops. Fen Hampson writes that "from a Western perspective, one of the main values of the accord is that it will make it impossible for any country to mass the forces needed to invade or intimidate another country without the operations being openly detected and challenged."[35] In addition, the agreement also allows for three on-site inspections per year for suspected violations. Recently appointed NATO Supreme Commander Galvin expressed his support for the accord and "believes NATO stands to gain more than the Warsaw Pact from increased exchanges."[36] As a member of NATO with forces in Europe, Canada was able to participate actively in the negotiations. NATO allies, especially Britain and West Germany, were instrumental in gaining American support for the pact. The successful conclusion of this agreement opened new opportunities in other areas, especially negotiations on conventional forces in Europe.

Negotiations for the reduction and balancing of conventional forces in central Europe have been a long-standing concern of the Alliance. Originating in the Harmel Report of 1967, formal negotiations did not begin until 1973. Since that time negotiations on Mutual and Balanced Force Reductions have been stalled. The confidence-building measures agreed to in 1986 and yet another Gorbachev initiative just may succeed in rejuvenating negotiations. The agreement reached in Stockholm in September 1986 achieved the first part of a 1978 French proposal for building confidence in Europe. The second phase of the proposal called for conventional disarmament.[37] Anxious to take advantage of this and launch another disarmament salvo, Gorbachev and his colleagues in the Warsaw Pact put forward the Budapest appeal in June 1986. Their proposal called for each side to remove between 100,000 and 150,000 troops "from the

Urals to the Atlantic." They also pushed to have the proposed force reduction talks expanded to include the thirty-five-nation Conference on Security and Disarmament in Europe. While NATO members, especially the United States, Britain, and West Germany were reluctant to expand the forum to include Europe's neutral states, many smaller countries and France supported it. The support is based on the greater possibility that neutrals will inject new ideas into the moribund negotiating practices that have marked these talks. In December 1986 NATO foreign ministers agreed to combine the two options by moving to the wider forum while retaining interalliance negotiations. While this provides no guarantee of success it will at least call an end to the long-dead Vienna negotiations on conventional forces. It may, however, merely create a new corpse in its wake unless the Alliance takes advantage of the opportunities Gorbachev is presenting.[39]

Support for conventional arms control has clearly intensified after the recent INF accord. As with any negotiated arms control agreement, however, negotiations on conventional arms have risks that may not yield effective security at lower levels of armaments. "The major risk is that deadlocked negotiations impose a 'planning blight' on NATO's Central Front . . . It would be unfortunate if the caution and inflexibility that can result from the actual practice of negotiating arms control, as well as from the regime that might eventually be agreed, were to constrain any possible changes and deny the Alliance the flexibility that it might need to rearrange its forces in a more sensible manner."[40] There have been, for example, a number of interesting proposals made for more defensive-oriented strategies. If linked to arms control such strategies may never be successfully implemented. It is quite clear that the Alliance and its principal adversaries in the Warsaw Pact have overarmed themselves to the point of making any future war between them mutually suicidal. Yet after years of negotiations we should be ready to agree with the former American negotiator who writes that, "In the longer run, the military confrontation in Europe seems as likely to shrink through independent actions on both sides taken to rationalize forces and to cope with economic stringencies as it is through agreed reductions. Not only the political confrontation in Europe, but the military confrontation, too, appears to have peaked."[41] Conventional arms control has shown few signs of being able to shake the stagnation that parity and reciprocity have brought to negotiations on nuclear arms. Unless such concepts are set aside for other, nonquantitative assessments of security, conventional arms control will have no future. In the final outcome, arms reductions in Europe are as likely to result from the growth of Canadian and American unilateralism as from a mutual arrangement with the Soviets. The possibility for transatlantic stability in the event of such actions by Canada and the United States are, however, remote. For this reason, continued Canadian involvement in East-West arms control negotiations requires a Canadian presence in Europe. Reducing Canadian forces in the future remains a possibility but should be linked to a multilateral approach that will enhance security and not to unilateral action. The Alliance has already suffered from too much unilateralism.

## CHAPTER FIVE

# Rambos and Euro-Wimps:
# The Roots of Global Unilateralism

What has come over you? What has caused this strange national self-exhaltation, this isolationism of the heart, these intrusions upon others' territories and cultures, these Rambo reflexes?

Terrorism is a word for things so terrible that it dulls the brain like alcohol. How can a nation which preens itself on its sensitivity to racism in its domestic arrangements behave with brutal racist indifference towards Libyans? . . .. People are asking, up and down Europe, whether this or that nation ought now to leave NATO. My own advice leads to a cleaner and simpler solution. Let the European NATO allies, with Canada, with courtesy and thanks, invite the United States to leave NATO. If she will not leave, then let them expel her. They can then attend to their own security needs in whichever way best suits them, and engage in their own negotiations for disarmament with the Soviet bloc.

We shall certainly feel safer when your F-111s, Poseidons and battle-fleets have gone home. You will probably feel safer also, and suffer from fewer rushes of ideological blood to the head.

> E.P. Thompson, "An Open Letter to Uncle Sam",
> *The Observer*, April 27, 1986.

## To the Shores of Tripoli

Shrouded in sea darkness, the planes came with no warning over the brilliantly lit North African city.

153

On the evening of April 14/15, 1986, three groups of American F-111 fighter-bombers took off from air bases in Britain on a mission against Moammar Gadhafi's Libya. It was, said President Reagan, a mission of self-defence, a mission fully consistent with Article 51, the self-defence provision of the United Nations Charter.[1] Few of America's allies agreed. The eighteen F-111s, twenty-eight tankers and several EF-111 electronic-warfare planes assembled over the English Channel and headed for Libya, nearly 3000 miles away on a route that avoided European airspace denied by France and Spain. Five hours later the U.S. Mediterranean Sixth fleet, which had recently engaged in hostile operations with Libyan forces in the Gulf of Sirte, launched carrier-based A-6 and A-7 fighter-bombers armed with radar-busting missiles, Combat Air Patrol F-14 and F/A-18 fighters, search and rescue helicopters, and two E-2C command-and-control aircraft to co-ordinate the raid. The target of the U.S. air-combat force from British bases was Tripoli, capital of Libya and reportedly the base of Colonel Gadhafi's international terrorist networks; the navy's principal objective was to pound military targets in the port of Benghazi, to the east of Tripoli. It was a declared venture in coercive diplomacy with the object of deterring state-sponsored terrorism against the U.S. and its allies. An unstated, though clearly central, aim of the U.S. mission was to kill Gadhafi himself or to bring about the destruction of his regime *pour encourager les autres*.

It was over in eleven minutes. The F-111s and their cargoes of laser-guided 2000-pound bombs arrived howling a few hundred feet over Tripoli at two in the morning. Simultaneously, the American fleet struck hard at Benghazi. Back in the U.S.A., at 7:00 p.m. EDT, people turned on the evening news and heard President Reagan put his case for the attack and threaten to strike again if necessary. While Defence Secretary Caspar Weinberger (who reportedly opposed the use of force against Libya) described the raid to TV viewers, American warplanes attacked the Sidi Bilal naval base and the Bab al Aziziya barracks, where Gadhafi and his family lived, and then swung round to demolish Tripoli's military airfield. A two-storey villa that stood next to the French Embassy in a residential area of Tripoli—reported to be the safe house in which Libyan security services met with extremist groups, such as the Abu Nidal Palestinian assassination squad—was a special, high-risk target of the U.S. jets. The low-level, night attack, coupled with the navy's disabling of Libyan radar and antiaircraft missiles, achieved complete surprise in both Libyan cities. Tripoli lay waiting for devastation like a beckoning Mediterranean resort, brightly lit up to welcome the American pilots; and for hours after the deadly tourists departed, Gadhafi's frustrated antiaircraft gunners fired volley after volley of wasted ammunition into the empty darkness of the city's harbour. It was like a drunken shout into the night, a gesture as futile as Gadhafi's own threats and rhetoric.

From a military standpoint, the raid was almost flawless. The Americans lost a single F-111 but inflicted massive damage on their military targets. Pentagon planners spoke reassuringly of a surgical strike and of measures to prevent civilian casualties, but warfare, especially air warfare, is harsh and remorseless and does not spare noncombatants—no more than does terrorism itself, which feeds on acts and threats against civilians. Gadhafi's adopted baby daughter was killed, two of his sons were badly wounded and there were about 160 other civilian deaths and injuries. Accounts such as the one filed the morning after the raid by Robert Fisk of *The London Times* had a major impact on allied reactions to the U.S. bombing:

> There was blood across the steps of the French Embassy and, on a stretcher down the road, lay part of a baby's body. They had already dug two corpses out of the wreckage of Mohamed Mahirgir's home. Several limbs lay in an ambulance beside a 30 foot wide water-logged bomb crater . . . The Americans had indeed bombed a heavily populated residential area of Tripoli and had killed and wounded civilians; if nothing else, it proved that all the talk of "surgical bombing" was, as usual in the Middle East, a myth.[2]

Even those inclined to support the toughest of antiterrorist policies paused in the face of such tragedy and the ugly enthusiasm of the American people over the bombings. Was it self-defence, or was it a powerful demonstration of the politics of revenge: a "Rambo reflex," as historian and peace activist Edward Thompson charged? Whatever the motives and *ex post facto* rationales, the Libyan raid and its casualties provoked a major transatlantic quarrel that raised fundamental questions about the purposes of the Western Alliance and the respective obligations of the United States and its European allies. Only Britain and Canada supported the U.S. action; without exception, America's allies on the continent condemned the bombings as imprudent and counterproductive. Italian Premier Bettino Craxi spoke for most of Western Europe when he said that "far from weakening terrorism, military action risked provoking explosive reactions of fanaticism." That sort of talk infuriated the Americans, many of whom accused the allies of cowardice and then promptly cancelled their vacations in Europe because of a fear of Arab reprisals. Reacting to European criticism, the secretary of the American navy remarked that the raid had been useful, if only to determine which allies "would come through— and the U.K. came through like gangbusters." It was a loyalty test, in other words, one of Mr. Reagan's oldest hobbies; a test the NATO Alliance had flunked.

NATO's secretary general, Lord Carrington, described relations in the aftermath of Libya "as bad between Europe and America as I can remember in the period I have been associated with the Alliance." Certainly there had been nothing quite as bitter since the scuttling of the Anglo-French invasion of Suez in 1956 by Eisenhower and Dulles. The stock exchange, that useful barometer of ruling opinion, reflected the division: the day after the Libya raid, an estimated 4.7 billion pounds was wiped off the value of companies listed on the British Stock Exchange, but stocks rose on Wall Street. The "Rambo mentality" of American investors made them "more optimistic" about Libya. "The feeling was that President Reagan had finally given investors what they wanted."[3]

The NATO states of southern Europe, such as Italy, Greece, and Spain, and several other members of the European Community, deplored the U.S. raid and the Thatcher government's decision to permit the use of warplanes based in Britain. The Mulroney government cautiously supported Reagan's use of force, but Canada's main interest in the wake of the raid was to prevent a deepening of the split in the Alliance. That split cut very deeply, and not just at the elite level. The early polls revealed massive popular support for Reagan within the United

States and equally massive opposition (seven in ten polled) in Britain and most of continental Europe to the bombing and Thatcher's complicity in the raid; curiously, the U.S. had strong popular support only in France, the government of which had denied overflight privileges to the Americans but whose population was less than sympathetic to either terrorism or North Africans and perhaps less chary of resorting to military force than some other Europeans.

On both sides of the ocean the split over Libya strengthened the hands of those who wanted disengagement and policies of unilateralism or neutralism. The quarrel was not so much over the need to oppose international terrorism (the Europeans have more experience in this than does the U.S.) as it was about the failure of the Europeans to support tough economic and diplomatic measures against Libya and the subsequent willingness of the United States to act unilaterally (albeit with British support, however reluctantly extended). The Europeans professed to favour economic sanctions instead of bombing, but it was not until April 21—a week after the raid—that the EEC adopted hard anti-Libyan measures and a Community-wide policy refusing sanctuary to proven Arab terrorists. Bitterly, Belgium's leading daily *Le Soir* commented that "Europe is little more than a banana republic in Washington's eyes." There was more than a little truth in this, as Europe's own incapacity to act collectively except in reaction to American unilateralism revealed. Mr. Reagan's message to Europe was *post factum nullum consilium*: when the deed is done, your advice is useless. Most Americans, outraged over European criticism and refusal to grant overflight privileges, asked: what are allies for? And the allies responded: what is this Alliance for?

The Libyan episode also raised the question as to whether an American president was entitled to the automatic support of the allies if he wished to operate from American bases on European soil against targets outside NATO's purview. Moreover, did the allies have the power to resist U.S. pressure? For once, the issue dividing the U.S. and Europe had nothing to do with conflicting views on communism, Soviet foreign policy or detente. Rather, the tensions concerned the Alliance's approach to what is known in NATO parlance as an "out-of-area" contingency: that is, the use of Alliance bases and forces for operations outside the European area, and for purposes that have nothing to do with NATO's original goals. Libya was by no means the first such out-of-area operation to generate controversy within the Alliance—the French war in Algeria in the late fifties, the Suez crisis of 1956, America's intervention in Vietnam, the war for the Falklands in 1982, and a long-standing concern over the interests of North America and Europe in the oil supplies of the Persian Gulf have all raised the issue of how allied interests beyond the treaty area are to be protected and by whom such interests are to be defined. France, for example, proposed in 1948 that much of North Africa, and especially Algeria, be covered by the North Atlantic Treaty, presumably as a hedge against a future Arab rebellion, but the U.S., Canada, and other states objected on the grounds that the Alliance should not be a vehicle to perpetuate a dying European colonialism.[4] Of recent years it has been the United States, reasserting its own imperial hegemony over Europe, that has sought to build consent around a policy that would stretch NATO's obligations geographically. We suspect that few Canadians or Europeans would concur with the 1979 definition of former Supreme Allied Commander Europe Alexander Haig that: "The entire globe is now NATO's concern."[5] The tendency of U.S. strategists to define all international conflict as part of the bipolar, ideological East-West struggle leads to the conclusion that either NATO must be prepared to fight America's battles in distant Third World "dirty wars" or else America must disengage itself from Europe and free up more forces to meet the global Soviet threat.

Can the Europeans resist American pressure for concrete support for out-of-area operations if the outcome is a growing isolationism and unilateralism in the U.S.? More precisely, *which* Europeans can say no to a formal request from the Americans, and in what circumstances? Could any British prime minister, for instance, ignore that island's deep-rooted economic and strategic dependence on the United States and deny a presidential request to use American bases in the U.K. for out-of-NATO purposes? Reagan's request to use the F-111s was made on the basis of an understanding reached between the Americans and British after the war: this simply states that under arrangements made for the common defence, the U.S.

has the use of certain bases in Britain and "that the use of these bases in an emergency would be a matter for joint decision by His Majesty's Government and the United States Government in the light of the circumstances prevailing at the time."[6] This does not give the U.K. a veto, only a right to be consulted if time permits. The phrase "joint decision" wholly begs the question as to whether a weak, dependent ally such as Britain (or Canada) is in any position to bargain on an equal footing with a superpower, especially in a moment of international tension.

Tony Benn, the left-wing Labour M.P., put the question to Britain's prime minister, Margaret Thatcher, in the aftermath of Libya. "Could the Prime Minister have refused the President's request?" Benn argued that Thatcher had acquiesced because she lacked power and because there was an unspoken debt to discharge: American support for Britain in the 1982 Falklands war. And Thatcher's nemesis on the Right, Enoch Powell, wondered aloud in the House of Commons whether Libya had not made it "clear to the people of this country how flimsy would be our protection against the use of bases on British soil for the launching of nuclear operations." Two former prime ministers, Edward Heath and James Callaghan, vowed they would have turned Reagan down, but the realities of the power relationship suggest otherwise.[7] Mrs. Thatcher, her critics said, had acted as the President's poodle, and—evoking a sombre fate usually reserved for Canada—turned Britain into the fifty-first American state.

If nothing else, the British reaction to the Libyan raid underlined the deep sense of unease over its entire relationship with the United States—a sense of its growing military and industrial dependence on the U.S. and a fear of the price that might be paid one terrible day for Soviet or American recklessness. For behind it all, as Powell's question indicated, there lay the issue of the recently deployed Euromissiles and their control during a crisis between the superpowers. Even Thatcher's parliamentary caucus, usually pro-American on foreign policy issues, was in an uproar over the implications of her decision. Tony Benn's demand that all American military bases in the U.K. be closed and that Britain disengage itself unilaterally from its alliances with America did not, in the context of the Libyan bombing, seem so extreme.

Standing squarely behind Article 51 of the UN Charter, Thatcher argued that since the Americans maintained over 300,000 troops in Europe to defend the West, it was "inconceivable" that Britain should refuse them the right to defend themselves against terrorist attacks. The *Times*, which supported Thatcher and Reagan, argued that British acquiescence was inevitable and necessary "even if the raid is judged imprudent." American public opinion was belligerently hostile to European allies "who both depend upon U.S. military assistance and yet persistently ignore American concerns. Britain, the beneficiary of U.S. military help during the Falklands, had a special interest and responsibility to ward off sentiments that might, if neglected, flower into isolationism."[8] In short, Britain lacked the power to refuse, much as Canada had lacked the power to refuse the American request to test the Cruise.

Nor should we exaggerate the power of other European states to deny the Americans their way on an issue such as Libya once it became an intra-Alliance issue, particularly if such a denial threatened to stimulate the furies of isolationism and unilateralism in the United States. The Europeans could refuse overflight privileges, hoping thereby to avoid Arab reprisals or the loss of their Mediterranean interests, but in the final analysis they would side with Reagan—much as he had sided with Thatcher instead of Argentina over the Falklands, and for the same reasons. European unity on defence questions was a chimera, an invention of armchair strategists, and all of the talk about going it alone, of kicking the Americans out of the Alliance, of removing the American bases, troops, and weapons was romantic bluff or anti-American rancour. Europe-without-America was still unthinkable. Despite the public outrage in much of Europe over the bombings, the governments of Western Europe very quickly acted to appease American anger through a series of anti-Libyan moves, and this indicated where real power lay. It lay in Washington.

The brutal reality of the whole Libyan episode is that the United States acted very much as all imperial powers have acted: it used force in defence of its interests. That it acted to appease domestic war fevers as much as in response to external threats is undeniable, but many powerful states have drawn the sword to placate mob passions in the past. Unquestionably, America attempted to intimidate Libya and probably succeeded in provoking the incident which it used as a pretext for the raid. It consulted its allies, but acted against their advice. Considerations of morality and justice entered little into America's calculations about the raid or the reactions of its allies. The issue was power and how it should be used. For it is concrete power that in the end settles great international disputes, and the final arbiter is armed force. The Americans might well have told the allies what the Athenians said in their notorious dialogue with the Melians—"that in human disputation justice is then only agreed on when the necessity is equal; whereas they that have odds of power exact as much as they can, and the weak yield to such conditions as they can get."[9] If the Libyan affair resolved nothing else, it did reveal the location of power in the western coalition. And it confirmed the old adage: alliances are not the friendships of international relations.

## Unilateralism, Ideology, and the New Right

The Libyan affair revealed three characteristics about American policy that are emblematic of the whole Reagan era: first, the militarization of foreign policy and an insistence upon dealing with complex political questions such as terrorism through coercive diplomacy; second, a willingness to act alone and to pursue a strategy of unilateralism in spite of strong allied objections to the use of force; and third, a heavy emphasis on the symbolism and ideology of American nationalism—what Edward Thompson calls the "whole hegemonic 'official' national ideology" that permeates not only the state but its liberal critics, the media, and even opposition groups within America. "There is nothing wrong with authentic American nationalism, if it is concerned with America's own cultural and historical traditions: but will it please go home and stay indoors?", pleaded Thompson.[10]

Libya signalled America's willingness to use force, to act alone and with impressive popular backing. Militarism, unilateralism, and the unifying glue of hegemonic nationalism—here, in a daunting eleven-minute demonstration of American strength, were three of the key ingredients of the New Right's foreign policy "consensus," a consensus that had its deeper roots in the Right's obsessions with America's defeat in Vietnam and the erosion of its military superiority over Russia. It resembled in some ways the older postwar consensus that had been built around America's imperial hegemony and the global containment of communism, but in its neoisolationist self-centredness, its hostility to postwar mulilateral institutions, and its deep suspicions of most of America's traditional allies it was quite different. The age of hegemonic leadership had given way to one of fragmentation, centrifugal nationalism and what the New Right was fond of calling "global unilateralism"—a tendency toward the aggressive assertion of supposed American interests everywhere on the planet without attention to the interests of America's allies. A volatile mix of know-nothing isolationism and messianic interventionism, this policy celebrates America's capacity to act alone, without the consent of allies and outside postwar international organizations. As we show in the following chapter, this unilateralist trend has divided the Western Alliance and alarmed some of America's oldest friends. Denis Healey, the British Labour Party's spokesman on foreign affairs and no leftist, suggests that the United States has changed beyond recognition as an actor on the world stage. "The danger today is not that the Americans will retire into post-war normalcy, but that they will opt for a policy of global unilateralism under which they intervene all over the world without trying to win the consent of their allies or of the countries in which they operate."[11] Another danger, reflected in the defence policy of Healey's own party, is that U.S. unilateralism will provoke a flight from multilateral co-operation across the whole Alliance.

Unilateralism on the American Right begins from a perception that there are growing security and political threats to the United States in the Third World, especially from the spread of Marxist revolution in Central America and state-supported terrorism and Moslem extremism in the Middle East, and that the postwar system of alliances and multilateral institutions no longer serves U.S. interests. The U.S. New Right wants to overturn the postwar settlement with the Soviet bloc, to repudiate the Yalta and Potsdam agreements, and to build up sufficient military and economic superiority over the Soviets to compel Moscow to make concessions to American hegemony. Spokesmen on the New Right reject the postwar strategy of containing communism as passive and defensive, and argue for a policy of "rolling back" and "liberating" Marxist regimes, especially in the Third World. If the European allies will not join the crusade for freedom outside Europe, then the United States should go it alone, withdrawing its forces from NATO for global duties. Irving Kristol, a prominent American neoconservative, argued in a prescient column written two months before the bombing of Tripoli that U.S. capacity to strike Gadhafi was constrained by NATO, "an entangling alliance" against which George Washington had warned the Republic, and by European vetoes over the use of American bases: "a risk-aversive Europe" was thus an encumbrance on America's globalism.

The U.S. bombing of Libya was an outgrowth of the pent-up resentments of the American Right and its quarrel with multilateral diplomacy and strategy: the raid was less an antiterrorist operation than it was a sharp demonstration of America's capacity to use force, and to act unilaterally, indeed in defiance of most of its NATO allies—allies who "always favor U.S. passivity," according to George Will, one of America's noisiest ultraconservatives. "Regarding Libya, U.S. policy toward the allies was correct. It was to listen very nicely, then go out and do precisely what U.S. interests required. In his sixth year Reagan is getting the hang of something important: selective unilateralism." For Will, the "Reaganization" of U.S. foreign policy involved these themes: first, support for anti-Marxist insurgencies in Nicaragua, Angola, and Afghanistan ("the Reagan Doctrine," discussed later in this chapter); second, demonstrating a willingness to use force, as in Libya, "even—no, especially—without allied consensus"; and third, displacing arms control as the central issue in Soviet-American relations. All three required a "healthy, even jaunty, disregard for 'world opinion'." Urging Reagan to abandon SALT II, Will thought this would be a useful test of the President's ability "to rise above unworthy concern for mere opinion."[12] Well, here was a president who was more than equal to *that* test. One is reminded of King George VI's relief on hearing news of the fall of France in June

1940: at least, he wrote to his mother, we no longer have allies to worry about.

The deeper origins of this mistrust of alliances and of international institutions, and of the messianic belief in the peculiarity and uniqueness of the American people and their role in world affairs, are questions well beyond the scope of this book. It is sufficient to say that American foreign policy and American imperialism have typically been cast in the language of universalist doctrines that emphasize such themes as anticolonialism, the extension of liberty and democracy, and the promotion of human rights. Interest, power, the balance of power—the permanent factors in international politics—have no place in this fairy tale. The United States is viewed as a moral exception in a world of power-brokering states, freedom's exemplar with no attachments to the old politics, the old diplomacy, the old Euro-centred system based on the idea of *raison d'état*—the European notion that the interests of the state endure and must have priority over the ideological fashions of the day. America's mission as a great power is not to provide order or to rule prudently over others, but to bring liberal improvements to those who fail to come up to American standards. "When men take up arms to set others free," declared Woodrow Wilson, "there is something sacred and holy in the warfare. I will not cry 'peace' as long as there is sin and wrong in the world." He was bound to be disappointed. On the occasion of one of his interventions in Mexico, Wilson told a skeptical British diplomat that, "I am going to teach the South American republics to elect good men." The great theologian, Reinhold Niebuhr, in his critique of the hypocrisy of U.S. imperialism, recalled how President McKinley, addressing a group of clergymen, justified his decision to occupy the Philippines: one night while praying for divine guidance, it came to him—"that there was nothing left for us to do but to take them all, and to educate the Filipinos, and uplift and civilise and Christianise them, and by God's grace do the very best we could by them . . . And then I went to bed and went to sleep and slept soundly."[13]

America's moral imperialism, which is typically expressed in a repugnance for colonialism, power politics, secret diplomacy and so on, has had few European admirers. The contempt of former German Chancellor Helmut Schmidt for Jimmy Carter's crusades on human rights in the late 1970s was common knowledge. General de Gaulle, who was fond of neither the United States nor its Anglo-Saxon satellites, once described American policy as the will to power cloaked in idealism. He may have had in mind a notorious conversation he had with President Franklin Roosevelt at the Casablanca Conference in early 1943, in the course of which FDR, deeply suspicious of de Gaulle and of French intentions toward Indochina, remarked that France was "in the position of a little child unable to look out and fend for itself," and that the wartime allies must therefore "hold the political situation in trust for the French people." Roosevelt, a moral imperialist on a grand scale, was at this same time urging Churchill to apply the wisdom of the American Founding Fathers in a British transfer of power in India. This naive populist, universalistic ideology, which derives from the early revolutionary ardour of Tom Paine and the messianic liberal interventionism of Wilson, gives American foreign policy an absolutist outlook that is ill-suited to the realities of the contemporary world. It is also dangerous.

The perils of moral imperialism and of utopianism in foreign policy have been lamented by political thinkers since Thucydides. Perhaps the greatest weakness of a foreign policy cast in universal doctrine is that it lacks an appreciation of the limits that attend foreign policy and strategy, even given the noblest of intentions. The limits to power correspond to the factor of "friction"—the tendency for a thousand unforeseen things to go wrong, "the force that makes the apparently easy so difficult"—which Clausewitz identified as the concept that distinguishes real war from war on paper. Power is finite; and it tends to evoke countervailing power. The realist thus emphasizes the limits of statecraft, the political as well as material limits.[14]

Ideology has a tendency to undermine empires because it leads the imperial state into an expansion of commitments and an overextension of power. It mistakes the periphery for the vital core of foreign policy, arguing in effect that there is no periphery, only a core. Realist critics of the ideological approach tend to be pessimistic about nations' capacity for disinterested behaviour (including small nations) and even more skeptical of claims that democratic communities are less aggressive and more pacific than undemocratic states. "It is not true that only kings make war," Niebuhr pointed out. "The common members of any national community, while sentimentally desiring peace, nevertheless indulge impulses of envy, jealousy, pride, bigotry, and greed which make for conflict between communities." And when such conflict acquires a doctrinal character, as it so frequently does, then all legal and moral limits are overturned and war becomes all-out war: total, remorseless, devoid of any rational political purpose.

These observations on ideology and foreign policy should be kept in mind as we approach the Reagan period and the trend toward unilateralism across the Western Alliance in the eighties. As we noted earlier, Reaganism represented in certain ways a rejection of the entire postwar settlement; even, to use Fred Halliday's phrase, "a comprehensive attempt to erode the consequences of the Second World War."[15] The postwar generation of American politicians, capitalists, and diplomats—the liberal internationalists—who constructed the Atlantic security system and the multilateral organizations that supported American economic dominance had by 1980 passed from the scene, together with their assumptions. Replacing them was a new elite, rooted in the Sunbelt states and preaching an odd blend of high-tech entrepreneurialism, religious fundamentalism, nationalism, and anticommunism. Its alliance with big business was based not so much on a nostalgia for laissez faire as on the promise of what some conservatives called the Economic Security State: economic growth via supply-side economics and massive military spending. The welfare state was to be replaced by the warfare state. The New Right's foreign policy lacked the postwar attachments to Europe and the North Atlantic system. Its focus was the Soviet threat in the Third World. The new elite, reflecting the shifting demographic patterns within the United States, was far more attuned to the impact of Hispanic immigrants and refugees from Mexico and Central and Latin America and of Asians from the West Pacific. Disorder in the Third World was the result of a failure by the West to use its strength; revolutions and Soviet influence flourished in a power vacuum.

As the coalition of conservatives, neoconservatives, the unborn and born-again formed into the New Right of U.S. politics in 1975-76, and then went into opposition to the presidency of Jimmy Carter, there was as yet no coherent rightist agenda on foreign and military policy. Certainly no new consensus had emerged: that had to be beaten out on the anvil as a response to international events in Angola, Ethiopia, Iran, Central America, and Afghanistan, and to the shifting and sometimes chaotic policies of the Carter Administration. From the outset, however, there were certain theses or propositions on international questions which the New Right set out to propagate, and these would form the ideological foundations of the new orthodoxy of the eighties. Of these higher articles of faith, four are worth some emphasis.

First, the New Right was preoccupied with the decline of America as a world power. It was evident to everyone that the U.S. had indeed declined, in part because of the impact of the war in Vietnam on America's economic position and the breakdown of postwar monetary arrangements; but the Right argued that it was the loss of U.S. military superiority and the buildup of Soviet military power that was the true source of the decline. The Right was concerned about America's economic weakness, which it blamed on state interference in the market, but the main index of a nation's power was its military power. What it wanted above all was a return to America's postwar military predominance. Detente had permitted the Soviets to achieve superiority, it was argued, and this must be reversed before any further relaxation of tensions was pursued. Deeply suspicious of arms control in general, and of the SALT process in particular, conservative pressure groups such as the influential Committee on the Present Danger argued that "to have the advantage at the utmost level of violence helps at every lesser level. In the Korean War, the Berlin blockades, and the Cuban missile crisis the United States had the ultimate edge because of our superiority at the strategic nuclear level. That edge has slipped away."[16] Beyond that call for "preponderance at any level," the Right wanted to use a large defence buildup to "race" the Soviet economy and thereby force Moscow into political concessions; in effect, a strategy of economic warfare.

Second, the New Right's view of the Soviet Union and of the Communist system was fundamentalist. The Soviets were dangerous because of what they were, not because of what they did. The struggle was a great ideological one between two incompatible social systems; it was not a traditional conflict be-

167

tween two great powers over territory, diplomatic disputes, or military balances. Soviet expansionism flowed from the peculiar internal makeup of a totalitarian state and was global in design. The Nixon-Kissinger strategy of detente had not merely failed, it was also an immoral policy that appeared to legitimate the Soviet system and its conquests. Emphasizing the need to return to (and in certain ways go beyond) the early cold war strategy of containment, the Right argued the need to use all measures short of war to coerce the U.S.S.R. and thereby to bring about internal changes to the Communist system. In the interval, one does not sup with the devil without a long spoon; detente was no longer on the agenda. There were many uses for anticommunism, but for the New Right it was not an ideology of convenience. It was a faith.

A corollary was that security and containment (and the peace) are indivisible. This was a familiar lesson drawn from the late 1930s. It meant that the global struggle between freedom and totalitarianism had to be waged on all fronts. Managua and Luanda were as important to the West as Berlin or NATO's northern flank. If you truly believed in the indivisibility of the peace and containment, then distinctions between vital and peripheral interests became academic. The New Right seemed, in fact, very preoccupied with the periphery and much less interested in America's postwar alliances. To dissolve the Vietnam syndrome (the public's deep reluctance to become involved militarily in the Third World) the New Right's well-financed think tanks, with their close connections to the Pentagon and the CIA, sought to promote new strategies of counterinsurgency, proxy warfare, and support for anti-Marxist insurgencies in countries such as Afghanistan and Nicaragua: this was the beginning of what would later be elaborated as the "Reagan Doctrine."

Third, the Far Right generally supported a unilateralist/isolationist approach, rather than a commitment to multilateral alliances, institutions, and interests. "It mirrors skepticism about the steadfastness and commitment of friends and allies, and it often reflects a sense of moral righteousness. As a member of Congress declared after the proclamation of martial law in Poland, this time the United States should proceed to do what is right without worrying too much about its allies."[17]

Distrust of Europe and European diplomacy is a very old theme in American foreign policy, of course, and it cannot be separated from the moral imperialism discussed earlier. An ideological grudge against European social democracy underlies much of the New Right's mistrust of its NATO allies. Whereas the United States was profoundly enmeshed in world politics, Irving Kristol wrote in 1979, the West Europeans, in contrast, "seem to have opted out of the strenuous game of world politics in order to pursue the comforts of domestic life." The "social democratization" of Europe, the placing of the welfare state before security, was producing a climate of defeatism and appeasement in the face of the Soviet threat. The U.S. was about to experience the "bourgeoning of a new American nationalism," Kristol correctly foresaw, and this presented the allies with a hard choice: if America had to operate overseas through unilateral military force (a reference to the Rapid Deployment Force then under consideration in Washington), a corresponding unilateral foreign policy would emerge. "From having been the centerpiece of American foreign policy, NATO will become an afterthought, and then a mere memory . . . the European partners in NATO will discover the partnership to have been dissolved, and that they are now allies of convenience—client states—on the order of South Korea, let us say."[18] Here was a nice example of the primacy of ideology over national interest. One selected one's allies on the basis of their ideological loyalty, not on the criterion of shared diplomatic and security interests. The NATO powers, America's major alliance relationships, and Europe, the central fulcrum of the cold war, can be dispensed with as allies of convenience and relegated to the status of South Korea; and further, this could happen without improving the power position of the Soviet Union or injuring the long-term security, political and economic interests of the U.S. and the West. It is a breath-taking delusion. Kristol's "global unilateralism" is little more than an updated variant of the 1930s case for isolationism: let us detach ourselves from Europe and the old games of power politics, and thereby free ourselves to expand our domain over the Western Hemisphere and the Third World.

Fourth, the New Right rejected liberal illusions about the obsolescence of force in international politics. In this, it was restating a traditional view that war and armed force are intrinsic in a system of sovereign states, and that neither the Vietnam War nor the development of complex webs of economic interdependence among the big capitalist countries had changed this fact. Nuclear weapons clearly had changed the nature of the military relationship between the superpowers to one of mutual deterrence, but the Right took the view that the Bomb had political utility beyond deterrence and that "if deterrence fails," the only reasonable thing to do was to win. Later, in its enthusiasm for the SDI, the Right rejected the entire structure of deterrence as immoral. But it was really the use of *conventional* armed force that the Right was promoting as a way of attacking the corrosive Vietnam syndrome and the related public impression concerning the irreversibility of America's decline in power. The New Right argued that the United States had lost in Vietnam only because politicians had placed undue restraints on the use of force and because the nation had fought a "limited" war without strong political support. Within the Right, a vigorous debate began over the reform of the military, the ways of using force in "low-intensity conflicts" in the Third World, and the need for conventional force doctrines aimed at winning. There was much less discussion about the real purposes of using force, or the costs of doing so unilaterally.

There was a final thesis or proposition implicit in almost everything the New Right said or wrote about post-Vietnam international relations, and it came to be deeply embedded in the practice of the Reagan Administration. The thesis was, simply, that there no longer existed an international order based on the principles of sovereignty, self-determination, nonintervention in the domestic jurisdiction of other states, and coexistence between rival ideologies and systems. These international principles, which derive from sixteenth and seventeenth century diplomatic practice, have been ignored by great powers in the past, sometimes to the point where international politics have degenerated into a nasty, brutish Hobbesian war of all against all. That world politics have usually not been like that is because most powers, large and small, acting from considerations of national interest, have respected the right of other states to exist and to determine their domestic affairs as they prefer. Most statesmen have understood that in following the principle of reason of state, they must act toward other powers as they would hope to be treated in the future: for instance, a power that constantly interferes in the domestic politics of other states can expect the same practice to be applied to it in the future. The point, then, is that we have had something called an international order, based upon certain fundamental customs and conventions that are supported, not because they are just or good, but because it is in the interests of the member states of the world political system to have such practices.

The American Right appears to deny the existence of such an order, and certainly it denies that America's Communist adversaries uphold the principles of sovereignty, self-determination, and nonintervention; since the Soviets violated the detente accords negotiated by Kissinger and Nixon, the argument goes, they uphold principles such as self-determination for tactical or propaganda purposes only. It follows that there is no functioning international order, and that there cannot be one so long as the bipolar, ideological struggle persists. It is this unstated but deeply held conviction of the Right that lies behind many of America's dubious experiments in global unilateralism and the retreat from multilateral diplomacy into "America first" foreign policies. It was this hegemonic nationalism that lay beneath the repudiation of the UN, the Law of the Sea Conference, UNESCO, the World Court, and the postwar multilateral economic organizations in Reagan's first term.

Such are the deeply embedded, unspoken assumptions of the New Right's global unilateralism. They underlay the Right's entire critique of the Carter presidency's foreign and defence policies in the late 1970s and formed the basis of the new orthodoxy of Reaganism in the eighties. That they sought a revolution in international affairs was freely admitted by the New Right's spokesmen. "We are different from previous generations of conservatives," remarked Paul Weyrich, the organizational genius of American right-wing politics. "We are no longer working to preserve the status quo. We are radicals, working to overturn the present power structure of this country." And they did.

## The Overthrow of Internationalism

Ideological doctrine is no substitute for *raison d'état*, yet it has plagued the international system of states for most of the past two centuries. The new cold war is not new. It is merely another chapter in an age of international revolution and civil war that opened in France in 1789 and expanded into a war without frontiers against the old order, the old diplomacy, the states system itself. Long before the Bolshevik seizure of power in Russia in October 1917, ideological civil strife—which the ancient Greeks called *stasis*—had subverted power politics, introduced fanaticism into diplomatic relations, and provided the motives for the all-out war, the Carthaginian peace, the republic of the guillotine. Though we think ourselves special, there is nothing particularly new about the war fevers or metaphysical dogmas of our own era. In retrospect, what seem unusual have been the interludes in the cold war when the faint melody of diplomacy and power politics could be heard above the din of ideological shouting.

The flight from power politics into utopianism has been happening across the Western Alliance, and not only in the United States. In other parts of the world, such as the Middle East, it is a veritable man-made plague. Among the socialist states, propaganda and doctrinal warfare maintain society in the state of an armed camp and the international system in a permanent condition of *stasis*. The effect on diplomatic practice and moderation has been dreadful, though hardly unprecedented. In his commentaries on the civil strife that broke out and introduced unheard-of atrocities into the warring states of Greece during the Peloponnesian War, Thucydides deplored how the ideological division of society into two camps affected the manners and customary language of a noble people. "To fit in with the change of events, words, too, had to change their usual meanings":

> What used to be described as a thoughtless act of aggression was now regarded as the courage one would expect to find in a party member; to think of the future and wait was merely another way of saying one was a coward; any idea of moderation was just an attempt to disguise one's unmanly character . . .

> Fanatical enthusiasm was the mark of a real man, and to plot against an enemy behind his back was perfectly legitimate self-defence.[19]

172

Thucydides believed that this was simply human nature flying its true colours, and not much has happened since he wrote to disprove the belief. Of course, the atrocities are no longer unheard-of.

We may find some solace in the evidence that reason of state tends over the longer run to win out over a doctrinal approach to world politics. Revolutionary ideologies appear in the night sky like novas, brilliant stars burning in intensity and brightness until they consume themselves in fire. The international theorist, Martin Wight, remarked that "international revolution has never for long maintained itself against national interest. Doctrinal considerations have always within two generations been overridden by *raison d'état*."[20] In the case of the Soviet Union, it took less than a decade for national interest to triumph over the delusion of imminent world revolution.

In the U.S. there has been a continuing debate over the nature of communism and the Soviet Union and how to deal with the "threat." One school emphasizes the Soviet system itself as the source of the threat to western values and international order. The ideology of the American New Right, discussed above, found its roots in the tradition of Wilsonian liberalism and the urge to bring improvements to the barbarians living under the yoke of communism. It was an updated version of the nineteenth century liberal opinion of the Ottoman empire and "the unspeakable Turk": sick and rotten to the core, the eastern despotism must either be reformed from without or destroyed. The "liberalization" and "democratization" of Soviet communism would come about in part through a strategy of external threats and pressures. Diplomacy has no real function. Through increased western military spending, technological and economic leverage, and support for anti-Marxist insurgents within the Soviet orbit (Afghanistan, Nicaragua, etc.), the West could foster the seeds of destruction within the Communist system. Richard Pipes, the Harvard historian who worked on President Reagan's National Security Council staff for two years, has argued that the Communist regimes face a deepening economic and political crisis and that "the West, in its own interest, ought to assist those economic and political forces which are at work inside the Communist bloc undermining the system and pressuring its elites to turn their attention inward." The Soviet Union, he adds, will be a partner in peace only if and when it makes peace with its own people. Only then will the danger of nuclear war recede.[21] Here the purpose of state policy is simply punishment and revenge. One suspects that Professor Pipes, an ideologue and romantic who believes that thought, however dogmatic, is but one step removed from action, and that actions have predictable, rather than unintended, consequences, would be the last to wish that danger of war to recede and also the last to perceive that the policy advocated—conceived in confusion, executed through amateurism—would end by weakening the United States, not communism.

Other American conservatives have downplayed ideology and stressed the geopolitical competition: to Colin S. Gray, known for his robust analyses of how the U.S. could fight and "win" a nuclear war with Russia, the superpower competition is not about who rules in Eastern Europe or any particular issues. "Rather, it is about the relative capabilities of the two superstates, analagous to the conflicts between Rome and Carthage and between Athens and Sparta."[22] The geopolitical school has emphasized the confrontation between the Soviet "heartland" superpower and the "rimland" coalition of barrier states allied with the U.S. The collision is one of two great empires for supremacy; ideology is secondary.

Correctly or not, in the years subsequent to the final Communist victory in Vietnam in 1975, influential American strategists and conservative commentators agreed on several fundamental points about the balance of power: one, that the relative strength of the U.S. was in decline while that of the U.S.S.R. was in ascendancy; two, that the Vietnam syndrome was undermining America's ability to intervene and to use force in support of political goals; three, that the growth of Soviet nuclear and conventional military capabilities had been immense; and four, that U.S. vital interests were shifting from the industrialized world to those parts of the Third World, notably the Persian Gulf, where access to crucial resources was threatened by local instability and external interference. The perception of American decline and loss of military superiority converged with a conviction that the rise of the Soviet Union as a military power was linked to all of the revolutionary unrest in the Third World (whereas it was probably closer to the truth to say that such unrest was related to the widespread impression of American weakness). In the eyes of many, the decline of U.S. power was accelerated by the strategic incoherence of Jimmy Carter's presidency, especially in Soviet-American relations, by conflicts within NATO, and by Carter's deep moral aversion to the use of force. The same perception of an incoherent, not to say incompetent, American foreign policy oscillating, shifting direction, and lacking both a clear strategy and the confidence to use its power was widespread throughout the Alliance as well by the end of the seventies. Carter's lack of credibility, especially with the stronger European allies, further undercut America's power position.

Postwar American internationalism and multilateralism enjoyed a strong base of domestic bipartisan support. Much of this has now evaporated. Behind the unilateralism that has characterized so much of American foreign policy and military strategy in the 1980s, and which has won strong bipartisan support from the Democrats in Congress as well as much of the society as a whole, there lurks not just far-right ideology, but also the politics of protectionism, resentment, and revenge. Nativism—the reaction against the immigrant and the outside world, the desire to recover the true American nation and to celebrate American nationalism, the urge to "win" and to stand tall, if only on a crowded beach in tiny Grenada—helped bring Reagan to power in 1980 and massively reelected him in 1984. Resentments from the defeat in Vietnam resurfaced in 1979 with the second energy crisis and, far worse, the taking of the American hostages in Teheran and Russia's move into Afghanistan. Add to these events two other volatile factors—the growing domestic forces of economic protectionism, and the fear and hostility of white Americans to the large numbers of Hispanics migrating illegally from Mexico and Central America to the Sunbelt states—and popular support for a platform based on nativism and nationalism was guaranteed. Extolled in the songs of Bruce Springsteen, Bob Dylan, and hundreds of lesser lights, buttressed by a popular culture that preached vigilantism and Rambo cults, standing up for America and getting even with an unfriendly world became the focus of Reagan's nationalistic foreign policy.

A further impetus to global unilateralism lies in policy makers' belief, noted earlier, that every foreign policy and military interest is of equal value, that each regional threat to the U.S. should be seen as part of an indivisible whole. Thus the curious obsession of American strategists and politicians with insignificant Third World states and leaders, whose identification with U.S. policy too often constitutes a current liability as well as a future test of credibility and resolve. As Walter Lippmann noted in his famous postwar critiques of containment, American foreign policy has suffered from a debilitating incapacity to make the crucial distinction between vital interests, defined as those which may require fighting to defend, and more peripheral concerns. Paul Nitze, a principal architect of containment as it evolved from Truman in the 1940s to Reagan in the 1980s, has explained that the world "is like a chess board. We can say that the rooks are more important than the knights and bishops, and the bishops more important than the pawns. But if you strip yourself of your pawns, you're lost . . . Similarly with our strategy, if we strip ourselves of our pawns, we're lost." This is the kind of reasoning that provides a never-ending demand for capabilities to match an ever-rising supply of commitments. Yesterday it provided the rationale for intervention in Indochina, today for Central America. The world is never short of pawns.

## Nicaragua and the Reagan Doctrine

In early 1987 *The New York Times* revealed that the single most damaging foreign policy episode of the Reagan presidency—the secret U.S. dealings with Iran, trading arms for hostages, and the diversion of the profits to the contras attempting to overturn the government of Nicaragua—had its origins in a worldwide program of covert activity aimed against Marxist states on every continent. The program, known as Project Democracy, was financed by private individuals, foreign governments such as Kuwait and Saudi Arabia, and U.S. government sources; and, as *The Times* commented, after it was set up in early 1983 Project Democracy "grew into a parallel foreign policy apparatus— complete with its own communications systems, secret envoys, leased ships and airplanes, offshore bank accounts and corporations."[23] About all that was missing was a national anthem. The secret side of the program was run by the National

Security Council's Lt.-Col. Oliver North, whose poverty of ideas was matched only by the extravagance with which he sought their realization: a sort of high-tech Lawrence of Arabia stirring up revolts within the Communist empire, North could turn a televised Congressional hearing into a covert operation. His central passion, and the goal for much of Project Democracy, was to overthrow the Nicaraguan state through antiinsurgent warfare. It was a textbook case study of what happens to a foreign policy based on conspiracy theory and run by fanatics.

The doctrine in question is known as the Reagan Doctrine of support to anti-Marxist insurgencies in states such as Afghanistan, Nicaragua, Angola, Cambodia, and Mozambique. In essence, the purpose of this doctrine is not simply the containment of Marxism, but the "bleeding" and overthrow of radical regimes in the Third World through the use of mercenaries and proxies, economic warfare, strategies of destabilization, and the use of armed force in what U.S. strategists call low-intensity conflict. America generously supplies everything but the corpses. Under the Reagan Doctrine, the avowed goal of U.S. policy is no longer to contain the spread of Soviet-supported communism but to undermine it, initially at the periphery. Nicaragua, which has been the litmus test of this doctrine of counter-revolution, was subjected to externally backed insurgent warfare from the opening of the CIA-Argentine "war without frontiers" in Central America in the early eighties. Inside the United States, this undeclared war had very modest support, however, and it was the decision of the Congress to cut off military aid to the contras in 1984 that prompted the elaboration of the Reagan Doctrine, with its rhetorical flourishes about the global democratic revolution, the rising "freedom tide," and the need to support freedom fighters such as the contras on every continent. The Democratic-controlled Congress, eager to be seen as "tough" as Reagan, fell in step behind the White House.

Like President Harry Truman in 1947, Reagan understood that politically controversial policies to support anti-Communist forces are more likely to gain public and Congressional support if justified on grounds of moral principle and cast in the universal language of democracy and self-determination. What the Orwellian language cannot conceal, however, is that the Reagan Doctrine is a great-power rationale for illegality, disorder, and the fomenting of civil wars: it proclaims an unlimited right to U.S.-instigated intervention in the Third World and denies the legitimacy of all socialist revolutions and of any Soviet or Cuban support for such revolutions. Moreover, it denies that America's senior allies have any legitimate interest in opposing a global strategy of rolling back Third World Marxist regimes, notwithstanding the neoisolationist implications of the doctrine or its impact on allied interests in, say, southern Africa or Central America. From the standpoint of the allies, the Reagan Doctrine is global unilateralism in practice; it overthrows postwar internationalism and multilateral diplomacy.

Behind the doctrine the United States has been pursuing two aggressive strategies, one regional and the other global in design. The regional interest involves the reassertion of American hegemony through the total destruction of the Nicaraguan revolution and the removal of any basis for Cuban and Soviet penetration of Central America or the likelihood of a further spread of Marxism to U.S. dependencies such as El Salvador, Guatemala, Honduras, or even Mexico. The U.S. wants a military, not a diplomatic solution in Nicaragua, and to get it direct American intervention will probably be inescapable. The global interest is in using aid to anti-Communist insurgencies as a weapon in superpower relations, as leverage to force the Soviet Union to make concessions. In the summer of 1985 Congress agreed to supply sophisticated antiaircraft missiles to rebel groups operating in Angola and Afghanistan, and a year later both the House and Senate voted to renew military aid to the contras. Reagan's administration viewed this global approach to anti-Communist insurgencies as a way of weakening the Soviet Union and its "client states"; bogged down in Afghanistan, overextended militarily, and confronting internal economic weakness, the U.S.S.R. was deemed to be "on the run now" and susceptible to pressure. Eager to shift the agenda of superpower relations away from arms control, Reagan and his advisors sought to use the supply of armaments to insurgents to "bleed" Marxist states in the Third World and to gain the upper hand over the Soviets. Some of Reagan's people even believed the successful defeat of a backward socialist country would begin the destabilization of the entire Soviet system of states.[24]

Leaving aside the point that it is people, not "client states," who bleed when great powers arm mercenaries and proxies in their power struggles (and we do not claim that the U.S.S.R. behaves differently), there is something to be said here about Mr. Reagan's doctrine and the international order. What is totally offensive and unacceptable about the Reagan Doctrine is that it destroys the fundamental basis of world order that makes freedom, democracy, and peace feasible. It assumes the right—which cannot be upheld on any reading of international law—to dictate forms of government to states which the U.S. defines as illegitimate and goes on to assert an unqualified right to interfere using force and to overthrow socialist revolutions through support for insurgencies anywhere in the Third World. Although Reagan's government refused to accept the Court's jurisdiction, the implication of the American doctrine of intervention was set out with great clarity in the World Court's judgement in June 1986 in the matter of U.S. military and paramilitary actions against Nicaragua. The World Court ruled that the U.S. was in breach of its legal obligations in mining Nicaragua's harbours, infringing its air space, imposing a trade embargo, and arming the contras. The Court stressed that "the principle of non-intervention involved the right of every sovereign state to conduct its affairs without outside interference. Intervention was wrongful when it used coercion, particularly force, directly as military action or indirectly as supporting subversive activities in another state." If one state, with a view to the coercion of another, supported and assisted armed bands in that state whose purpose was to overthrow its government, that amounted to an intervention in its internal affairs, and the U.S. support to the contras thus constituted a clear breach of the principle of nonintervention.[25] In short, the Reagan Doctrine violated both international and domestic U.S. laws.

Any great power that turns over its foreign policy to fanatics and mercenaries probably deserves its fate. Machiavelli, who believed that a reliance on mercenaries had ruined Italy, warned his prince that they were disunited, thirsty for power, undisciplined, and disloyal; they were brave among their friends, cowards before the enemy; they avoided defeat just so long as they avoided battle. He could have been writing of the contras. It is clear that if the United States wants to overthrow Marxist states it will have to do the job itself, using American combat forces rather than venal and incompetent insurgents, and then face the political and diplomatic consequences. Like most foreign policy doctrines, the Reagan Doctrine has its roots in ideological delusions, and as such it is a symptom of confusion as well as illegality.

### *Achille Lauro* and Grenada

"We did this all by our little selves," exulted President Reagan in October 1985 after he had ordered the U.S. military to force down an Egyptian aircraft carrying Palestinian terrorists in international airspace over the Mediterranean and then dispatched a Delta team to capture them in Italy. Thus spoke the jeering voice of postinternationalist America. The *Achille Lauro* affair, which involved the seizure of an Italian cruise liner on the high seas, the taking of the passengers as hostages by a group of terrorists determined to force Israel to release fifty detained Palestinians, and the brutal murder of a handicapped American tourist, is an excellent illustration of the Reagan administration's substitution of action for thought in diplomacy. It also nicely brings out the American approach to allies involved in extraalliance crises and the contempt of the U.S. for international norms since 1981. American warplanes intercepted an Egyptian flag airliner carrying the terrorists and forced it to land in Italy where a U.S. Delta team attempted, despite Italian jurisdiction, to seize the Arabs. This appalling operation, reportedly conceived and directed by Reagan's "cowboys" on staff in the National Security Council, flagrantly violated crucial international laws and established a precedent for the use of force against lawful flights and the invasion of the airspace and jurisdiction of other powers. That this flouting of the rule of law occurred at the expense of the sovereignty of two of America's most important allies in the Mediterranean region, Egypt and Italy, and was still hugely popular with the U.S. public, might well give Canadians pause. For why should we, facing similar circumstances, expect to receive different treatment from those who act first "by our little selves" and only use diplomacy after the fact to repair the damage?

Isn't such unorthodox action justified to counter international terror? No. The desire to avenge the atrocities of murdering terrorists is human and understandable, but it cannot be the basis of state policy. Statecraft and strategy must be based on the public interests of the state, which cannot be equated with the private interests and values of those who are temporarily in charge of policy or with the momentary passions and prejudices of domestic opinion. This is especially the case for great powers that have the responsibility of upholding international order— not least against the disorder of terrorism. It is not that multilateral solutions are always better or that the resort to force is invariably mistaken; but a power cannot overthrow the interests of important coalition partners or the conventions of diplomacy and law without impairing its own international interests or encouraging more terrorism. Popular at home, America's actions nonetheless constituted piracy. They humiliated the governments of two strategic allies. They deterred no one. The best friends of the terrorists who seized the *Achille Lauro* were the rabid amateurs in Mr. Reagan's White House basement, with their ignorance of five centuries of diplomatic and legal practice and their contempt for the national interests of allies.

Part of the explanation for this dubious behaviour can be traced to America's morbid preoccupation with its "credibility" after its great defeat in Vietnam. If it could not use military intervention with success and strong domestic backing in, say, Central America, then, Mr. Reagan and the Kissinger Commission argued, U.S. credibility would collapse, its alliances would crumble, and nations in the Persian Gulf would turn elsewhere for their security. This self-imposed credibility argument is an old one that can be used to justify almost any intervention. Hegel wrote in his *Philosophy of History* that the only thing history teaches us is that people and governments have never learned anything from history. Still, Mr. Reagan's conservative coalition did deduce from the history of the Vietnam War one lesson: not that it may have been wrong or inexpedient, but that future military interventions in the Third World must be quick and cheap, not protracted or costly in blood and treasure. The tinier the targets, the lower the risks. Grenada was invaded in October 1983, ludicrous though it sounds, to alert the American public and the international community that the day of the Vietnam syndrome had passed. America was standing tall again. The American Far Right had seen nothing so magnificent since Iwo Jima: "U.S. soldiers' boot prints on Grenada's soil have done more than the MX [missile] will do to make U.S. power credible," wrote columnist George F. Will, the scourge of Libya, who also wants American boot prints on the soil of Nicaragua and Cuba as a sort of retribution for what happened to the United States in Vietnam. It was of course the same obsession with "credibility" that kept the U.S. fighting the Vietnamese revolution for more than twenty years, at a cost of 200,000 American and a million Vietnamese casualties.

American unilateralism is interventionist and ideological; it is not a withdrawal into an inactive isolationism. What we have termed the overthrow of liberal internationalism has gone hand in hand with the antirevolutionary obsessions of the New Right, and, as the U.S. attack on Libya demonstrated, this has seriously complicated life for America's allies in NATO. On one hand, many influential Americans say they want to deemphasize Europe and the Atlantic Alliance, to promote global unilateralism, and to force the Europeans to spend more on their own conventional defences. On the other hand, the U.S. has a vast strategic stake in Europe, including a huge array of communications, intelligence, and air force bases—many of which are nuclear weapons facilities. As intermediate- and short-range nuclear missiles are withdrawn from Europe under arms control accords with the Soviets, the U.S. grip on these facilities must tighten. The U.S. is also anxious to preserve its option of using its many European bases for global operations outside the NATO area, and it wants to prevent any NATO member from setting a precedent by negotiating a withdrawal of American military bases. The U.S. regards the phrase "joint decision" as meaning consultation, but it does not admit any right of its allies to veto the use of its overseas facilities or weapons—including its nuclear weapons. This is a great deal to ask. Whatever Canadians may decide about their own future in the Alliance, Europeans can perhaps be forgiven for wondering whether the costs of having the Americans on their soil—what one critic calls the "burdens, obligations, constraints and complicities of the most diverse kind"[26]—do not now outweigh the benefits of a lifetime membership.

## CHAPTER SIX

# Europe: Who Killed Atlanticism?

> After Yalta, which had enabled Stalin's Russia to annex
> Central Europe and the Balkans automatically at the time of
> the collapse of the Third Reich, a further extension of the
> Soviet bloc was certainly to be feared, and in the event of
> such an aggression the Western States of the Continent could
> not by themselves offer sufficiently powerful resistance . . .
> Hence nothing could have been more justified and perhaps
> more salutary than the American aid which, through the
> Marshall Plan, enabled Western Europe to re-establish its
> means of production and saved it from drastic economic, so-
> cial and political upheavals, while protecting its security
> under the atomic umbrella. But an almost inevitable conse-
> quence had been the inauguration of NATO, a system of secu-
> rity whereby Washington controlled the defense and
> consequently the foreign policy and even the territory of its
> allies.
>
> Charles de Gaulle,<br>Memoirs of Hope: Renewal 1958-62

## Retreat from Power Politics

In the autumn of 1986, just a few months after the blow up in
Anglo-American relations over the use of the F-111s against
Libya, the British Labour party convened its annual conference
in the resort town of Blackpool. This would be the final such
event before the next general election, expected in 1987. Since
the Libyan bombing, party members had been demanding a
sharp response from the leadership and they ensured that the
central issues at Blackpool revolved around peace and defence:
Britain's future role in NATO, Labour's nonnuclear defence pol-

icy, and Anglo-American military relations. After a fractious and often bitterly anti-American debate, Labour voted overwhelmingly to scrap Britain's own nuclear submarine deterrent and to evict U.S. nuclear missiles, nuclear-armed aircraft, and nuclear bases from the U.K. But Labour leader Neil Kinnock, resisting anti-NATO attacks from the party's Left, won support from the conference for his pledge to keep Britain in the NATO Alliance and to permit the U.S. to maintain its intelligence, communications, and conventional air force bases in the U.K. Having demanded the removal of all nuclear weapons from the U.K., he vowed he would never ask the United States for its nuclear guarantee: "I would, if necessary fight and give my life for my country. I would die for my country. But I could never allow my country to die for me." For Kinnock, the shrewd Welsh pragmatist whose personal commitment to nuclear disarmament stretched back to the fifties, the vote balanced the party's deep antipathy to nuclear weapons and deterrence against the need to reassure Britain's allies, particularly the United States. He spoke from conscience, but he was also driven by the political necessity of containing his radical opponents on the Labour Left. His greatest difficulty was that he could no more raise the prospect of a nonnuclear Britain without alienating the NATO Alliance than he could send peace signals to the White House without declaring war on a substantial—and very active—portion of his own party. It was this, more than any other issue, that would keep him in opposition and out of office.

Viewed by many as a tactical compromise between the "soft" and "hard" Labour positions on defence, Blackpool was actually a victory for Prime Minister Margaret Thatcher's Con- servatives and her right-wing allies in Washington—some of whom had gone to the trouble of flying to London on the eve of the Labour conference to utter dire threats about the likely im- pact of Labour's antinuclear policy on NATO and on U.S. isola- tionist sentiment. If Labour were elected and carried out its unilateralist program, warned U.S. Defence Secretary Caspar Weinberger in a BBC interview, NATO would be weakened and politically split, Britain would risk losing the American nuclear guarantee, while many Americans would demand the with- drawal of U.S. forces from Europe. Weinberger's assistant,

Richard Perle—known to his admirers around the Alliance as the Prince of Darkness—added the threat that the United States itself might withdraw from NATO if Labour tried to implement its defence policy, though he did not explain how this would serve American interests. Kinnock attacked the "offensive and bullying tactics" of these two guardians of the American empire, yet the blunt warnings were bound to disturb many of Labour's potential supporters. To drive home the point that Weinberger spoke with strong bipartisan support in the U.S., Senator Sam Nunn (D-Georgia) told the BBC that "if the British decide they are going to jerk the rug out from under a very carefully constructed NATO policy, that would erode the whole NATO Alliance."[1] The issue that now had to be faced was whether the election of an antinuclear, unilateralist Labour government would set in motion a chain reaction of events across the Western Alliance, strip the U.K. of any bargaining power in its dealings with Washington, and leave her with neither allies nor sufficient coercive power to discourage her adversaries.

It was worth Weinberger's weekend to come to Britain and meddle in its internal politics. If implemented by a future Labour government Kinnock's program of unilateral nuclear disarmament would have large repercussions on the U.S. and the rest of the NATO coalition. Labour, though protesting its fidelity to NATO, was unwilling to link the abandonment of the British nuclear deterrent to reciprocal disarmament by the Russians; nor would it agree to make the removal of American cruise missiles and nuclear-armed F-111s subject to multilateral negotiations with the allies affected. There was more than a touch of the Campaign for Nuclear Disarmament's fundamentalism in the policy of the Labour party: what was needed was not a better defence policy but a once-for-all act of will to rid the British Isles of the nuclear plague—no matter what the impact upon other countries. Even if it did not produce a domino-like rejection of U.S. nuclear arms and bases on the continent, this unilateralism was sure to complicate NATO's strategy of flexible response—a strategy that the British Labour Party now disparages as outmoded because of the arrival of nuclear parity between the superpowers.

Within NATO, Britain is a key staging area and forward base for Alliance forces operating in the eastern Atlantic and North

Sea; a main base for operations in the Channel; and a support base for both British and U.S. forces stationed on the European continent. British nuclear forces, all of which are committed to NATO—though under British control—consist of: the Polaris submarine deterrent; eleven RAF strike-attack squadrons of Tornado and Buccaneer aircraft based in the U.K. and West Germany and capable of delivering free-fall nuclear bombs; and theatre nuclear weapons used by the British Army of the Rhine. (The BAOR has a peacetime strength of about 55,000 or three armoured divisions which form part of NATO's Northern Army Group, defending northern Germany from the Ruhr to the coast). Under Labour's blueprint, all of these nuclear swords would be beaten into ploughshares or converted into conventional military power.

Labour's defence policy also demanded the removal of all U.S. nuclear weapons systems and bases from the U.K., a step that would bring about a fundamental change in Anglo-American relations. The Reagan administration was at this time involved in negotiations with other allies (such as Greece, Turkey, and Spain) to renegotiate the terms of its base-leasing agreements, including rights to equip U.S. forces with nuclear warheads or to use bases for out-of-area operations in, say, North Africa and the Middle East. In NATO's Southern Region, the United States had been unable since the 1973 Arab-Israeli War to obtain agreement for the use of American installations for missions not clearly related to NATO or the security interests of the respective host nation. As the Libyan bombing demonstrated, Thatcher's Britain was far more pliable. However, Washington worried that if a future British Labour government was able to carry out its antinuclear program, a domino effect would be felt throughout NATO; the defence relationships between the U.S. and its allies across the continent would be complicated and America's hegemonic position in the Mediterranean Basin subject to new challenges and demands from its erstwhile friends in such capitals as Madrid, Athens, and Ankara.

A good deal of the domestic political debate in the U.K. over defence has been created by Labour's plans to scrap Britain's own nuclear deterrent by decommissioning the aging Polaris nuclear submarines and cancelling the expensive Trident D5 replacement (in 1980 the Thatcher government decided to replace Polaris with a force of four nuclear-powered submarines armed with Trident ballistic missiles). Trident is so powerful and costly that it seems beyond the means or needs of any medium power, and defence critics have questioned whether it would contribute very much to the existing framework of East-West deterrence; but that question is basically unanswerable since so much ultimately depends upon one's assumptions about the reliability of the American nuclear guarantee to Western Europe.

Let us consider Labour's case against Trident. To begin with the gloomiest case: if U.S. neoisolationists were to gain strength in the Congress and presidency in the years ahead; and if this led to further U.S.-European tensions and major reductions in the American military presence in Europe over the longer run; and if in turn this weakened the U.S. nuclear guarantee to its European allies, then Britain's own deterrent might make strategic, if not economic sense. As the previous chapter suggests, it was plausible that the Americans would gradually reduce their military commitments in Europe in favour of a stronger global maritime strategy, especially if the U.S. became more deeply involved in extra-NATO conflicts, such as Central America or the Persian Gulf, but proved unable to pressure the allies into increased defence spending. Because of such uncertainties, the size of the British defence effort has been shaped politically by the need to keep the Americans in Europe, while simultaneously getting ready for their possible departure. Using the worst-case assumptions about future U.S. unilateralism and the Alliance, Trident's advocates are able to construct a case for higher defence spending and a "nationalist" independent deterrent:

If it is assumed, for example, that current trends in NATO are potentially irreversible and that Atlantic tensions will worsen rather than abate, then a weakening of the U.S. commitment to Western Europe becomes a possibility that must be taken very seriously by defence planners. Yet this argues for a more nationalistic approach: rather than shape its defence efforts to fit in with Alliance priorities, the United Kingdom should adopt policies and maintain a national order of battle which have a validity and coherence that goes beyond the

NATO framework. The implication of this is that the long-term case for Trident is particularly powerful.[2]

The Labour Party rejected this logic (although former Prime Minister James Callaghan, Denis Healey, and others reportedly agreed with it) on the grounds that it was inconsistent with a nonnuclear approach to defence.

Against Trident, it can be argued that the British and French deterrents have added little to the overall stability of the nuclear balance, and that it is possible to hold a more relaxed view of U.S. policy. The Americans still have vital interests in Europe, and these dictate that U.S. forces be maintained there—notwithstanding current ideological trends and the temptations to withdraw from entangling alliances. In fact, the Reagan administration itself resisted pressure from U.S. unilateralists and acted much as every administration since Truman's had acted: to protect the United States' stake in Europe and the Alliance, it rejected Congressional calls for a reorientation of U.S. global strategy away from NATO. This continuity, based as it is upon enduring American national interests, arguably is likely to persist. Even in the event that most or all of the 325,000 U.S. troops were sent home—and how would such a decision benefit America?—the Soviets could never be certain that if trouble came in central Europe the United States would not fight for its vital interests. And if the Russians were not deterred by that uncertainty, why would they fear the British or the French? If West Germany already had reason to question the credibility of the U.S. nuclear guarantee, would it put its trust in a cheque signed in London or Paris?

France's Gaullists are fond of the nationalist maxim: *le nucleaire ne se partage pas*, which is to say that, ultimately, nuclear weapons protect only those who possess them. Britain's long history of avoiding continental commitments—perfidious Albion—did not inspire confidence among her allies that she would prove to be the exception; was it credible that any British politician would ever order the firing of Trident's missiles, knowing that doing so would be followed by the certain obliteration of the United Kingdom? On strategic grounds, as the Labour party rightly said,[3] the case for independent nuclear deterrents within the Western Alliance was not compelling. Trident in particular was so exorbitant, so clearly built to the specifications of a superpower, and so much in conflict with Britain's conventional military commitments in NATO, that even some right-wing opinion in the U.K. was uneasy about going ahead with the project.

However, the debate on Trident could not be resolved solely on strategic grounds: military considerations alone had never determined postwar British policy on nuclear weapons. Rather, it was Britain's declining status among the powers and its dependence on the United States that heavily influenced the thinking of both Labour and Tory politicians. The debate over nuclear weapons was inextricably tied to nationalist concerns over the collapse of British power and influence after the war, concerns that cut across traditional party lines. The initial decision to make a British atom bomb—made in early 1947 by the Attlee Labour government—was motivated less by fear of Russia or by strategic concerns (though Attlee's advisors understood the arguments for a retaliatory deterrent) than by considerations of great power status and Anglo-American relations. Britain had lost its empire, its economic supremacy, and was about to lose its place at the table where the great powers confer. To restore its prestige and status, and above all to lessen its dependence on a fickle United States, it was imperative for Britain to gain the price of entry to the nuclear club: this was the conclusion of the entire political establishment of the day, including the Labour party. American efforts to preserve the U.S. atomic weapons monopoly by sabotaging the British bomb production effort—by, among other methods, getting exclusive rights to all Canadian uranium and plutonium—only reinforced the conviction in London that foreign policy influence and independence demanded a costly struggle to become an atomic power. The motives were not unlike those of General de Gaulle a decade later. The hopes of the foreign secretary of the Labour government, Ernest Bevin, were to sustain a war-shattered Western Europe against Russian pressure through "a Western European system organized by Britain and backed by the material aid of the United States, a system which should develop a power and influence equal to that of the United States and Russia. Bevin believed strongly that it was for the British as Europeans to give the lead, spiritually, morally and politically in Western Europe, to help in forming what he himself called a Third Force. The Western European Union remained a dominant theme of Bevin's policy, but he always saw it within the framework of an alliance with the United States."[4] For Attlee and Bevin, the atomic deterrent represented a necessary investment in Britain's future as a great power. Unfortunately, Britain turned out to be a great power without a future, bomb or no bomb.

By and large, the same arguments prevailed in debates in the later 1950s over the decision to build a thermonuclear weapon: renunciation of the H-bomb would reduce Britain to "the wholly dependent satellite of the United States" and send the British foreign secretary "naked into the conference chamber," argued Labour. The Tories concurred. Prime Minister Harold Macmillan, speaking in the aftermath of Britain's humiliation by the U.S. in the 1956 Suez crisis, defended the H-bomb decision on purely nonmilitary grounds. "The independent contribution gives us a better position in the world, it gives us a better position with respect to the United States. It puts us where we ought to be, in the position of a great power. The fact that we have it makes the United States pay a greater regard to our point of view, and that is of great importance." Support for "Atlanticism"—junior partner of the United States within the multilateral framework of NATO—went hand-in-hand with the recognition that influence and independence within the Alliance had to be paid for; the alternative, believed the politicians of the day, would be a Britain reduced to the status of a complete satellite. But we could well argue that Britain's pursuit of nuclear status as compensation for her lost power was precisely one of the main drives behind her growing docility and dependence on the United States. That was underlined in the late 1950s when plans for a British-made ballistic missile were abandoned and President Eisenhower promised to sell Britain the Skybolt missile in return for a base for U.S. nuclear submarines at Holy Loch, Scotland. The Skybolt program was suddenly cancelled in late 1962, exposing the extent to which nuclear weapons were deepening Britain's dependence on the United States rather than becoming a source of influence. Macmillan had to fly to Nassau for a hastily convened summit with U.S. President Kennedy (who had hardly bothered to consult the British two months before during the Cuban missile crisis). A deal was struck which allowed the British to purchase the Polaris submarine-launched missile from the United States, though only on condition that it would be used "for the purpose of international defence of the Western Alliance in all circumstances."[5] The illusory pursuit of "independence" through the development of nuclear weapons only accelerated Britain's decline and subordination to American policy.

The link between the possession of one's own nuclear strike force and "a nation's place in the world" is now part of the symbolism of Thatcherism, Labour having opted in 1980 for the peace movement's conception of a strictly conventional military posture—albeit one closely tied to NATO (Kinnock referred to this as his "Canada Option"). The Tories are unabashedly pro-nuclear from nationalist conviction: Margaret Thatcher and the "neo-Gaullist" wing of the Conservative party have stressed the need for a beefing-up of Britain's navy and the modernization of the country's nuclear forces—i.e., to push ahead with the Trident D5—for without it, as one ranking Tory expressed it, "the British people would be too exclusively at the mercy of every American missile on British soil."[6] This mealy-mouthed Gaullism, which hints at but never declares the belief that the American umbrella is leaking, links the Trident symbol—made in the U.S.A.—to the tarted-up patriotism of America's most enthusiastic subaltern, Mrs. Thatcher. With its several hundred multiple, independently targetted warheads, Trident is far more than Britain needs or can afford; but it is what the Americans are selling and therefore what the British must buy if they want to keep the U.S. link. Deploying arguments very similar to those of the U.S. neoisolationists, some Tories with a bad case of Falklands Fever have supported major cuts in Britain's continental army and air commitments in order to shift resources to a maritime strategy and to the deterrent; and like their counterparts in America they have proposed to do so unilaterally. The sheer cost of the Trident acquisition makes cutbacks in British conventional military expenditure a certainty.

If Labour's defence policy drew heavily upon the ideas of Europe's peace groups, Thatcherism, with its heavy stress on the coercive state, enterprise, and technological progress, was a variant of what German sociologist Ralf Dahrendorf has called Europe's new conservatism à l'americain. The new European conservatism emerged in the latter 1970s, partly as a response to the collapse of the decade of detente but also as an answer to the unravelling of the postwar social democratic consensus. It sought to revitalize the economies of France, Britain, the Netherlands, Scandinavia, and West Germany through an all-out assault on the welfare state and the pursuit of technological modernization. Though often influenced by North American models and values, this new conservatism has had an inward, nationalistic orientation in much of Western Europe—a self-regarding "new patriotism" which preaches the Europeanization of a Europe now equidistant between "the two superpowers." Among Western Europe's conservative governing classes, Atlanticism has all but vanished as a transnational system of ideas and values:

> Thatcher is popular in the United States—but is she an Atlanticist? French technocrats seem quite close to Americans in their thinking—but are they really intent on promoting the Alliance? Or does the new conservatism in all its brands espouse an international Darwinism as well, including the deliberate attempt to hold one's own against the great ally across the Atlantic?[7]

The ruling elites of Western Europe, whether social democrat or conservative, Protestant or Catholic, retain a strong interest in supporting the North Atlantic Alliance—if not the early cold war enthusiasm for Atlanticism. By contrast, the European peace movement that emerged after 1979 went into the streets not only to rid the continent of nuclear weapons but to shatter the consensus of the Western Alliance. The new cold war polarized West European politics, and one of the outcomes was that most of Europe's socialist and social democratic parties shifted to the left on war and peace issues (they did not do so in Italy or France, and in those countries the peace movement remained small and ineffective).

This was partly a matter of conviction and partly an attempt to capture the electoral muscle of a thriving peace movement out to dismantle both the "Euromissiles" and Europe's nuclear-dependent security policy.

Seeking to contain the threat of radicalism from the Left, the leaders of European social democracy—notably in the northern,

Protestant part of the continent—found themselves accommodating the antinuclear revolt or being shoved aside. West German Chancellor Helmut Schmidt, who had helped to orchestrate the 1979 NATO decision on INF deployment, was ousted from the leadership of his party, the SPD, in 1982 because he could not hold back the tide of nuclear protest. Denis Healey, the British Labour party's senior spokesman on defence and an architect of NATO's nuclear strategy, supported Labour's drift after 1979 into the circle of the unilateral disarmers. As a substitute for traditional approaches to security, the disarmers advocated territorial defence, hostility to the NATO Alliance and its Euromissiles, support for nuclear-free zones, and apologetics for the Soviet Union. Here was a heady ideological brew of neutralism, pacifism, and utopianism: a short cut to electoral suicide, it was a testament to the power of romantic ideas (or the threat from the "hard" Left) that social democrats such as Healey could bring themselves to support it. Doing so, they virtually handed political power to the Right across the "Arc of Angst": throughout northern, Protestant Europe the parties that linked their fortunes to the peace revolt were reduced to marginal status. "At the end of the day, every Labour (or Liberal) party that had sought to absorb or outflank the protest movement ended up not in power but on the opposition benches."[8]

The political liabilities of unilateral disarmament were especially evident in Britain. The British Labour party ran a very slick and effective campaign in the 1987 general election, but neither it nor the SDP/Liberal Alliance were able to prevent Margaret Thatcher from winning a third term. She won for many reasons, not the least of which was Neil Kinnock's handling of unilateral nuclear disarmament. What would happen, asked a TV interviewer, in a clash between a nonnuclear Britain and a nuclear-armed enemy? Kinnock replied that the country would lose the flower of its youth if it resisted, and that the best defence would be to retreat and use "all the resources you have to make any occupation totally untenable." The war in Afghanistan, he said later, "surely demonstrates the point." The Polaris submarine deterrent would be decommissioned within a couple of weeks of his election, and he did not want the U.S. to include Britain within its extended nuclear deterrent. The Tories quickly brought out a poster showing a British soldier with his hands raised in surrender.

The image of hundreds of thousands of protesters marching through the streets of London, Brussels, or Berlin from 1979 to 1982 was powerful enough to inspire unilateralists on both sides of the Atlantic to write NATO's epitaph. Many on the European Left were convinced that the 1979 decision by NATO to deploy cruise and Pershing missiles in Western Europe represented a deliberate move by the United States to prepare for a "limited" nuclear war confined to the European theatre. This paranoia was fed by the increased East-West confrontation of the later 1970s and early 1980s and by the rather blood-curdling rhetoric of the Reagan administration about the possibility of prevailing in a nuclear war. In West Germany especially, the Euromissile deployment—which, ironically, had been agreed to by a reluctant Jimmy Carter as a way of reassuring the Europeans about the commitment of American power to their security—was interpreted by the Greens and other peace groups as "a great power plot to turn Germany into a neatly demarcated arena for nuclear proxy war, with the two Germanys as its battlefield and victims."[9]

The Federal Republic's consensus on the need for nuclear deterrence, its trust in the Alliance and in U.S. leadership, its willingness to suppress discussion of uniquely German national interests: these values were severely challenged in the crisis of the Euromissiles. Having repudiated Chancellor Schmidt and voted against INF deployment, the SPD ran in the 1983 election on the slogan, "In the interest of Germany." Suddenly Europe's old nemesis, the German question, reappeared along with the recurrent dream (or nightmare) of a neutralized, reunited Germany. This mixture of antinuclear pacifism and German nationalism, represented particularly in the fundamentalist wing of the Green party, was not produced merely by a fear of the Pershing and cruise missiles; rather it emerged from a deep resentment over Germany's lack of sovereignty, its dependence on nuclear weapons under *foreign* control. Not simply nuclear weapons but foreign nuclear weapons were stirring the bright coals of neutralism. Deployment of the INF missiles in 1983 only heightened the West German sense of dependence and insecurity.

Deployment dramatized the deepest issue. It suddenly made Germans realize their dependency, the limits of their autonomy, the extent of their vulnerability. It also made them feel a certain chilly isolation: many Germans feared that the new missiles added to Germany's insecurity rather than security. They thought themselves misunderstood: as they became more conscious of the special vulnerabilities of the FRG, they thought that the great protector, the U.S., was heedless of them—and that circumstances had left the West Germans exposed and dependent.[10]

By 1987, however, the centre-right of German politics, in the past a bastion of loyalty to NATO and the U.S., was deeply concerned over the proposed "double zero-option" INF arms control agreement which would eliminate all intermediate- and short-range nuclear missiles in Europe. Coming as it did as part of the October 1986 summit at Reykjavik, Iceland, where President Reagan, acting without consulting U.S. allies, had proposed the elimination of all nuclear missiles—missiles on which the NATO security guarantee is thought to depend—the double-zero INF proposal held out the prospect of the European states in NATO being confronted with "denuclearization" at a moment of conventional inferiority vis a vis the Warsaw Pact. Behind this concern lay a deeper psychological fear, a fear of abandonment by the allies and of West Germany's interests being dealt away in a bargain between the superpowers. Whether nuclear weapons are being deployed or removed, the constant is that the decisions are not being made by Germans on the basis of German interests. A loss of confidence, a deepening sense of vulnerability, produced in West German policy what one writer has called a new "cycle of anxiety" in which fears of abandonment by the U.S. compete with opposing fears of being entrapped in a superpower confrontation.[11]

One response to this sense of vulnerability is German neutralism, an idea which had strong popular appeal in the early 1980s. It is estimated that in 1983 about a third of West Germany's population (and more than half of those under nineteen) thought it better for the Federal Republic to be neutral between the eastern and western blocs rather than continue to be part of the western defence alliance. Some advocate neutrality as a way of attaining German reunification, others want it in conjunction with disarmament, while still others see it as a necessary step on the road to a powerful, unified Europe. In the German context, neutralism is an illusion, a dream of opting out of the harsh everyday practice of world politics. It is illusory because neutrality must be based on independence, and independence in turn must be assured by tangible power: i.e., a strong military. "As the world is shaped more by power than by law the concept of neutrality as a policy of survival is only viable in connection with a credible defence capacity."[12] To acquire such a capacity for defence the Federal Republic would have to engage in measures that would be totally unacceptable to her neighbours and to the great powers who have guaranteed the postwar settlement. Already alarmed by the spread of neutralist sentiment in West Germany, states such as France and the U.S.S.R. share an interest in preventing any revival of German militarism.

The trend to neutralism notwithstanding, large majorities of West Germans and other West Europeans continue to favour membership in NATO: even at the height of the Euromissile conflict seventy-two per cent of Norwegians and Dutch and seventy-eight per cent of West Germans indicated support for the Atlantic Alliance. It was not NATO that was the target but its new nuclear arsenal. Anti-Americanism, never far beneath the surface in most of Western Europe, was on the rise in the 1980s, especially in Britain, where by 1983 fully seventy per cent had little or no confidence in American "ability to deal wisely with present world problems," and in the Netherlands, where distrust in American policy rose sharply from thirty-one to fifty per cent in 1982. But nowhere in Western Europe was there any parallel increase in mass support for the Soviet Union. What the opinion polls suggest is a triad of popular fears: 1) fear of the new generation of theatre nuclear weapons; 2) fear over the collapse of detente and of a war caused by rising East-West tensions; 3) and fear or uncertainty about the direction and methods of U.S. foreign policy.

Whatever else the Euromissile affair did to relations within NATO, it revealed that people do not feel reassured by the delegation of their defence to nuclear weapons under the exclusive control of an unpredictable and unilateralist superpower. If many Americans accused their allies of undercutting U.S. interests outside the NATO area and of taking a "free ride" on the common defence, many Europeans thought that Washington's hard line on detente and arms control was dangerous and short-sighted.

## The Burdens of Empire

European resentment and anxiety over the Reagan administration's policies toward the Soviet Union on issues such as Afghanistan, Poland, East-West trade, and arms control only reinforced those Americans who wanted the United States to abandon a Eurocentric approach and go its own way. Anti-European sentiment grew strongly in the U.S. in the wake of the hostage crisis in Iran and the Soviet invasion of Afghanistan in late 1979, reviving an instinctive American suspicion of "free riding" allies and fresh proposals from Congress to reduce the U.S. military presence in Europe. Walter Laqueur asked in early 1982, "What can America do to satisfy those who want equidistance from the two superpowers, who want defense (but not too much of it), who are more afraid of American sanctions than of events in Poland, more apprehensive about American than Soviet missiles, who want to be allies and mediators at the same time?"[13] In this conservative view, the European states in NATO were undermining the contract or understanding that formed the basis of the Alliance: i.e., that in assuming the obligation to protect Western Europe from the threat of Soviet power, the U.S. was to be accorded the support of its allies in determining how NATO should be protected.[14] In the absence of such deference to the dominant ally, it was argued, the United States should assert its global prerogatives and redeploy its ground forces away from Europe, thereby administering some "mild shock therapy for the more lethargic and complacent Europeans," as President Carter's former national security adviser delicately put it.[15] That the American Right could no longer see the advantages to the U.S. of a coalition strategy in dealing with the Soviets during a cold war revival was itself an augury of the unruly state of the Alliance in the eighties.

Seeking to reassert U.S. military power and to revitalize containment outside Europe, particularly in Southwest Asia, Washington attempted after 1980 to mobilize the resources of the Western Alliance in a collective response to security threats that lay beyond its traditional defence perimeter, and to fashion a new division of responsibilities that would free up U.S. forces for interventions in the Middle East, the Gulf, or Central America. Thus, it was the burden of empire, not just of the Alliance, that the Europeans (and Canadians) were now being asked to shoulder.

## The Allies Engulfed

In NATO's formative years, it was the Europeans—especially the French and the British—who attempted to use the Alliance and its front-line forces in support of out-of-area colonial objectives in Algeria, Suez, Indonesia, and Indochina. In 1948-49, some of the original twelve signatories even sought to have their overseas colonies included within the North Atlantic Treaty's boundaries; but the United States, Canada, and others were unwilling to have the Alliance underwrite any resuscitation of Europe's dying colonial empires, and only France's Algerian "departments" were included in NATO's defence perimeter in 1949 (and this lapsed when Algeria gained its independence). The Americans, who were in the process of superseding British and French predominance from the strategic crossroads of the eastern Mediterranean to the giant oil fields of Arabia, would not permit the Europeans to threaten U.S. interests in the Middle East by reconstituting their colonial empires under NATO's banner. However, the roles began to reverse in the 1960s as the United States deepened its involvement in the Vietnam War. Like France before it, the U.S. complained bitterly that it was bearing the brunt of the West's struggle with communism but receiving no assistance from its NATO allies: the battle of Saigon was really a battle for Berlin. The allies were largely unmoved. Since the Vietnam intervention, it has typically been the United States that has attempted to stretch NATO's obligations, arguing with General Haig that the entire globe is now the concern of the sixteen allies, while Canada and the Europeans have opposed NATO's involvement in out-of-area disputes. "There has been concern lest such involvement could lead to NATO being dragged into a conflict, or at least into significant diversion of scarce resources from what Europeans naturally see as their primary concern—the defence of Europe. The growth of Warsaw Pact capabilities against NATO itself has enhanced these worries, and led Europeans to fear diversion of U.S. resources as well."[16] Canada shares those worries and fears. Because of them the states of NATO Europe have insisted that out-of-area action must be a matter of individual national decision; yet, as we saw in the case of the 1986 air raid on Libya, such actions retain the potential to tear the Alliance apart. NATO cannot be isolated from the rest of the world.

Tensions within the Western Alliance over how to cope with security questions beyond the NATO area have focused for a decade on the troubled oil-rich Persian Gulf. Long a safe haven of Anglo-American hegemony, control of the Gulf was suddenly thrown into question in 1978-79 by the internal radicalization of Iran and the fall of the Shah, a key regional ally of the United States. There followed in bewildering succession the seizure of U.S. diplomatic hostages in Teheran, the invasion of Afghanistan by the U.S.S.R., occupation by Islamic fundamentalists of the Grand Mosque in Mecca, the opening shots by Iraq in what was to become a prolonged and cruel war of mutual attrition with Iran, and President Carter's declaration in January 1980 that an attempt "by any outside force to gain control of the Persian Gulf region will be regarded as an assault on the vital interests of the United States of America, and such an assault will be repelled by any means necessary, including military force." This "Carter Doctrine," as it was called, was a response to the political outcry in the U.S. over events in Kabul and Teheran, and had little to do with short-term oil supplies or the threat of resource wars. Rather it was part of the revitalization of the postwar policy of containment, a policy based on the premise that the crisis in the region was being driven by the exigencies of worsening East-West relations, not by local conditions. Soviet expansionism and U.S. military weakness in Southwest Asia had destabilized the Gulf and created a power vacuum that would eventually be filled, possibly by the U.S.S.R. As one well-respected American conservative put it, resorting to an economic determinism that would make a Marxist blush, this could spell the end of the West's alliances:

If the Gulf is eventually controlled, whether directly or indirectly by the Soviet Union, the post-World War II political structure will suffer sudden destruction. The loss of the Gulf could be expected to form an almost certain prelude to the effective end of the American position in Western Europe and Japan. Dependent as they would then be on the Soviet Union for oil, these nations would adjust their policies and actions to Moscow's wishes. Even if the Soviet Union did not immediately insist that they break their security ties with the United States, these ties would be deprived of any substantive meaning. In these circumstances, no real purpose would be served by the retention of an American security presence in Europe, even if this presence were not asked to leave.[17]

The view that the Europeans and Japanese would, in the last analysis, put their oil supplies and economic interests above their overall security relationship with the U.S. was about as sensible as the assumption that the Soviets, who were neither energy importers nor likely to risk a world war, were about to occupy the Persian Gulf. These were worst-case assessments driven by anti-Soviet paranoia and prejudiced intelligence, and yet they were widely believed in the United States. Responding to such fears and to the vagaries of domestic politics, the Carter administration swung sharply in early 1980 toward a hard-line policy of confronting the Soviets in Southwest Asia. A line was to be drawn in the Persian Gulf, despite the lack of any existing U.S. or allied military capability to enforce Carter's new doctrine; the allies would be informed, not consulted, and expected to fall in line; there was much discussion of a new division of labour within the Alliance that would demonstrate western commitment to secure the Gulf yet not detract from NATO's credibility in Europe. A key premise of the new U.S. strategy was that America had rich allies who could afford to defend Europe while the United States shifted more of its resources into the defence of its interests in Southwest Asia. From the strategic point of view, the collapse of the Shah's regime in Iran and instability throughout the Gulf had undermined one of the ruling principles of U.S. foreign policy: namely, that American interests could be safely entrusted to local satellites installed, armed, and advised by the United States (the 1969 "Nixon Doctrine"). To reassert U.S. hegemony in the region, Washington would have to abandon indirect methods of intervention.

The American approach, with its deeply ideological assumptions about the situation in the Gulf and the need for military rather than diplomatic solutions, was received skeptically in most European capitals, and usually for good reason. There was general consensus that events in the Gulf did indeed affect western security, but few of the European members of NATO had the resources to act directly beside the U.S. This meant that, even if they agreed to the policy, they would have no influence over it. In effect, they would be paying to support U.S. intervention outside Europe. The Europeans did not expect Soviet aggression in the Gulf, nor did they believe that military intervention by the western powers would do anything but exacerbate the existing instability in Iran and other Gulf states. Unlike the Carter administration, the governments of NATO Europe doubted that oil supplies could be secured through the threat of military force; the problems in the region were basically political in nature, stemming from indigenous rather than external forces, and they required a political response. The West Europeans were especially concerned not to align themselves with the Americans and Israelis in actions against the Arab states that *would* jeopardize their oil supplies. In the worst case, the Europeans worried over the prospect of the Americans attempting to preempt Soviet aggression and thereby setting off a superpower confrontation that would automatically involve Europe.

But on the other hand, the allies were already under attack in the United States for having done so little to help the American hostages and for failing to condemn Soviet expansionism, and the political climate in Washington was becoming poisonous to European interests as Congress rumbled about American boys dying for Europe's oil. The Carter initiative had placed the Europeans in an awkward predicament, and in the end most decided to put Alliance politics—i.e., the need to avert a major rupture with Washington—before their growing misgivings about American policy.[18]

In May 1980, the NATO allies struck a bargain over a new division of labour between the defence of Europe and the defence of western interests in the Gulf. "By implication," writes Christopher Coker, "the Alliance for the first time in its history defined a security interest which lay outside its traditional defence perimeter."[19] This NATO decision committed the Americans to assume most of the burden for establishing a military presence for intervention in the Gulf/Indian Ocean, via measures discussed below, and the Europeans and Canadians "to do their utmost to meet additional burdens for NATO security which could result from the increased United States responsibilities in South West Asia."[20] In effect, the Europeans agreed that, as a matter of Alliance policy, they would contribute to the U.S. buildup in the Gulf and the Indian Ocean even if this threatened to weaken NATO Europe's own defences, and they would do this in three ways. First, they could facilitate American measures by granting overflight privileges, refuelling rights, and so on. Second, they could compensate for U.S. actions by spending more on conventional defence in Europe itself. And third, those states with the capability (France or Britain) could send military forces into the Gulf or Indian Ocean to support the U.S. But there was a deficiency in these commitments: the Europeans did not agree to make new expenditures or to add new resources, only to reshuffle existing priorities.[21] Britain and France were in the process of expanding their own out-of-area capabilities for intervention in Africa and elsewhere, but they were unlikely to co-ordinate them except on an ad hoc basis, while the West German state is under constitutional constraints that prohibit its armed forces from operating outside the Federal Republic. The remaining allies had no capability for out-of-area operations, although it was open to them to provide more liberal use of European bases, en route access to U.S.-based airborne forces, and heavier contributions to combat service support in NATO to compensate for the reinforcements diverted away from Europe.

For its part, the United States intended to acquire its own force for rapid deployment to the Gulf—10,000 kilometres from the U.S. by air—in a crisis, while strengthening its small existing forces in the region. A Rapid Deployment Force was activated by Carter in 1980, and in 1983 this force became the U.S. Central Command, with headquarters in Florida and responsibility for "security and defence" in a vast area from the Horn of Africa to the borders of Pakistan and Afghanistan. Drawing on nearly 400,000 personnel, including five army divisions, seven air force wings, three aircraft carrier battle groups, special forces, marine amphibious forces, and much else, the U.S. Central Command's mission is to maintain an increased deployable military presence which can deter Soviet efforts to gain power and hegemony in the region; to promote regional stability via security assistance; and to maintain access to an unhindered use of Persian Gulf oil resources.[22] The broad security objectives of the new command imply that it could be used to intervene wherever a threat to western oil supplies or "regional stability" is thought to exist; there is no requirement for prior Soviet intervention. And although the primary purpose of this formidable military power is deterrence, in order to maximize their chances of a successful intervention in the Gulf it might well be necessary for U.S. armed forces to arrive before the Soviets. A *preemptive* U.S. intervention during a crisis, with the related risks of global escalation, is thus a logical possibility.

In U.S. strategic planning, the term "rapid deployment" refers to the quick movement of conventional forces based in the United States to areas of vital interest where the American military presence is minimal. The forces drawn upon are not new but are already assigned to other missions—e.g., the reinforcement of NATO. Rapid deployment is envisaged in the event of a "limited contingency" in the Third World requiring a multiservice force against a sophisticated adversary—Soviet, "Soviet-proxy," or Soviet-equipped. The literature mentions as examples the early U.S. intervention in Vietnam; the Korean War; the 1973 Middle East War; and the possibility of a Soviet thrust into the Persian Gulf.[23] What is being planned for, in other words, is not counterinsurgency but NATO-scale conventional warfare aimed at rapid victory. Post-Vietnam U.S. military doctrine has stressed the need for American forces to avoid divisive, protracted interventions in the Third World and to "play to win" by using their military power in a highly concentrated fashion before the corrosive Vietnam Syndrome (public and Congressional opposition to new military interventions in the Third World) can set in.

Whether the United States actually *could* mount a large-scale intervention in the Gulf area, given the glaring deficiencies in airlift and sealift capability, the immense distances, the political uncertainties over the use of bases and staging areas from the Mediterranean to the Indian Ocean, and the lack of forward-deployed U.S. forces, is another question entirely. The rapid deployment of a multidivision force from the U.S. to a distant region in the Third World would involve enormous logistical, refuelling, supply, and other problems. Much would depend on the co-operation of America's NATO and non-NATO allies in facilitating the movement of men and equipment across Western Europe, the Middle East, and Africa. A nation that nearly botched the invasion of tiny Grenada might find the Persian Gulf a tough testing-ground for its concepts and strategies of rapid intervention. The United States might overreach the limits of its power again. Yet it would be a grave mistake to conclude that America lacks the capability to intervene with force in those Third World nations it deems security threats. U.S. rapidly deployable combat services are already formidable, and they are growing.

American preparations and plans for military intervention in the Gulf region impose major costs on the Western Alliance. To be sure, there are some benefits as well (e.g., U.S. improvements to the rapid-deployment forces also improve the capability to reinforce Europe in a crisis). Most of the forces designated for U.S. Central Command missions in Southwest Asia would be drawn from those already committed to the reinforcement of NATO, though not from U.S. forces already deployed in Europe. In theory, Europe would have first priority for U.S. reinforcements in the event of simultaneous crises in the Gulf and Europe; but theory would be of little use in the event that U.S. forces were dispatched to Southwest Asia in response to a conflict which later escalated to involve Europe. U.S. airlift capacity would be virtually used up by a large-scale intervention to the distant Gulf; ground force reinforcements for NATO would be cut by a third. Combat service support forces available to NATO would be reduced by up to 70,000 men. One military analyst has noted that "committing the entire pool of rapidly deployable forces to South Asia could undercut later U.S. reinforcements to Europe significantly, not only by absorbing units that might otherwise be deployed to Europe directly but by draining mobility assets in transferring these forces to, and sustaining them in, the Gulf region."[24] A study by the Congressional Budget Office argued that the cost to NATO Europe of "compensating" for the U.S. forces that might be diverted to the Gulf region would be as high as U.S. $40 billion over five years. That would require an additional three to four per cent annual increase in real defence expenditures by the non-U.S. allies as the financial cost of supporting the reassertion of U.S. power in Southwest Asia: America's is not an empire on the cheap.

The political cost of an intervention could be immeasurably greater. As the Gulf war of Iraq's Saddam Hussein and Iran's Ayatollah Khomeini dragged into the second half of the 1980s, the risks of an internationalization of the conflict began to expand as the superpowers, half in concert and half in competition, began to deepen their involvement. The ostensible interest they were defending was the need to protect the right of free international navigation through the waters of the Gulf and the Straits of Hormuz in the face of the "tanker war" that had sent about 250 ships to the bottom between 1984 and 1987. The tanker war was begun by Iraq and its Gulf allies in a desperate attempt to broaden the conflict and bring it to an end by threatening the oil supplies of the great powers. But Gulf oil, though vital in the long run to the industrialized world, remained in plentiful supply throughout the course of the Iran-Iraq conflict, and substantial excess productive capacity outside the Gulf provided room for the powers to manoeuvre diplomatically. Then in late 1986 Iraq's ally, Kuwait, worked out an agreement with Moscow to have three Kuwaiti tankers leased to the U.S.S.R and protected under the Soviet flag—i.e., "reflagged." The U.S., which had turned down a similar bid, promptly agreed to place the Stars and Stripes on eleven Kuwaiti-owned tankers and to provide air and naval cover. Thus commenced a major U.S. buildup in the Gulf and the Indian Ocean, directed at both Iran and the Soviet Union. The spectre of a Soviet-dominated Gulf, used so adroitly by Kuwait in playing off the two superpowers, rattled windows in the White House. "Once we knew that the Kuwaitis were negotiating with the Soviets, it sped up the process tremendously and we said, "Let's do it all," said one administration official. "We didn't want the Soviets coming into the gulf en masse."[25] If the U.S. didn't respond to Kuwait, warned Defence Secretary Weinberger, "then you are creating a vacuum and the Soviets will be very quick to rush into that." This logic produced some bizarre decisions. The deadly (allegedly accidental) Iraqi air attack on the American frigate *Stark* in May 1987 was used by the Reagan administration as a pretext for beginning an intervention on behalf of, not the Iranians, but a *de facto* U.S.-Kuwait-Iraq alliance. By aligning itself with the fortunes of the Iraqi side, the United States (which had sold arms to Iran a year earlier) risked losing whatever credibility it still had as a potential mediator. Worse still, the internationalization of the war had the potential to turn the Gulf into a cockpit of Soviet-American rivalry, and it was that prospect, much more than concern for short-term oil supplies, that bothered the governments of Western Europe. The Europeans did not want an escalating naval buildup in the Gulf, for that would increase the risks of war and might leave the superpowers in control of access to its resources.

There were strong domestic political pressures on the Reagan White House to drag the allies—including Japan—into some type of multilateral involvement and burden-sharing in the Gulf. The U.S. Senate overwhelmingly opposed the risky reflagging operations of the navy unless Britain, France (each of whom had small naval forces in the Gulf), and other allies provided warships and air cover: why shouldn't the Europeans and Japanese, who were more dependent on Gulf oil than the U.S., share the risks of protecting free navigation and access to the resource? As a precondition for Congressional support, the NATO allies must back American action in the Gulf. "European allies must understand," one American senator exclaimed shortly after the *Stark* attack, "that the United States alone cannot defend the Persian Gulf indefinitely. It is time we made some arrangements for a West German, French, and British naval presence in the Persian Gulf so the United States does not have to bear the entire burden." But the Europeans were more interested in moderating U.S. belligerence and in using diplomacy in place of gunboats to bring the war to an end, and thus acting on the basis of individual national decisions rather than through NATO. Initially, they resisted most of the American pressure. Eventually, in the interest of their relationships with Washington, they began to make concessions. The French and British did dispatch additional naval forces to the region. They were later joined by Belgium, the Netherlands, and Italy. In spite of this support the European allies vetoed all proposals to turn the Gulf crisis into a test of NATO's solidarity or to link it to burden-sharing debates within the Alliance. In doing so, they risked incurring the wrath of U.S. public opinion in the event of a serious escalation of the Gulf conflict, and they also risked losing what leverage they had had to shape the course of American policy. The oil resources of the Gulf were a vital national long-term interest for every member of NATO, yet it was clear that the Alliance could not act collectively to defend that interest. It was also clear that a major crisis in the Gulf could make the Libyan affair look like a schoolyard row; indeed, it could destroy NATO altogether.

## The Power to Deny

European reluctance to support U.S. foreign policy goals in the Persian Gulf was rooted less in short-run concern over world oil supply than in fundamental disagreements over the new cold war assumptions of postdetente America. Foremost among these was a basic difference about the nature of communism and the implications of American foreign policy for Europe's relations with the U.S.S.R. and the eastern bloc. The governments of NATO Europe objected to the unreconstructed anticommunism that animated U.S. policy around the globe after the invasion of Afghanistan, and they protested Washington's habit of linking East-West relations in Europe to, say, events in Central America or the Gulf. If Nicaragua got a cold, must the Germans freeze? To say the least, there was no consensus in NATO that western interests in the Third World were really under a Soviet-sponsored attack; nor could the allies agree that American, French, and British forces for power projection or intervention in areas such as the Gulf were inferior to those of the Soviets. In fact, most of the allies would agree that U.S. power projection capabilities "far exceed those of the Soviet Union,"[26] especially if we compare the two powers' worldwide alliances and bases, seapower, airlift forces, and so on. U.S. and allied perspectives on out-of-area military interventions are, however, so at odds that it is evident NATO cannot function as an alliance in this field: in effect, the allies exercise a kind of veto power over out-of-area actions, and in practice this means that the U.S. is unable to organize the collective resources of the West in support of its hegemonic objectives in the Third World, particularly in the Middle East and the Gulf where the European states retain important economic and political interests.

The manifest inability of the United States to mobilize Canada, Japan, and the states of NATO Europe behind its diplomatic and military actions in the Third World reminds us of the limits of American power and of the pervasive role of national interests in coalition politics. Though they depend on U.S. security guarantees and must frequently defer to Washington on many issues, Canada and the European allies have been able to moderate some of the worst excesses in American policy; working in the Alliance with like-minded states, smaller powers such as Canada can gain a leverage over U.S. diplomacy and strategy which they could never hope to achieve acting on their own. Left-wing critics of NATO in Canada and Europe, exaggerating the extent of allied dependence on the U.S., ought to pay more attention to the American Right: the argument made by U.S. neoconservatives is that the Alliance acts as a brake on global unilateralism, a check on the unrestrained use of America's power.

Even on crucial East-West issues the allies may have enough power to frustrate Washington. Soon after taking office in 1981, the Reagan administration sought to mobilize the NATO allies behind a policy of economic sanctions against the Soviet Union. The stated objective of the U.S. policy was to force Moscow to alter its course in Afghanistan and Poland, but prominent officials in the American government were on the record as favouring economic sanctions—collective sanctions by all western states—against the U.S.S.R. in the hope that this would produce internal changes in the Soviet *system*. Through the Coordinating Committee for Multinational Export Controls, the United States and its allies have for many years applied security controls to certain strategic exports, such as technology that could advance weapons development, but in 1981-1982 the U.S. sought to restrict a broad category of industrial goods and technology deemed not sensitive by Canada and the Europeans.

Moreover, it tried to obtain European compliance with its sanctions through the extraterritorial application of U.S. domestic law to the overseas subsidiaries of American multinationals. The target of these unilateral steps was Europe's commercial participation in the construction of the 4500-kilometre Soviet natural gas pipeline from Siberia to West Germany—a project opposed by the Reagan administration for two reasons: first, to deny the Soviets hard currency, and second, to stop Europe from becoming dependent on supplies of Soviet gas. The Europeans (supported by Canada) bitterly objected to the use of extraterritorial legal powers as an attack on their sovereignty and ordered their firms not to comply with the U.S. measures. NATO, a divided house, adopted the position it typically takes on such controversies: each of the allies would act according to its own situation and laws. Where there is no collective interest national interest reigns. By late 1982 it was clear that the United States had badly damaged its relations with Paris, Bonn, Rome, and London on the pipeline issue, and President Reagan, proclaiming another victory, dropped the sanctions.

A further example of allied veto power over U.S. strategic decision making can be drawn from NATO's Southern Region, the five member states from the Mediterranean area—Portugal, Spain, Italy, Greece, and Turkey (France is not designated a Mediterranean power here). The Southern Region states are linked together militarily through a large number of U.S. bases and associated installations, including sophisticated communications and intelligence-gathering activities, that are under an American command structure. While most of these facilities are associated with NATO commands, they have nearly all been established since the late 1940s through bilateral defence agreements between the United States and the individual host countries. At issue, especially in Spain, Greece, and Turkey, have been the rights and conditions attached to the base use agreements struck between the U.S. and its Mediterranean allies, whose leaders have well understood the significance of the bases to America's strategic position in the world. American military bases are a potent source of popular opposition to the U.S. and NATO throughout the Mediterranean region, yet host governments of every ideological stripe have found them to be a most useful bargaining chip in negotiating with Washington for generous security assistance and political concessions. Unlike Thatcher's docile Britain, the NATO states of the Mediterranean attach strict conditions to the use of their territory by U.S. forces; in some instances they have denied it altogether. A 1986 Congressional report on the Southern flank pointed out that:

> It is important to understand that a host country does not, as a rule, waive its sovereignty over installations and facilities that it has permitted the United States to establish and utilize within its territorial boundaries—although it is a common practice to refer to an overseas base used by the United States as an "American base" or a "U.S. installation". Rather, host countries grant operating rights through specific base use agreements that are usually subject to conditions spelled out in associated implementing agreements . . . It is legally permissible for a host nation to object to the use of military facilities on its soil by the United States for military purposes not authorized by specific governing agreements.[27]

Much as it was for the older British empire, control of the Mediterranean is a vital strategic interest of the United States and its allies. Virtually by definition, the great power or coalition that commands the gates to the Mediterranean—Gibraltar, Suez, the Turkish Straits—can control Europe's short route to the Persian Gulf and beyond, project its power in the Middle East and North Africa, and challenge Soviet naval forces operating from the Black Sea. Since 1947, when the Truman administration began to move American economic and military assistance into Greece and Turkey to fill the vacuum left by the collapse of British power, the U.S. has enjoyed a position of hegemony in the Mediterranean part of its post-1945 role as the world's dominant sea power. This hegemony is based on military power and the provision of security assistance to the regional states. Thus the sprawling complex of U.S. and NATO air and naval bases, intelligence facilities and communications installations across the northern Mediterranean, together with the mobility of the Sixth Fleet, supplies the real infrastructure of America's predominance in the region. However, since the mid-1970s American hegemony in the Mediterranean has been challenged on two fronts: from the buildup of the rival Soviet Mediterranean fleet, the Fifth Escadra, as a lever of influence with states such as Libya, Syria, and Egypt; and from America's allies, who began to chip away at U.S. access to its network of Mediterranean bases and installations.

It is mostly the actions of the U.S. itself that have caused the latter political challenge and the erosion of its control. Its pro-Israeli policy, its interference in Greece's domestic affairs, its "tilt" toward Turkey over Cyprus and the disputed air space of the Aegean, its reckless disregard of Italian sovereignty over the *Achille Lauro* affair, and the bombing of Libya—these have been highly unpopular among the five Mediterranean NATO states; their response has been to deny the U.S. the use of their bases, territory, and airspace for unilateral military acts.

During the 1973 Arab-Israeli war, Greece, Turkey, and Italy adopted neutral stances and refused to allow the use of bases in their countries by the United States for the resupply of Israel. Spain, which had important U.S. bases on its territory but was not at the time in NATO, also declared its neutrality and with-held diplomatic clearances for these installations to be used in the American military airlift to Israel. Though Spain became NATO's sixteenth member in 1982, there has remained a very significant domestic opposition to the American-operated bases, to NATO, and to the foreign policy of the United States: traditional Spanish isolationism, a deep-seated hostility toward military alliances, and anti-Americanism combined in a powerful peace and anti-NATO movement that is well to the left of the ruling Socialist party. But the Americans, responding to rapid growth of Soviet military capabilities worldwide, insisted that Spain become fully integrated in the Western Alliance and that the U.S. retain unrestricted control over its naval and air bases at Cadiz, near Gibralter, and its large air bases at Torrejon, near Madrid, and at Zarazoga. In March 1986, Socialist Prime Minister Felipe Gonzalez (like Ed Broadbent, a closet supporter of the NATO Alliance) put a referendum to the Spanish people that was not a simple vote for or against membership in NATO, but whether Spain should stay in the Alliance on the basis of certain conditions that were inserted by the government. The three conditions on Spain's decision to remain in NATO, were that 1) it would not be part of the integrated military structure of the Alliance; 2) nuclear weapons would continue to be prohibited on

Spanish territory; and 3) the U.S. military presence in Spain would be progressively reduced. These reflected the political situation in Spain, and the referendum carried. One month later, Spain turned down overflight privileges for the F-111s on their way from Britain to bomb Libya, and it is plain that no Spanish government would risk allowing the United States to strike at out-of-area targets or to intervene in another MidEast or Gulf conflict from Spanish bases. Membership in NATO gives Madrid a stronger position to demand that military operations from Spain conform strictly with the purposes of the Alliance. Spanish national interest acts as a constraint on American unilateralism.

The Eastern Mediterranean and the Turkish Straits would be a vital *point d'appui* or fulcrum of any military conflict between the superpowers. In the earliest stages of a conflict both powers would attempt to secure control of the straits and command of the Mediterranean itself. Dominance of the Mediterranean theatre would be essential to the U.S. objective of overall military supremacy in the opening of a war with Russia. Turkey's vital geographic location and possession of the straits—in accordance with the 1936 Montreux convention—allow it to deny transit to Russian military forces; and it is also well-positioned to complicate Soviet air operations in the Middle East.

Since 1952, the United States has maintained a series of intelligence-gathering installations in Turkey that collect data on Soviet space, missile and military force and systems development, research, operations, and strategic nuclear activities. At Sinop, on the Black Sea coast in north-central Turkey, the National Security Agency of the United States keeps secret watch on Soviet missile-testing, air, and naval activity in the Black Sea, and domestic Soviet communications, while the Diyarbahir Air Station in southeast Turkey monitors Soviet military movements through long-range radar. Turkey also hosts a major tactical fighter base for the U.S. Air Force and plays a key role in NATO's Airborne Early Warning Force; and it maintains the second largest military force of the NATO powers. Such is its strategic importance that successive Turkish governments have been able to extract large financial and military concessions through bilateral agreements with Washington; when the U.S. Congress imposed an arms embargo in reaction to the 1974

Turkish invasion of Cyprus, the Turks took control of all military bases and installations in Turkey used by the United States. This forced the closure of the major intelligence facilities used by the U.S. in Turkey until President Carter succeeded in having the Turkish arms embargo lifted in 1978. In 1980, after much bargaining, the two countries signed a Defence and Economic Co-operation Agreement (DECA), a "synthesis of years of negotiation aimed at achieving a defence agreement that permits effective U.S. use of Turkish military installations while providing assurances to Turkey that these facilities will not be used for missions it is not prepared to support."[28] The agreement specifically limits U.S.-Turkish defence co-operation to "obligations arising out of the North Atlantic Treaty"; there would be little support in Turkey, NATO's only Moslem country, for the use of its territory and bases for American military operations in the Middle East or the Gulf (in 1983 Turkey refused to approve transit of U.S. military equipment and supplies to American forces then in Lebanon).

In 1981, Andreas Papandreou's nationalist movement swept to power in Greece on a platform of radical change in Greek foreign policy. Like many other Greeks, Papandreou was passionately anti-American because of U.S. involvement in the 1967 coup that installed a military junta in Athens; because Washington supported the junta while it was in power; and because of the failure of the United States and NATO to prevent the Turkish invasion of Cyprus in 1974. Papandreou had pledged to remove all U.S. military bases from Greece and to withdraw the nation from NATO (after the Cyprus affair Greece had removed its armed forces from NATO's integrated military structure; Greece rejoined the military wing of NATO in 1980). Greece provides the U.S. and NATO with four large bases and facilities on the mainland and on Crete, of which the Hellenikon Air Base near Athens and the Souda Bay naval complex on the northwest side of Crete and two large intelligence and communications sites are the most important. As of 1986-87, Greece received U.S. $343 million in military credits and aid for hosting these agencies of American hegemony.

In 1983, Athens negotiated a five-year bases agreement with Washington. Greece depicted it as notice to the U.S. to leave, but the Americans portrayed it as an agreement to keep the bases. Both were negotiating positions. If Greece withdrew from NATO or evicted the American bases and personnel, it would lose most of its leverage over Washington as well as its vehicle for restraining Turkey's ambitions. American military assistance to Greece and Turkey is informally fixed at a 7:10 ratio, but if Greece left the Alliance the U.S. would almost certainly expand Turkey's military role to offset the loss of Greek bases such as Souda Bay. Greece's departure from NATO might thus facilitate Turkish militarism and expansionism. Greece outside NATO and without U.S. bases might have greater internal autonomy, but it would also be exposed to a predatory Turkey and cut off from further American military assistance. Such developments would displease the U.S.-trained Greek military, and the Americans have used the Turkish threat to remind Athens of that fact. Thus it would seem to be in Greece's national interests to remain in the Alliance and to keep the U.S. connection, just as it is in the American interest to have a Papandreou in power in Greece—"a left-winger who accepts the U.S. bases, and thus makes American hegemony in Western Europe appear unchallengeable."[29] But as in Spain and Turkey, the United States has little chance of using its Greek military bases for purposes beyond those of the NATO Alliance. Greece is pro-Arab in its foreign policy and successive governments have denied the use of its territory to facilitate U.S. resupply operations to Israel and Lebanon.

There is little the United States can do but accept these political constraints. Notwithstanding its worldwide power and its dominance within NATO, America remains dependent on its allies. A multilateral—or coalition—strategy is a necessity; unilateralism is a fiction of ideology that bears little resemblance to the world in which U.S. policy makers must choose and act. They must think of their alliances as Pericles warned the Athenians they must shoulder the burdens of empire: "Your empire is now like a tyranny: it may have been wrong to take it; it is certainly dangerous to let it go." The emphasis on necessity rather than choice is well-placed. The United States has allies because it needs them; it cannot act in detachment from the changing alignments of world politics, nor can any other power. Martin Wight argued in *Power Politics* that "no power is able to make its policy wholly without reliance on some other powers, even if it relies only on their neutrality. Dominant powers like Napoleonic France or Nazi Germany acted with much arbitrariness and contempt for their allies, but always took a certain trouble to ensure either a servile compliance or non-interference. The United States at the beginning of her history, predominant on a distant continent, could repudiate European entanglements; but when there was a danger of European intervention in South America she accepted an entente with Britain as the basis of the Monroe Doctrine."[30] In spite of a diplomatic tradition to which all alliances were anathema, alliances with Europe especially so,[31] the United States today is a world power enmeshed in a security system based on alliances. This is at once a source of America's strength as well as a profound limiting force on the unilateral exercise of its power.

# Where to Now?

Before the last war, the spectre haunting Canadian policy-makers was that the United States would remain aloof from British and French efforts to protect the peace against Nazi and Fascist aggression. Today the spectre is that the United States may feel it necessary to pursue policies inside our coalition which the other members cannot wholeheartedly follow; or that inadequate cooperation from the other members may discourage American effort and leadership to the point where Washington may decide to "go it alone." Any Canadian government is bound to do what it can to exorcise these dangers; and this may mean at times expressing its own views forthrightly in London or Paris or, above all, in Washington, where the center of power now lies. This is the first principle of Canadian diplomacy. It is founded on the inescapable fact that no country in the world has less chance of isolating itself from the effect of American policies and decisions than Canada. If Washington "went it alone," where would Ottawa go?[1]

Lester Pearson, 1951

## Old Problems, New Directions

The cover of the 1987 white paper on defence displays a polar projection of the world with a virginal white Canada shining like a beacon amidst the rest of the countries of the world coloured green—with envy, no doubt. The radiance of the Canadian image shines away from the rest of the world, across the United States toward the lower left corner of the cover where it forms a reflection of the Canadian Arctic. The image is striking and its message as clear as the contents of the paper are subtle.

Canada's armed forces will stay close to home. This theme is emphasized by Prime Minister Mulroney who writes in his introduction to the white paper that: "Canada must look to itself to safeguard its sovereignty and pursue its own interests. Only we as a nation should decide what must be done to protect our shores, our waters, and our airspace. This White Paper, therefore, takes as its first priority the protection and furtherance of Canada's sovereignty as a nation." Independence and self-interest have become the order of the day.

After three years and four defence ministers, the Mulroney government produced Canada's first defence white paper in sixteen years. Somewhat ironically, given the paper's emphasis on a new strategic reality, the Tory defence proposals closely resemble those of the Trudeau government outlined in the 1971 policy document, "Defence for the 70s." The Trudeau white paper emphasized the role that the armed forces would play in defending the realm. Once again, under the current proposals the Canadian armed forces will be devoted to the home front. Stressing the need for the military to protect Canadian sovereignty and echoing Trudeau's refrain that Canada is a "three-ocean country," the defence policy outlined in the most recent white paper, "Challenge and Commitment," suggests a realignment of Canadian defence priorities, northward and westward. Robert Fowler, the assistant deputy minister responsible for policy in the Department of National Defence, provided the following summary of the white paper:

> I think if you take the sum total of everything that's in that white paper I think it's fair to say that the centre of gravity of Canadian defence policy has shifted westwards and slightly northwards. I think you'll see more of that in the changing shape of the navy, the reserves, the development of an effective Canadian defence capacity, vital point defence etc . . . I don't think we are in any way abandoning Europe. I think there's no doubt that both our land and our air commitments are going to be made more credible, enhanced and more credible. Equally however, there's no doubt that there is a slight Canada firstism—which I will insist is very different than isolationism—to the basic thrust of the paper.[2]

The "Canada firstism" of the Mulroney government's defence proposals is partly a response to the shifting strategic priorities of the superpowers, partly designed as a political tactic to win support for higher levels of defence spending, and partly a sop to the anti-European sentiment that has grown in this country. The implementation of the proposals, however, will be first and foremost a matter of dollars and it is the shortage of these dollars that will force the government to make some hard choices from the military wish-list presented in the white paper.

The strategic rationale for the realignment of Canadian defence commitments rests on shifting strategies in the Soviet Union and the United States that have emphasized the Arctic and the Pacific. Combined with the widely shared view within the Canadian military that it was the "navy's turn," to be re-equipped, the white paper outlines a significant shift of capital resources to the navy and especially to the construction of a fleet of nuclear-powered submarines to patrol Canada's three oceans. The largest expenditure will be for these new submarines which are primarily a response to growing concern about superpower activities under the icepack. In the words of the white paper, the Arctic is now prime territory and "Canadians cannot ignore that what was once a buffer could become a battleground." In subsequent appearances before the House of Commons Committee on National Defence, Defence Minister Perrin Beatty maintained that the submarines were not selected solely for the Arctic. Indeed, they were not: NATO wants them for duty in the Atlantic. It is obvious, however, that it is primarily their ability to travel under the icepack that makes nuclear-powered submarines so desirable. As discussed in chapter Two, the strategic rationale for nuclear submarines is highly suspect. It is unlikely that the Soviets have been or will become dependent on the Canadian Arctic. It is also unlikely that Canadian submarine patrols in the area would be able to detect American or Soviet submarines even if they were there. Finally, the net effect of the deployment of Canadian submarines in the Arctic would be to make them mere appendages of American vessels in the region. The governing strategic guidelines will be made in Washington, not Ottawa. Faced with the potential for Soviet threats to trans-atlantic shipping, Canadians would make a more cost-effective contribution to collective defence by supporting a mixed fleet of surface vessels and new generation diesel submarines that would not only enhance coastal security but would also serve the collective interests of the Alliance by offering a better protection of the sea lanes of communications. Not incidentally, this could also serve to raise the nuclear threshold by enhancing the Alliance's ability to sustain its conventional military capabilities.

The emphasis on territorial defence is not based solely on strategic assessments. It is also based on a premise that local defence will be more politically palatable and thus create and maintain popular support for higher levels of defence spending. This explains why the government has sought to justify such high-priced items as the acquisition of nuclear-powered submarines on sovereignty as well as security grounds. By mixing the motives of sovereignty protection and strategic deterrence, the government hopes to create a consensus by playing to the fears of anti-Sovietism and anti-Americanism by allegedly freeing the Canadian Arctic from the grasp of both. The political rationale responds to the demands that neutralists and isolationists have been making for some time, that Canada should cut its military commitments to Europe and concentrate its resources on the defence of the North American continent. Continentalist options were rejected in the immediate postwar period because of their profound implications for Canada's sovereignty and political independence, given its geography and its strategic position for the United States. But today, continentalism is once again in vogue in commercial as well as in security policy, although the dangers inherent in such an orientation remain. The emphasis given to the protection of Canadian sovereignty in the white paper assumes that activities designed for sovereignty protection will necessarily complement those designed for security, but as Charles Doran notes: "Sovereignty and security are not identical. Indeed, the search for the former may lead to the decline of the latter."[3]

When the Trudeau government in the late 1960s returned Canadian forces from Europe to meet threats to internal security and coastal sovereignty, the policy was criticized by historian Jack Granatstein who in 1971 wrote:

Sovereignty is a fraud, a patently phony defence priority. There is no physical threat to our sovereignty in the north. There is no enemy there against which our forces can operate. There is simply no justification whatsoever for using troops in this role that only political weapons, firm leadership, and united public opinion can handle. The public is being gulled in a very skilful fashion. Skilful, because sovereignty sounds good today, attuned as we are to the neo-nationalism of our press, academics, and young people.[4]

In practice, Trudeau's policy seriously weakened Canada's position within NATO, forcing him to make subsequent gestures to the Europeans in a bid for their support for Canadian economic and diplomatic initiatives. Trudeau also recognized that military force was an inappropriate response to allies challenging Canadian sovereignty claims in the Arctic. Rather than call out the forces he had recalled from Europe in response to the voyage of the *Manhattan* in 1969, the Trudeau government adopted the Arctic Waters Pollution Prevention Act and through this functional measure secured legal support for Canada's jurisdictional claims in the region. The current emphasis on military measures to meet challenges to Canadian sovereignty overlooks this earlier experience and the essentially political and commercial character of these challenges. A military response is a blunt instrument not well-suited for dealing with allies encroaching on our sovereign territory.

Politics aside, the emphasis on national interests, narrowly defined, is also indicative of a growing resentment among Canadians toward the commitment of Canadian forces to the forward defence of Europe. Such isolationist sentiments are not unique to Canada but suggestive of a disturbing go-it-alone tendency that is apparent throughout the Western Alliance. The white paper's discussion of sovereignty interests and territorial defence does not argue that these should replace Canada's commitment to the defence of western interests through NATO. The implication is that we can have it all. The reality is that we must make choices. Priorities must be set in the formulation of defence policy.

The economic reality in which defence policy must be implemented will force the government to make some hard choices.

Some have apparently already been made. Financial resources to support defence programs have been in short supply. The first three years of the Mulroney government showed no significant deviation from the politics of restraint that devastated the Canadian armed forces during Trudeau's tenure as prime minister. The political and economic realities that will govern future defence spending in this country make it imperative for the government to sort out its defence priorities before it gets locked into expensive programs that will do little to enhance Canadian security, do even less to ensure sovereignty and imply that Canada will withdraw even further from its commitment to NATO. A Canadian defence policy that seeks to assert sovereignty claims against American challenges through military means will not only be unsuccessful, but will also leave scarce funds remaining with which to meet Canada's main security requirements. As a result of the excessive concentration of expenditure on local defence as outlined in the white paper, the government has already curtailed a significant (although, with current levels of funding, militarily risky) commitment to Norway. While the government offered some sound strategic justifications in cancelling the Canadian commitment to send the CAST brigade to Norway in times of crisis, the rationale of insufficient material support is specious when the government proposes to pour billions of dollars into a submarine fleet and undertakes a commitment to send the brigade to central Europe, raising the same logistical, support, and sustainment problems that were used to dismiss the commitment to Norway. It is not difficult to see why the paper and the political arguments mounted in its defence may lead some to conclude that it portends an eventual withdrawal of Canadian forces from Europe. Unless the political will is there, the funds will not be available.

## The Allure of Neutralism

Canada needs NATO more than NATO needs Canada. The North Atlantic Alliance would not collapse if Canada withdrew. It would be weaker, politically and militarily, and the member states may be even more prone to the unilateralism that is already creeping into policy debates throughout the Alliance. The greater loss would, however, be for Canada. Its security would be impaired. More importantly, it would lose a vital political balance to its bilateral relationship with the United States. Canada, freed from its position within the Alliance, would become even more subservient to American strategic designs than it is already. This is a view widely shared among advocates of neutrality, such as journalist Gwynne Dyer, who admits that a neutral Canada would need to reassure the Americans that they would not be threatened by the lack of Canadian action. It has become quite clear, however, that the United States is not easily "reassured" when its security is at stake. Making the Americans feel secure is an expensive proposition. It is also likely to lead Canada into supporting activities that it would otherwise wish to avoid such as the forward deployment of offensive systems in the Arctic, increases in the resources devoted to active air defences and an increase in the amount of military activity in waters adjacent to the Canada. The Alliance has deflected much of this activity across the Atlantic. Once outside NATO, Canada would become militarily more significant for the Americans.

Neutralists commonly lament Canada's inability to conduct a more progressive foreign policy and blame this lack of success on our involvement in NATO. Frequently this implies a critique of Canadian support for American foreign policy. Yet it is nowhere a requirement of the Alliance that a member country support the foreign policy of any other member state. The lack of opposition to American foreign policies is more a question of lack of political will or, in some cases, an agreement-in-principle with American objectives, than a result of Canada's Alliance membership. Freed of our Alliance commitments, Canadian governments may be no more or less inclined to criticize American policies than they have been in the past. More importantly, there is no compelling evidence to indicate that Canada would be more successful in influencing the United States or any other state once it withdrew from the Alliance. As Prime Minister Trudeau discovered at the time of his peace intitiative, influence outside the Alliance on East-West questions was at least in part a result of the fact that we were allied, not neutral.

Membership in the Alliance also provides Canada with an otherwise unavailable opportunity to participate in East-West negotiations of fundamental importance. The failure of superpower negotiations to secure meaningful strategic arms control has temporarily at least given way to an agreement to eliminate medium-range missiles from Europe and also encouraged potentially more useful negotiations on confidence-building measures and other measures for reducing the East-West confrontation in Europe. Canadians retain a strong interest in arms control, despite their limited success. The opportunities for Canadian input are, however, limited and revolve principally around our NATO membership. The opportunities for productive arms control may grow more important as the Soviet Union under Mikhail Gorbachev's leadership intensifies its efforts to secure a more permanent settlement of the military and political balance in central Europe. If our commitment to arms control means anything, Canada needs to be involved in the various negotiations underway in Europe. But its presence is only possible if we remain a full-fledged member of the Alliance and retain forces in Europe. As a neutral state we would lose not only influence but our seat. To be frank, Canadians must admit that their opportunities for influencing matters such as Soviet-American arms control negotiations inside or outside the Alliance are limited. But influence has not been the hallmark of neutral states either. Neutral states are not at the forefront of East-West relations except when it comes to hosting summits. This might be a sound tourist policy but it makes little sense as a basis of one's security policy.

Other concerns about the restraints of our Alliance commitments have also been raised. The New Democrats argue, in their defence proposals, that once out of NATO they would be more active in supporting peacekeeping around the globe. Yet where is the peacekeeping mission that Canada has not supported? Peacekeeping operations have been fully consistent with Canada's Alliance objectives, which is one reason why this country has been such a consistently active supporter of these operations. Those who favour neutrality for Canada argue that withdrawal from NATO will suddenly and mysteriously unleash an as yet hidden element in Canadian foreign policy that is more just, less bellicose and more effective in bringing peace and prosperity to the far corners of the world. Why would this be an inevitable result of a declaration of Canadian neutrality? Why would a neutral Canada be more progressive? Most neutrals are no more progressive than Canada. Indeed, if anything they tend to be more isolated from the more important aspects of international politics. "Neutrals are states without an active foreign policy at all," wrote Martin Wight, "their hope is to lie low and escape notice."

## Do We Need NATO?

The emphasis on local defence may prove to be politically popular in Canada. As discussed in chapters Five and Six, it is an idea that is gaining popularity in other parts of the Alliance. These developments raise some fundamental questions about the future of the Alliance and Canadian security policy. Should territorial defence be Canada's prime security mandate? Is it worth risking Canada's support for NATO to send submarines under the Arctic ice? Is this country willing to confine ourselves to a continentalist defence policy? Have Canadian interests changed to such an extent that we can safely reject the solutions of the late 1940s? Most importantly, have the threats to peace that led to the creation of NATO in 1949 disappeared?

Frequently, one encounters comments that support for NATO is like living in the past as if nothing forty years old could still be relevant in our world of constant change. Yet, Canadian interests are not as fluid as these comments would suggest. Neither are the patterns of international politics. The North Atlantic Treaty Organization was formed in response to the threat that the Soviet Union posed to the unstable political situation that existed in Western Europe in the late 1940s. Since that time Canadians, along with their allies, have benefitted from a stable peace in Europe. The collective armed forces of NATO members and the demonstrated commitment of mutual support restored the balance of power in Europe and deterred the Russians from upsetting this stable peace. The stability that NATO has brought to Western Europe has over time reduced (although probably not eliminated) the Russian interest in securing military control over the continent. As important, the security and stability that NATO provides makes it possible to pursue a mutually advantageous relationship with the Soviet Union.

Western Europe without NATO and without American and Canadian involvement would be less secure and less stable than it is today and the risks of war would be much greater. NATO was designed to serve many different objectives. Among the most important of these was to contain the militant European nationalism that had dragged Canada and the rest of the world into two devastating wars in this century. The postwar alliance system has had considerable success in containing these tendencies on the European continent over the past forty years by reassuring all member states that their security needs were being met. Its very success in responding to the potential resurgence of German nationalism, for example, makes it easy to forget the important role that the Alliance has played in this area. The disintegration of the Alliance is as likely, indeed more likely, to foster the historical suspicions and animosities and increase the prospects for Soviet intervention than a continuation of the status quo. By reassuring the West, NATO has also provided a degree of reassurance to the East. While the Russians might prefer a European order in which they were dominant, some European order is better than none at all.

There is much speculation in Canada and throughout the West about the new wave of thinking that has infected the Soviet Union since Mikhail Gorbachev came to power and its implications for East-West relations. It is evident that many in the West see in Gorbachev's approach to foreign policy an opportunity to restructure the hostile bipolar system that has dominated much of international politics since the end of the Second World War. It is too early to determine whether Gorbachev will succeed in his plans to reform Soviet domestic and foreign policy. It is clear, however, that until there is a fundamental change in Soviet foreign policy, the need for NATO will remain. Soviet foreign policy is still conditioned more by its historic interests and great power status than by ideology or the idiosyncracies of its leaders. Russian expansion has been more the result of opportunism than ideological zeal but like all great powers they have displayed a persistent willingness to use force when their security interests have been threatened. Whatever changes Gorbachev is able to implement, the continuity of Russian interests and its position as a great power will remain unchanged. Security will continue to be protected by the largest military force in the world and like all great powers the Soviet Union is unlikely to respect weaker states. The West will need to maintain cohesion to support the weak and deter the strong. This cohesion is also necessary, however, to support what former West German Chancellor Helmut Schmidt calls the "double-track philosophy," that being "to make whatever effort is necessary to feel secure against Russian pressure or blackmail or attack, and, with that security as a foundation, to co-operate with them."[5] NATO helps to guarantee the security that the West requires to explore and expand the opportunities for co-operation that Gorbachev's Russia may provide. It is important to remember the foundation of security that will make an easing of tensions possible.

Another objective in pursuing a transatlantic alliance for Canadians was to limit the adverse effects of American pressure as the superpower pursued its cold war politics with the Soviet Union. The government's proposals to reorient Canadian defence policy to focus more on territorial defence collide with a similar interest emerging in the United States. Recent shifts in American strategy at both the nuclear and conventional level will have profound implications for Canadian security and sovereignty. In the past, as argued in chapter Two, bilateral co-operation for the purpose of continental defence has tended to distort Canadian defence priorities by involving the Canadian military in ancillary tasks for American strategic forces. It has also discouraged Canadians from comprehending a role for their armed forces that is not merely an appendage of the Pentagon. Yet supporting the white paper's proposals would lead us on a similar course. The next logical step for the government to meet the alleged security threats in the Arctic might be a bilateral arrangement with the American military. This is already being proposed by some who see it as a possible exchange for American guarantees of Canadian sovereignty. On purely strategic grounds, one must question the idea, given the potential for recent American strategies to threaten Canadian security interests. One must also acknowledge that if pursued, bilateral defence arrangements with the Americans make it more likely that the government will lose control over its defence policy. François de Rose, a French security analyst, has a few words of advice that are of relevance to Canada: "It would be the height of absurdity if the single-minded (not to say obsessive) pursuit of military independence were to lead to the loss of political independence and sovereignty."[6]

It is evident in reviewing the preceding chapters that Canadian defence policy cannot be discussed in isolation from developments in other parts of the world, and especially developments within the Western Alliance. It is also imperative to recall the events that initially led Canada into the Alliance. Canada's security commitments to Western Europe were not based on sentiment or pity for the war-devastated Europeans but on the realization that Europe would have to remain at peace if Canada were to prosper. A European war would be a Canadian war whether we wanted it or not. That fact became the foundation of Canada's defence policy throughout the postwar era. Canadian interests led Canada into NATO in 1949. Canadian interests have kept us there since. Pierre Trudeau realized this in the 1970s, just as Lester Pearson had in the 1940s. Although Canadian interests have expanded to include other states and other regions of the globe, Europe remains the centre stage for a few simple reasons. Canada's security rests on the peace and stability of the international order. A European balance remains of paramount importance in preserving this.

Why Canadian troops in Europe? This has become the central point of both isolationist and neutralist critiques of Canadian defence policy. The neutralists argue that Canadian forces, while virtually meaningless, do contribute to the ever-escalating arms race in central Europe that is leading us ever closer to Armageddon. Isolationists see these forces as a major drain on our defence capabilities; they want them returned to this country to look after matters closer to home. For the average Canadian there is the persistent question: why spend a billion dollars a year to keep forces in central Europe? Canadians have always faced a tension between commitments to NATO in Europe and commitments to continental defence. Many Canadians seem inclined to echo the Americans' refrain—the Europeans are now rich enough to look after their own defences. The rich Europeans should allow their poor Canadian cousins to bring their troops back home; as if it had been merely a matter of dollars all these years that kept Canadian and American forces in Europe. When the Alliance was established nearly forty years ago the allies were not satisfied with a paper commitment from Canada and the Americans. Subsequently Canadian and American forces were deployed in Europe to aid the Europeans and to make the North Americans' commitments explicit. Today those forces have taken on more political significance but they continue to reflect Canada's military commitment to support the European peace. A European war remains the most likely scenario in which Canadian forces would be engaged and by committing these forces beforehand Canada helps to support the European balance of power that reduces the likelihood of war on that continent. Even at the price of a billion dollars annually it is cheaper to pay for this stability than to suffer the costs of war.

## Summing Up

We have shown that Canada played an active role in the founding of NATO because security interests demanded a multilateral rather than bilateral framework. In what was a variant of the old idea of balancing American and European power in a North Atlantic triangle, the King and St. Laurent governments seized upon the concept of an Atlantic security pact as a way of deflecting American pressure for free trade and continental defence arrangements. As Lester Pearson noted in 1951 (see the prefatory quote to this chapter), Canadian interests were shaped as well by the fear of American unilateralism—a phenomenon discussed throughout this book—and the need to limit it through webs of interdependence and collective defence.

Today, however, unilateralism is on the rise in almost all of the NATO states. The sharp conflicts within the Alliance on strategy and diplomacy and the quick resort to unilateral rather than collective actions stem in part from economic tensions and the division of the world capitalist system into regional blocs, but ideological differences over the nature of the Soviet Union and the future of East-West relations are also behind many of the problems in the Alliance. While we do not share the perception, expressed in Canada's 1987 white paper, that the Soviets wish to divide and conquer NATO and encourage the U.S. and Canada to withdraw from Europe—something that would profoundly destabilize central Europe and threaten Moscow's vital interests

—we do think it is crucial for Canada to take a far stronger role within the Alliance as an advocate of a longer-term settlement of the conflict in Europe. That would challenge the U.S.S.R. and its allies to enter into reciprocal measures with the West that would embrace Canada's territorial and sovereignty concerns, especially in the Arctic. As an alternative to a very expensive effort in building up a military surveillance and control capability through nuclear-powered submarines, Canada should adopt the ideas of some arms control specialists and try to work for an Arctic security regime involving confidence-building measures that would limit and stabilize military activities in the North. As an active member of NATO, Canada's diplomats should be able to pursue such a policy most effectively multilaterally through the Alliance's councils.

This sort of approach would return Canada to the philosophy of the 1967 Harmel Report, which, it will be recalled, stressed the need for the Alliance to follow two tracks: deterrence and defence *plus* a policy of East-West detente. The two-track approach has come to be identified with arms control but the original objective of Harmel was less concerned with controlling arms than with a "just and lasting peaceful order in Europe." In the excitement of pushing ahead with arms control this longer-term objective should not be slighted lest it be derailed by the arms control process itself. In the last decade it has often seemed as though the U.S. and its allies have been on separate tracks, the former emphasizing a massive military buildup in the name of deterrence, the latter attempting to hold onto the idea of reducing cold war tensions via diplomacy. The Canadian white paper's underlying philosophy is given away in its primitive, cold war view of the Soviet threat, and there is precious little in the document that strengthens the Harmel second track.

The white paper is thus a rejection of the ideas that drew Canada into the Alliance in the late 1940s. Implicitly, Canada is turning its back on the old notion of building counterweights to enhance both security and political independence. Canadian military planners—full of ambivalence about NATO—are frantically trying to get on the North American bus, and their worst fear is that they will be left out of any role in continental strategic planning. To get the back seat on the bus they will gladly give up the rest of the world.

# Notes

## Introduction

1. Josef Joffe, "Europe's American Pacifier," *Foreign Policy* (Spring 1984).

## Chapter One

1. Frank Underhill, Canada and the Organization of Peace, cited in R.A. MacKay and E.B. Rogers, *Canada Looks Abroad*, Toronto: Oxford University Press, 1938. p. 269 and a review of James Minifie's Peacemaker or Powdermonkey, *International Journal*, Summer 1960. p. 250.
2. James Eayrs, *In Defence of Canada, Growing Up Allied*, Toronto: University of Toronto Press, 1980. p.30.
3. J. Bartlet Brebner, "A Changing North Atlantic Triangle," *International Journal*, Autumn 1948. p.314.
4. Cited in David Dilks, "The British View of Security," in Olav Riste, ed. *Western Security: The Formative Years*, New York: Columbia University Press, 1985. p.40.
5. Eayrs, op.cit. p.18.
6. Cited in Escott Reid, *Time of Fear and Hope*, Toronto: McClelland and Stewart, 1977. p.108-9.
7. Nicholas Tracy, *Canada's Foreign Policy Objectives and Canadian Security Agreements in the North*, Ottawa: ORAE Intramural Paper No. 8, 1980. p. 105.
8. Cited in Reid, op.cit. p.16.
9. D.V. LePan to L.B. Pearson, memorandum, "The North Atlantic Community," September 6, 1951. DEA, file 50105-40. Cited in Reid, op.cit., 1977. p.241.
10. Harald von Reikhoff, *NATO: Issues and Prospects*, Toronto: CIIA, 1967. p.109.
11. T.C. Davis cited in Eayrs, op.cit. p.325.
12. Cited in New York Times, April 2, 1952.
13. Cited in Eayrs, op.cit. p.224.
14. John Gellner, *The Defence of Canada: Requirements, Capabilities, and the National Will*, Toronto: Behind the Headlines, 1985. p.3.
15. Cited in Eayrs, op.cit. p.52.
16. Andrew Brewin, "Canada Within the North Atlantic Community," in *Debate on Defence*, Toronto: Ontario Woodsworth Memorial Foundation, 1960. p.10.

17. James Eayrs cited in Bruce Thordarson, *Trudeau and Foreign Policy*, Toronto: Oxford, 1972. p.22.
18. *Ibid*. p.140-1.
19. *Ibid*. p.141.
20. John Holmes, "The Dumbbell Won't Do," *Foreign Policy*, No. 49, 1983. p.5.
21. R.B. Byers, et.al., *Canada and Western Security, the Search for New Options*, Toronto: Atlantic Council of Canada, 1982. p.29.
22. Reid, op.cit. p.163.
23. "The Future Tasks of the Alliance: Report of the Council," *NATO Final Communiques, 1949-1970*, Brussels: NATO, 1971.
24. Henry Kissinger, *White House Years*, Boston: Little, Brown and Co., 1979. p.129.
25. Ulrich Strempel, "Bonn-Ottawa: Idyll Slightly Marred," *Aussenpolitik*, Volume 34 Number 3, 1983. p.228.
26. Dutch Defence Minister Jan Houwelingen Cited in *International Canada*, October/November 1984. p.20.
27. John Halstead, Behind the Headlines, 1983. p.13.
28. John Gellner, *North America and NATO*, Behind the Headlines, Volume 24, 1964. p.8.

## Chapter Two

1. Recounted in *Mike, The Memoirs of Lester B. Pearson, Volume II*, Toronto: University of Toronto, 1973. p. 75.
2. John Kirton, "Comments on the Green Paper," *Behind the Headlines*, Volume V and VI, 1985. p. 32.
3. Daniel Deudney, "Forging Missiles Into Spaceships," *World Policy Journal*, Spring 1985. p. 272.
4. E.P. Thompson, "Folly's Comet," in E.P. Thompson, ed., *Star Wars*, London: Penguin, 1985. p. 139.
5. David Watt, "Wishful thinking on a star," *The Times* (London), February 15, 1985.
6. James Schlesinger, "Rhetoric and Realities in the Star Wars Debate," *International Security*, Summer 1985. p. 5.
7. Douglas Ross, *Coping with Star Wars: Issues for Canada and the Alliance*, Ottawa: Canadian Centre for Arms Control and Disarmament, 1985. p. 9.
8. Colin Gray in a submission before the House of Commons Standing Committee on External Affairs and National Defence, March 29, 1973.
9. Christoph Bertram, "Strategic Defences and the Western Allies," *Daedalus*, Summer 1985. p. 292.
10. Cited in Donald L. Hafner, "Assessing the President's Vision," *Daedalus*, Spring 1985. p. 94.
11. *Toronto Globe and Mail*, July 24, 1985.

12. James Schlesinger, "Rhetoric and Realities in the Star Wars Debate," *International Security*, Summer 1985. p. 5.

13. David Frum, "In Defence of Strategic Defences," *Saturday Night*, January 1986. p. 14.

14. Charles Murphy, "The U.S. as a Bombing Target," *Fortune*, November 1953. p. 121.

15. David Cox, *Canada and NORAD, 1958-1978: A Cautionary Retrospective*, Ottawa: Canadian Centre for Arms Control and Disarmament, 1985. p. 9.

16. Cited in R.D. Cuff and J.L. Granatstein, *Ties That Bind*, Toronto: Hakkert and Co., 1977. p.108.

17. Memorandum from the Minister (Bliss) at the American Embassy in Ottawa, April 3, 1951, *Foreign Relations of the United States*, 1951, Volume II. p. 878.

18. Jon Mclin, *Canada's Changing Defence Policy*. Baltimore: John Hopkins, 1967. p. 28.

19. Cited in James Eayrs, *In Defence of Canada: Growing Up Allied*, Toronto: University of Toronto Press, 1981. p. 248.

20. L.B. Pearson, "A New Look at the 'New Look'", Ottawa, Department of External Affairs, Speeches and Statements, 54/16. p. 7.

21. *Financial Post*, May 14, 1955.

22. Joseph Jockel, "The Military Establishments and the Creation of NORAD," *American Review of Canadian Studies*, p. 5.

23. Canada. House of Commons, Special Committee on Defence Expenditures, Minutes of Proceedings and Evidence, May 17, 1960. p. 88.

24. Cox, op.cit. p.27-8.

25. *New York Times*, December 16, 1986.

26. *New York Times*, May 3, 1987.

27. Henry L. Stimson and McGeorge Bundy, *On Active Service*, New York, 1948. p. 506.

28. Admiral James Watkins, "The Maritime Strategy," *Supplement to U.S. Naval Institute Proceedings*, January 1986. p. 11.

29. Alfred Thayer Mahan, *Naval Administration and Warfare*, Boston: 1906. p. 229.

30. John Honderich, "The Arctic Option," *Canadian Forum*, October 1987. p.9. Also see his *The Arctic Imperative*, Toronto: University of Toronto Press, 1987.

31. Cited in James Eayrs, *In Defence of Canada: Peacemaking and Deterrence*, Toronto: University of Toronto Press, 1977. p. 344.

32. Barney Danson, "Arctic military threat a red herring," *Toronto Globe and Mail*, May 29, 1987. p. 7.

33. For a discussion of the role of submarines in contemporary strategy see Kurt Lautenschlager, "The Submarine in Naval Warfare, 1901-2001," *International Security*, Winter 1986-87. p. 109. For a skeptical commentary on the Maritime Strategy see John Mearsheimer, "A Strategic Misstep," *International Security*, Fall 1986. pp. 3-87.

34. *Toronto Globe and Mail*, June 7, 1987.

35. Kurt Lautenschlager, "The Submarine in Naval Warfare," op. cit. p.109.
36. *New York Times*, March 19, 1987.
37. *Toronto Globe and Mail*, June 7, 1987.
38. *Toronto Globe and Mail*, June 8, 1987.
39. Brian Cuthbertson, *Canada's Military Independence in the Age of the Superpowers*. Toronto: Butterworths, 1977. p. 114.
40. Nicholas Tracy, *Canada's Foreign Policy Objectives and Canadian Security Agreements in the North*, Ottawa: Department of National Defence, ORAE, 1980. p. 16.

## Chapter Three

1. Reprinted in Eayrs, *Growing Up Allied*, pp. 374-5.
2. Alfred Grosser, *The Western Alliance*, New York: Vintage Books, 1982. p. 154.
3. See David Dilks, "The British View of Security: Europe and a Wider World, 1945-1948", in O. Riste, (ed.), *Western Security: The Formative Years*, New York, Columbia University Press, 1985.
4. Robert Osgood, *NATO: The Entangling Alliance*, Chicago: the University of Chicago Press, 1962. p. 30.
5. *Ibid.*, p. 47.
6. Bradley's speech of April 1949 is quoted in, *Ibid.*, p. 44.
7. Cited in Phil Williams, *The Senate and U.S. Troops in Europe*, New York: St. Martin's Press, 1985. p. 35.
8. See Williams, *op. cit.*, pp. 56-111; and U.S. House of Representatives, Committee on Foreign Affairs, *Congress and Foreign Policy —1984*.
9. Osgood, *op. cit.*, p. 78.
10. Cited in Osgood, *op. cit.*, p. 78.
11. Robert A. Divine, *Eisenhower, and the Cold War*, Oxford University Press: Oxford, 1981. pp. 33-9.
12. The document is discussed by Lawrence Freedman, *The Evolution of Nuclear Strategy*, St. Martin's Press: New York, 1981. pp. 81-3.
13. Divine, *op. cit.*, p. 37.
14. *Ibid.*, p. 110.
15. Eayrs, *Growing Up Allied*, *op. cit.*, p. 252.
16. *Ibid.*, p. 254.
17. Pearson's memorandum is reprinted in Eayrs, *Ibid.*, pp. 379-82.
18. *Ibid.*
19. Grosser, *The Western Alliance*, p. 165.
20. Based on Osgood, Chap. 5; and J. Record, *U.S. Nuclear Weapons in Europe*, Washington: The Brookings Institution, 1974.
21. Michael Howard, *The Causes of Wars*, 2nd ed., Cambridge: Harvard University Press, 1984. pp. 252-3.

22. For a lucid analysis of Soviet doctrine in this period see Michael MccGwire, *Military Objectives in Soviet Foreign Policy*, Washington: The Brookings Institution, 1987. Chap. 4.

23. Raymond Aron, *The Century of Total War*, Boston: Beacon Press, 1955. pp. 153-4.

24. Osgood, *op. cit.*, p. 164.

25. George F. Kennan, *Russia, the Atom and the West*, New York: Harper, 1957. pp. 62-3.

26. "International Control of Atomic Energy," January 20, 1950, *Foreign Relations of the United States*: 1950, I. p. 38.

27. Eayrs, *Growing Up Allied*, p. 327.

28. See Osgood; and Michael M. Harrison, *The Reluctant Ally*, Baltimore: Johns Hopkins University Press, 1981.

29. Osgood, *op. cit.*, p. 98.

30. Alain C. Enthoven and K. Wayne Smith, *How Much Is Enough?* New York: Harper and Row, 1971. p. 161.

31. Enthoven and Smith, *op. cit.*, p. 118.

32. *Ibid.*, p. 138.

33. *Ibid.*, p. 140-1.

34. *Ibid.*, p. 138.

35. David N. Schwartz, "A Historical Perspective," in J.D. Steinbruner and L.V. Sigal, eds., *Alliance Security: NATO and the No-First-Use Question*, Washington: The Brookings Institution, 1983. p. 14.

36. *Ibid.*, p. 15.

37. Robert S. McNamara, "The Military Role of Nuclear Weapons: Perceptions and Misperceptions," *Foreign Affairs*, Fall 1983.

38. Cf. Leon V. Sigal, "No First Use and NATO's Nuclear Posture", in *Ibid*.

39. International Institute for Strategic Studies, *The Military Balance 1986-87*, London, 1986. p. 225.

40. Howard's 1982 letter to *Foreign Affairs* is reprinted in William P. Bundy, ed., *The Nuclear Controversy*, New York: Meridian, 1985. pp. 39-40.

41. William W. Kaufmann, "Who is Conning the Alliance?", *The Brookings Review*, Fall 1987.

42. Barry R. Posen, "Measuring the European Conventional Balance," *International Security*, Winter 1984-85; and Posen and Stephen Van Evera, "Defense Policy and the Reagan Administration: Departure From Containment," *International Security*, Summer 1983.

43. John J. Mearshimer, "Why the Soviets Can't Win Quickly in Central Europe," *International Security*, Summer 1982.

44. *Jane's Defence Weekly*, November 1987.

# Chapter Four

1. Harold Nicolson, *The Evolution of Diplomatic Method*, London: Constable and Co., 1954. p.42-3.
2. Stanley Hoffmann, "An Icelandic Saga," *New York Review of Books*, November 20, 1986.
3. Cited in *New York Times*, October 22, 1986.
4. James Schlesinger, "Reykjavik and Revelations: A Turn of the Tide," *Foreign Affairs*, Volume 65 Number 3, 1986. p.437.
5. *The Economist*, October 18, 1987.
6. Christoph Bertram, "Europe's Security Dilemmas," *Foreign Affairs*, Summer 1982. p.950.
7. Theodore Draper, "Nuclear Temptations," *New York Review of Books*, January 19, 1984.
8. Lawrence Freedman, *Arms Control*, London :Routledge and Kegan Paul, 1986. p.4.
9. Lawrence Freedman, *The Evolution of Nuclear Strategy*, London: St. Martin's, 1983. p.356.
10. Michael MccGwire, "Dilemmas and Delusions of Deterrence," *World Policy Journal*, Summer 1984. p.750.
11. *Manchester Guardian Weekly*, May 31, 1981.
12. House of Commons. Debates, March 6, 1987. p.3909.
13. Jane Sharp, "Arms Control and Alliance Commitments," *Political Science Quarterly*, Winter 1985-86. p.654.
14. *London Times*, November 3, 1981. (letter)
15. Thomas Schelling "Abolition of Ballistic Missiles," *International Security*, Summer 1987. p.181.
16. Freedman, *Arms Control*, op.cit. p.46.
17. *New York Times*, October 14, 1986.
18. Cited in Michael Gordon, "INF: A Hollow Victory?," *Foreign Policy*, Number 68, Fall 1987. p.176.
19. *Globe and Mail*, May 1, 1987.
20. *Washington Post*, April 26, 1987.
21. Helmut Schmidt, "The 1977 Alastair Buchan Memorial Lecture," *Survival*, January-February 1978. p. 4.
22. Gordon, op.cit. p.164.
23. See the discussion on entrapment and abandonment in Jane M.O. Sharp, "After Reykjavik: arms control and the allies," *International Affairs*, Spring 1987. pp.240-248.
24. For a discussion of these proposals see Matthew Evangelista, "The New Soviet Approach to Security," *World Policy Journal*, Fall 1986.
25. *Ibid*. p.567.
26. Cited in Tsuyoshi Hasegawa, "Soviets on Nuclear-War-Fighting," *Problems of Communism*, July-August 1986. p.70.
27. *Ibid*. p.71.
28. Michael MccGwire, *Military Objectives in Soviet Foreign Policy*, Washington: The Brookings Institution, 1987.

29. Jane M.O. Sharp, "Are the Soviets Still Interested in Arms Control?," *World Policy Journal*, Summer 1984. p.819.
30. MccGwire, op.cit. pp.30-1.
31. Sharp, op.cit. p.825.
32. C.G. Jacobsen senior researcher at the Stockholm International Peace Research Institute cited in John R. Walker, "Nuclear Disarmament: The Gorbachev Initiative," Canadian Institute for International Peace and Security, Background Paper No. 11, January 1987. p.6.
33. Canada. House of Commons Debates. January 23, 1986.
34. Canada. Standing Senate Committee on Foreign Affairs, June 9, 1987.
35. Fen Osler Hampson, "Arms Control and East-West Relations," in Brian Tomlin and Maureen Appel Molot, eds. *Canada Among Nations*, 1986. Toronto: Lorimer, 1987. p.45.
36. *Manchester Guardian Weekly*, October 11, 1987.
37. *New York Times*, November 5, 1986.
38. For a commentary on these talks see Chalmers Hardenbergh, "The Other Negotiations," *Bulletin of the Atomic Scientists*, March 1987. pp.48-9.
39. Freedman, *Arms Control*, op.cit. p.52.
40. Jonathan Dean, "Military Security in Europe," *Foreign Affairs*, Fall 1987. p.40.

## Chapter Five

1. Article 51 of the Charter states in part that "nothing in the present Charter shall impair the inherent right of individual on collective self-defence if an armed attack occurs against a member of the United Nations . . ."
2. *The London Times*, April 16, 1986.
3. *The London Times*, April 16, 1986.
4. See Escott Reid, *Time of Fear and Hope*, Toronto: McClelland and Stewart, 1977 and James Eayrs, *In Defence of Canada: Growing Up Allied*, Toronto: University of Toronto Press, 1981.
5. Cited in Christopher Coker, *The Future of the Atlantic Alliance* London: Macmillan, 1984. p. 96.
6. Joint Communique by Churchill and Truman, January 9, 1952. State Department Bulletin, January 21, 1952.
7. See excerpts from the House of Commons debates in *The London Times*, April 16-17, 1986 and *The Manchester Guardian Weekly*, April 27, 1986.
8. *The London Times*, lead editorial of April 18, 1986.
9. As recorded by Thucydides in his history of the Peloponnesian War (Book V, 89); translation is by Thomas Hobbes. *Hobbes's Thucydides*, ed. by Richard Schlatter. Rutgers University Press, 1975.

10. E.P. Thompson, *The Heavy Dancers*, London: Merlin Press, 1985. p.38-9.
11. Denis Healy, *Labour and a World Society*, London: Fabian Tract 501, January 1985, p. 3.
12. George Will, "Let Reagan Be Reaganized," *Newsweek*, April 28, 1986.
13. Reinhold Niebuhr, *Moral Man and Immoral Society*, New York: Charles Scribner's Sons, 1934. p. 102.
14. Robert W. Tucker, "Isolation and Intervention," *The National Interest*, Fall 1985. p. 23.
15. Fred Halliday, *The Making of the Second Cold War*, 2nd ed., London: Verso Books, 1986. p. 242.
16. Paul Nitze is cited in Jerry Sanders, *Peddlers of Crisis*, Boston: South End Press, 1983. p. 286.
17. A. Dallin and G. Lapidus, "Reagan and the Russians: United States Policy Toward the Soviet Union and Eastern Europe," in K. Oye, et. al., eds., *Eagle Defiant*, Boston: Little, Brown Co., 1983. p. 210.
18. Irving Kristol, "Does NATO Exist?", in *Reflections of a Neoconservative*, New York: Basic Books, 1983. p. 246.
19. Thucydides, *The Peloponnesian War*, Middlesex: Penguin, 1972. pp. 236-45.
20. Martin Wight, *Power Politics*, Middlesex: Penguin, 1979, pp. 92-93.
21. Richard Pipes, *Survival is Not Enough*, New York: Simon Schuster, 1984. pp. 13-14 and p. 278.
22. Colin S. Gray, "Maritime Strategy," *U.S. Naval Institute Proceedings*, February 1986, p. 36.
23. *The New York Times*, February 15, 1987.
24. See Larry Pratt, "The Reagan Doctrine and the Third World," *The Socialist Register*, 1987.
25. Summary of the World Court ruling in *The Times* (London), June 28, 1986.
26. Ralph Miliband, "Freedom, Democracy and the American Alliance", *The Socialist Register*, 1987, p. 498.

## Chapter Six

1. W.B. Messmer, "If Labour Wins," *Foreign Policy*, Summer 1987, p. 147.
2. Phil Williams, "Meeting Alliance and National Needs," in John Roper, ed., *The Future of British Defence Policy*, London: Gower, 1985. p. 22.
3. See Labour's White Paper, *The Power to Defend Our Country*, London: December 1986.

4. Margaret Gowing, *Independence and Deterrence: Britain and Atomic Energy, 1945-1952*, Vol. 1, London: Macmillan, 1974. p. 242.

5. See Lawrence Freedman, *Britain and Nuclear Weapons*, London: Macmillan, 1980; and Richard Neustadt, *Alliance Politics*, New York: Columbia University Press, 1970.

6. Christopher Coker, *A Nation in Retreat?* London: Brassey's, 1986. p. 78.

7. Ralf Dahrendorf, "The Europeanization of Europe," in Andrew J. Pierre, ed., *A Widening Atlantic? Domestic Change and Foreign Policy*, New York: Council on Foreign Relations, 1986. p. 27.

8. Josef Joffe, "Peace and Populism," *International Security*, Spring 1987. p. 12.

9. Josef Joffe, "Squaring Many Circles: West German Security Policy Between Deterrence, Detente and Alliance," in J.A. Cooney et. al., eds., *The Federal Republic and the United States*, Boulder, Col.: Westview Press, 1984. p. 187.

10. Fritz Stern, "Conclusion," in *Ibid*.

11. Jane M.O. Sharp, "After Reykjavik: arms control and the allies," *International Affairs*, Spring 1987.

12. Marcell von Donat, "Neutralism in Germany," *Government and Opposition*, Autumn 1986. p. 407.

13. Walter Laqueur, "Poland and the Crisis of the Alliance," *Wall Street Journal*, January 4, 1982.

14. Robert W. Tucker, "The Atlantic Alliance and Its Critics," *Commentary*, May 1982.

15. Zbigniew Brezezinski, *Game Plan*, New York: Atlantic Monthly Press, 1986. p. 205.

16. Robert W. Komer, "Problems of Over-extension: Reconciling NATO Defence and Out-of-Area Contingencies: Part II," in *Adelphi Papers*, Spring 1986. p. 61.

17. Robert W. Tucker, *The Purposes of American Power*, New York: Praeger, 1981. p. 65.

18. A useful European summary of these events is in: Simon Lunn, *Burden-sharing in NATO* in *Chatham House Papers*, No. 18, London: Royal Institute of International Affairs, 1983. Chapter 3.

19. Christoper Coker, *The Future of the Atlantic Alliance* London: Macmillan, 1984. p. 95.

20. NATO Defence Planning Committee, *Final Communique*, May 13-14, 1980.

21. Simon Lunn, *op. cit.*, p. 24.

22. U.S. Senate, *Hearings Before the Committee on Armed Services on S. 2199 Part 2: Unified Commands* 99th Congress, 2nd Session, March 11-12, 1986.

23. See Robert P. Haffa, Jr., *The Half War: Planning U.S. Rapid Deployment Forces to Meet a Limited Contingency. 1960-1983*, Boulder Col.: Westview, 1984.

24. James R. Blaker, "The Out-of Area Question and NATO Burden Sharing," in Linda P. Brady and Joyce P. Kaufman, eds., *NATO in the 1980s*, New York: Praeger, 1985. p. 46.
25. *The New York Times*, May 26, 1987.
26. James H. Wyllie, *European Security in the Nuclear Age*, Oxford: Basil Blackwell, 1986. p. 154.
27. Congressional Research Service, *U.S. Military Installations in NATO's Southern Region*, Report for the Subcommittee on Europe and the Middle East, U.S. House of Representatives, Committee on Foreign Affairs, October 1986.
28. Congressional Research Service . . . *op. cit.*, p. 53.
29. Manchester Guardian Weekly, December 28, 1986.
30. Wight, *Power Politics*, p. 157.
31. Eayrs, *Growing Up Allied*, p. 78.

## Conclusion

1. "The Development of Canadian Foreign Policy," Foreign Affairs, October 1951. p.25-6.
2. Interviewed, August, 1987.
3. Charles Doran, "Sovereignty Does Not Equal Security," *Peace and Security*, Autumn 1987, p. 9.
4. J.L. Granatstein, in *Behind the Headlines*, October 1971.
5. Helmut Schmidt, *A Grand Strategy for the West*, New Haven: Yale University Press, 1985. p.27.
6. Francois de Rose, *European Security and France*, London: Macmillan, p.53.

# Selected Bibliography

Calleo, David P., *Beyond American Hegemony: The Future of the Western Alliance*, New York: Basic Books, 1986

Coker, Christopher, *The Future of the Atlantic Alliance*, London: Macmillan, 1984

Cuthbertson, Brian, *Canada's Military Independence in the Age of the Superpowers*, Toronto: Butterworths, 1977

Eayrs, James, *In Defence of Canada, Growing up Allied*, Toronto: University of Toronto Press, 1980

Freedman, Lawrence, *The Evolution of Nuclear Strategy*, New York: St. Martin's 1983

Garthoff, Raymond, *Detente and Confrontation: American-Soviet Relations from Nixon to Reagan*, Washington: Brookings, 1985

Grosser, Alfred, *The Western Alliance: European-American Relations Since 1945*, New York, Vintage Books, 1982

Hertzman, Lewis, et. al., *Alliances and Illusions: Canada and the NATO-NORAD Question*, Edmonton: Hurtig, 1969

Holm, Hans-Henrik and Petersen, Nikolaj, eds., *European Missile Crisis: Nuclear Weapons and Security Policy*, London: Francis Pinter, 1983

Howard, Michael, *The Causes of War*, 2nd Ed., Cambridge: Harvard University Press, 1984

Jockel, Joseph and Sokolsky, Joel, *Canada and Collective Security: Odd Man Out*, New York, Praeger, 1986

Komer, Robert, *Maritime Strategy or Coalition Defense?*, Cambridge: Abt. Books, 1984

MccGwire, Michael, *Military Objectives in Soviet Foreign Policy*, Washington: Brookings, 1987

McLin, Jon, *Canada's Changing Defense Policy, 1957-1963*, Baltimore: John Hopkins, 1967

Osgood, Robert, *NATO: The Entangling Alliance*, Chicago: University Press, 1962

Pierre, Andrew, ed., *A Widening Atlantic? Domestic Change and Foreign Policy*, New York: Council on Foreign Relations, 1986

Pierre, Andrew, ed., *Nuclear Weapons in Europe*, New York: Council on Foreign Relations, 1984

deRose, François, *European Security and France*, London: Macmillan, 1983

Reid, Escott, *Time of Fear and Hope*, Toronto: McClelland and Stewart, 1977

Riste, Olav, ed., *Western Security: The Formative Years*, New York: Columbia University Press, 1985

Wyllie, James, *European Security in the Nuclear Age*, New York: Basil Blackwell, 1986

# Acknowledgements

We have benefitted from the assistance of many people in the production of this book.

We would especially like to thank Sharon Hobson who conducted most of our research in Ottawa and to the many officials in Ottawa who shared their ideas with her and us. For their assistance in conducting research in Edmonton we thank Shawn Kernaghan, Lorna Dawson, Todd Nelson, Anita Mathur, and Deborah Alford. The Central Research Fund of the University of Alberta and the Canadian Institute of International Peace and Security provided generous financial support for this project. We also owe a debt of thanks to Pam Ouimet and Ruth Koenig who sifted through various drafts of the manuscript and under considerable pressure worked beyond the call of duty to type the manuscript to meet the deadline. We would also like to acknowledge the assistance of our editors Maryhelen Vicars and Barb McCord who offered many helpful comments and added greater clarity to the final manuscript. Finally we would like to acknowledge our intellectual debts to James Eayrs, John Holmes, Robert Osgood, and Michael Howard whose writings on the North Atlantic Treaty Organization, past and present, have greatly influenced our own ideas about the Alliance and Canada's place in it.

We also wish to express special thanks to our families who suffered through too many weekends and evenings that were devoted to completing this task.

# Index